India Ebook's

ASSAM GK 2023-24
FOR COMPETITIVE EXAM

FOR APSC, GRADE-III, GRADE-IV & OTHER COMPETITIVE EXAMS OF ASSAM

Covers – Concepts with 450 MCQs Assam's Geography, Economy, Polity, History, Art & Culture, Misc. Topics & Various Maps

Author: JANMEJOY
C-Author: KRISHNA KAMAL

INDIA EBOOK PRESS

Contents

1. ASSAM'S GEOGRAPHY

GE-1: Administration & Demography
GE-2: Physiography, Drainage, Soils and Climate
GE-3: Bio-diversity
GE-3: Protected Areas

1.1: GE-1: Administration & Demography

➢ GE-1.1: Assam Maps, Boundaries and Key Information

ASSAM AT A GLANCE

Location: Latitude **24'3 N** and **27'58 N**

Longitude **89'5 E** and **96'1 E**

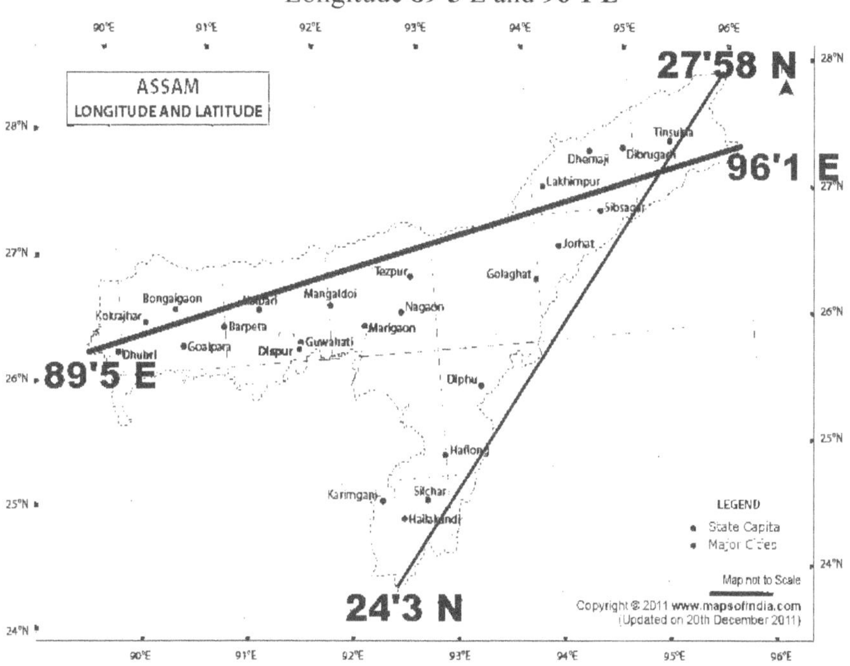

Capital: Dispur

Total Area: 78,438 square kms.

Area-wise Position: **17**[th] in India and **2**[nd] in Northeast(NE)

(Largest State of NE is Arunachal Pradesh)

Population: **3,12,05,576** (2011 Census)

Population-wise Position: **14**[th]

Official Languages: **Assamese, Bengali, Bodo**

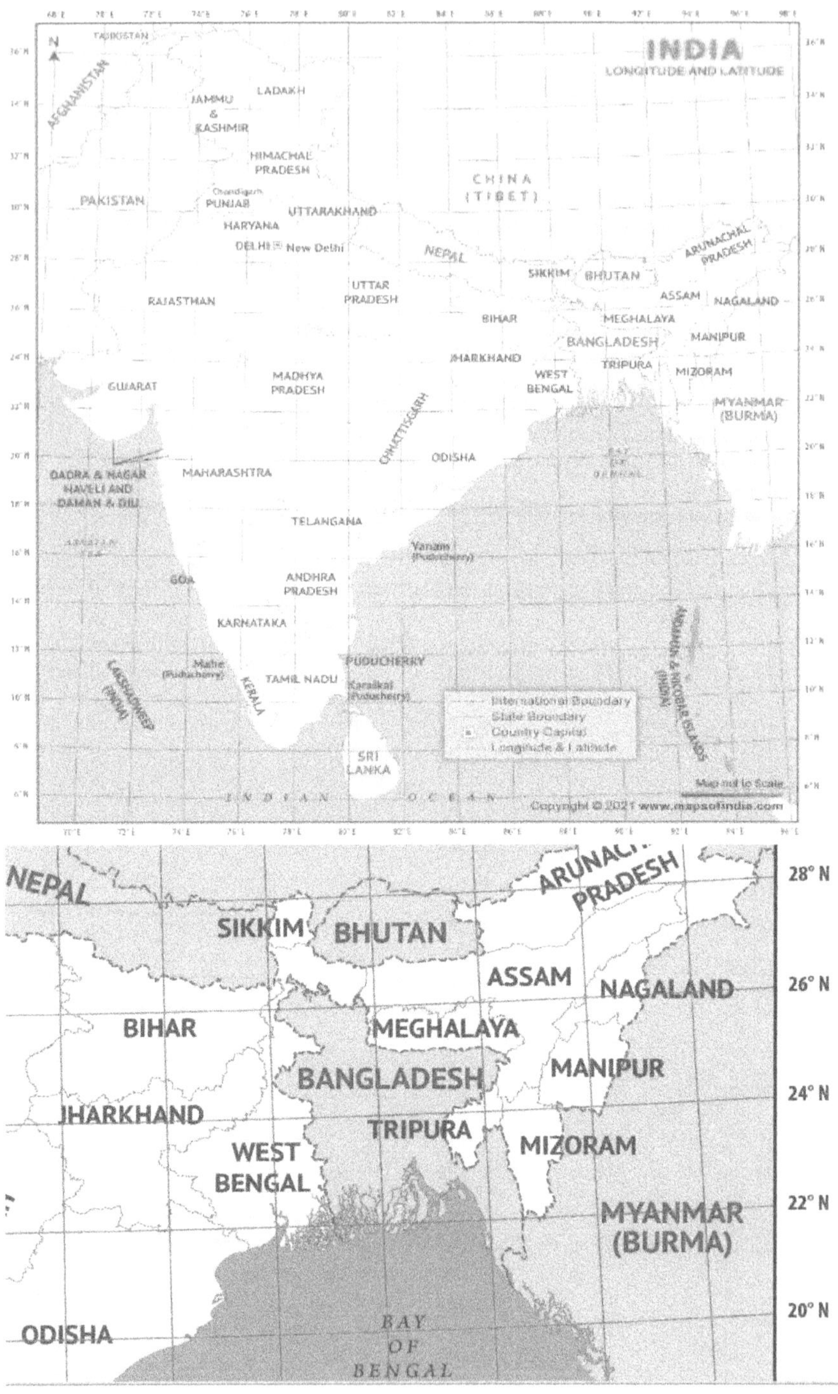

INDIA
LONGITUDE AND LATITUDE
TAJIKISTAN
AFGHANISTAN
JAMMU & KASHMIR
LADAKH
HIMACHAL PRADESH
CHINA (TIBET)
PAKISTAN
PUNJAB
Chandigarh
UTTARAKHAND
HARYANA
DELHI New Delhi
NEPAL
SIKKIM
BHUTAN
ARUNACHAL PRADESH
ASSAM
NAGALAND
UTTAR PRADESH
RAJASTHAN
BIHAR
MEGHALAYA
MANIPUR
BANGLADESH
JHARKHAND
TRIPURA
MIZORAM
WEST BENGAL
GUJARAT
MADHYA PRADESH
CHHATTISGARH
MYANMAR (BURMA)
ODISHA
BAY OF BENGAL
DADRA & NAGAR HAVELI AND DAMAN & DIU
MAHARASHTRA
TELANGANA
ANDAMAN & NICOBAR ISLANDS (INDIA)
GOA
ANDHRA PRADESH
Yanam (Puducherry)
KARNATAKA
PUDUCHERRY
Mahe (Puducherry)
Karaikal (Puducherry)
LAKSHADWEEP (INDIA)
KERALA
TAMIL NADU
International Boundary
State Boundary
Country Capital
Longitude & Latitude
SRI LANKA
INDIAN OCEAN
Map not to Scale
Copyright © 2021 www.mapsofindia.com
NEPAL
ARUNACHAL PRADESH
28° N
SIKKIM
BHUTAN
ASSAM
26° N
NAGALAND
BIHAR
MEGHALAYA
MANIPUR
BANGLADESH
24° N
JHARKHAND
TRIPURA
MIZORAM
WEST BENGAL
22° N
MYANMAR (BURMA)
20° N
ODISHA
BAY OF BENGAL

BOUNDARIES

➤ **International Borders with 2 Countries**

1. Bhutan
2. Bangladesh

(Assam **doesn't have border** with **China & Mynmar**)

Seven (7) Districts of Assam shares with international Borders

Bhutan- Baksa, ~~Tamulpur~~, Chirang, Kokrajhar, Udalguri

(**Note:** As Tamulpur merged with Baksa)

Bangladesh- Karimganj, Cachar, Dhubri, South Salmara

➤ **Inter-State Borders with 7 States:**

Meghalaya (884.9 kms), Arunachal Pradesh (804.1 kms), Nagaland (512.1 kms), Manipur (204.1 kms), Mizoram (164.6 kms), West Bengal (127 kms) & Tripura (46.3 kms).

24 Districts Shares Inter-state Boundaries.

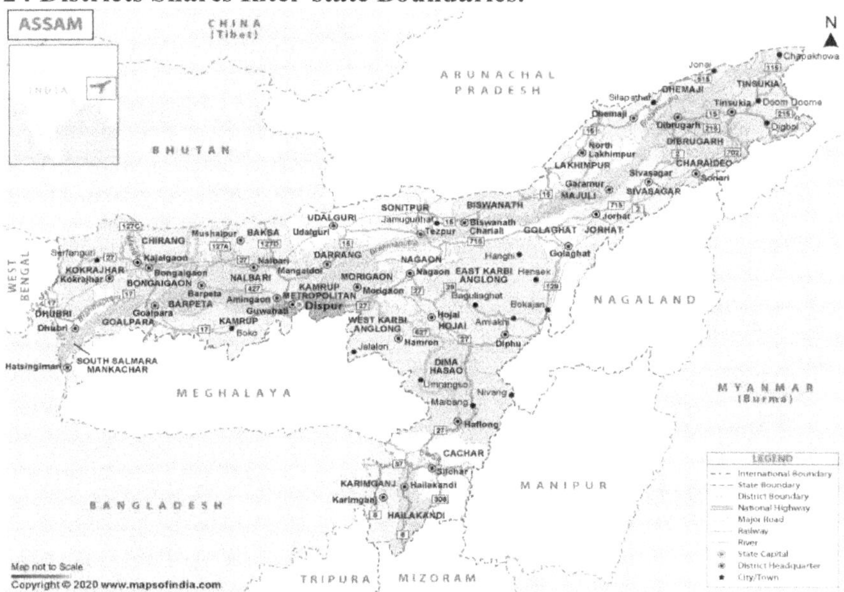

ASSAM & INTERNATIONAL BORDER

Total Length of International Border : 533.3 km

1. Assam-Bangladesh	**: 267.5 km**
Karimganj-Bangladesh	: 92 km (3 km)
Cachar-Bangladesh	: 70 km
Dhubri-Bangladesh	: 90 km
S Salmara Mankachar-Ban	: 63 km

6) **West Bengal** – Kokrajhar, Dhubri

7) **Tripura** – Karimganj

IMPORTANT BORDER DISTRICTS

Tinsukia- Arunachal Pradesh : Largest Inter-State Border – 282 km

Karimganj- Mizoram : Shortest Inter-State Border – 12 km

Dima Hasao Border with **3 states** (Nagaland, Manipur & Meghalaya)

Cachar- Border with **Bangladesh** and **3 states**- Manipur, Mizoram, Meghalaya.

GENERAL INFORMATION OF LEGISLATIVES

Legislative Assembly

Total Number of Legislative Constituencies = **126**

Reserved Seats:

Schedule Caste (SC) = **8**   Schedule Tribes (ST) = **16**

Legislative Council

No Legislative Council in Assam. **Assam is a Unicameral** State. <u>Only 6 States of India</u> have **Legislative Councils**: (Bicameral)

1. Uttar Pradesh   –   2. Bihar

3. Maharashtra   –   4. Karnataka

5. Andhra Pradesh   –   6. Telengana

Lok Sabha (Lower House)   Seats = Fourteen (14)

Karimganj, Silchar, Autonomous Districts (ST), Dhubri, Kokrajhar, Barpeta, Gauhati, Mongoldoi, Tezpur, Naogaon, Kaliabar, Jorhat, Dibrugarh, Lakhimpur

Rajya Sabha (Upper House) Seats = Seven (7)

These are elected by Member of Legislative Assemblies (MLA)

Total Number of Autonomous Councils **(in Assam)** under the **6**th **Schedule** of the Constitution of India = **Three (3)**

NOTE: There are *10 Autonomous Councils* **in India** under the **6th Schedule** as "other Schedule Areas". All are in Northeast.

MEGHALAYA
- Khasi Hills Autonomous District Council
- Jaintia Hills Autonomous District Council
- Garo Hills Autonomous District Council

MIZORAM
- Chakma Autonomous District Council
- Lai Autonomous District Council

- Mara Autonomous District Council

TRIPURA
- Tripura Tribal Areas Autnomous District Council

ASSAM
- Dima Hasao Autonomous Council
- Karbi Anglong Autonomous Council
- Bodoland Territorial Council

Total Number of Autonomous Councils under State Act = Six (6)

Total Number of Development Councils = 33

Total Number of Autonomous Councils under State Act = **Six (6)**

- Rabha Hasong Autonomous Council
- Mising Autonomous Council
- Tiwa Autonomous Council
- Deori Autonomous Council
- Thengal Kachari Autonomous Council
- Sonowal Kachari Autonomous Council

Autonomous Councils under the 6th Schedule of the Constitution of India = Three (3)

North Cachar Hills District

Karbi Anglong District

Bodoland Territorial Areas District

➢ GE-1.2: Assam's Administrative Divisions

CATEGOGY	TOTAL NO	HEADED BY
Divisions	5	Commissioner
Districts	35	Deputy Commissioner (DC)
Sub-division	80	SDO
Revenue Circles	184	Circle Officer or SDC
Development Blocks	219	Block Development Officer
Towns	214	Guwahati – Municipality Corporation Others – Municipality Boards or Town Committees
Census Towns	126	
Villages	26,395	

Hon`ble Governor of Assam
GULAB CHAND KATARIA
View Profile >

Hon`ble CM of Assam
Dr. Himanta Biswa Sarma
View Profile >

THE ADMINISTRATIVE DIVISIONS IN ASSAM

⤻ **North Assam (Headquarter – Tezpur)**

Udalguri, Darrang, Sonitpur, ~~Biswanath~~ = **3** Districts

   (**NOTE:** Biswanath merged with Sonitpur)

⤻ **Lower Assam (Headquarter – Guwahati)**

Dhubri, Kokrajhar, Bongaigaon, Goalpara, Baksa, ~~Tamulpur~~, Chirang, Barpeta, ~~Bajali~~, Nalbari, Kamrup (R), Kamrup (M), South Salmara Mankachar = **11** Districts.

(Note: Bajali merged with Barpeta & Tamulpur merged with Baksa)

⚜ <u>Hills & Central Assam (Headquarter – Nagaon)</u>

Dima Hasao, East Karbi Anglong, West Karbi Anglong, Nagaon, Morigaon, ~~Hojai~~ = **5** Districts

NOTE: Hojai is merged with Nagaon.

⚜ <u>Upper Assam (Headquarter – Jorhat)</u>

Lakhimpur, Dibrugarh, Dhemaji, Tinsukia, Sibsagar, Charaideo, Jorhat, Majuli, Golaghat = 9 Districts

⚜ <u>Barak Valley (Headquarter – Silchar)</u>

Cachar, Hailakandi, Karimganj = 3 Districts

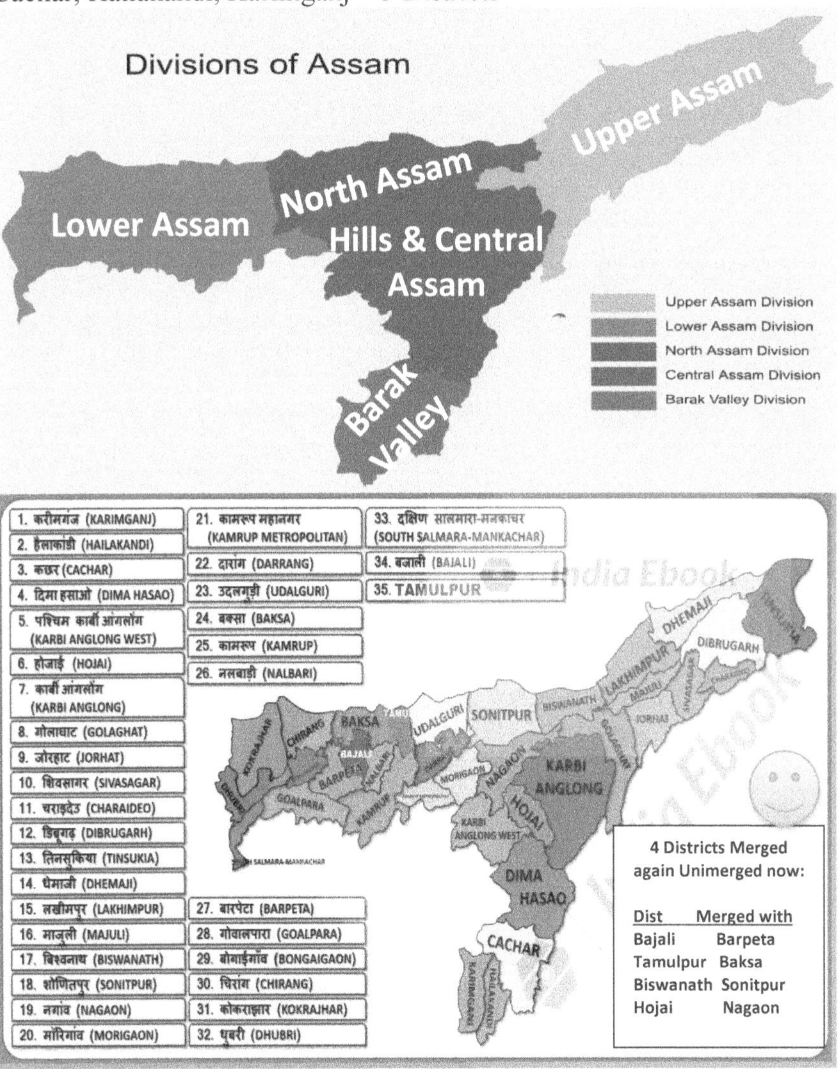

> **GE-1.3: Demographic Information (based on Census) - Population, Density, Literacy Rate etc.**

KEY DEMOGRAPHIC INFORMATION – CENSUS 2011

Total Population	: 3,12,05,576
Population Growth Rate (2001 to 2011)	: 17.1 %
Population Density (per sq. km.	: 398
Sex Ratio (Female per 1000 Male)	: 958
Overall Literacy Rate	: 72.19 %
Birth Rate (per 1000)	: 22.4
Death Rate (per 1000)	: 7.2
Maternal Mortality Rate (MMR) 2014-16	: 237
(It is highest MMR in India) National MMR	: 130
Infant Mortality Rate (per 1000 live birth)	: 44 (2016)
Below Poverty Line (BPL) Population	: 1.01 crores
	: 32%(2011-12)

LITERACY RATE : 72.19 %

Male Literacy : 77.85%	Female Literacy 66.27 %
Urban Literacy: 88.47 %	Rural Literacy: 69.34 %

RANK OF ASSAM AMONGST THE STATES OF INDIA

Total Population	14th
Population Density	15th
Sex Ratio	15th
Area	17th India 2nd Northeast
Literacy Rate	26th

CATEGORY	POPULATION	Million	Billion	PERCENTAGE %
Total Population	3,12,05,576	31.2	0.312	
Male	1,59,39,443	15.9	0.159	51 %
Female	1,52,66,133	15.3	0.153	49 %
Rural	2,68,07,034	26.8	0.268	86 %
Urban	43,98,542	4.39	0.0439	14 %
S C				7.15 %
S T				12.45 %

Category	Highest/ Largest	Lowest/ Smallest
Area	Karbi Anglong	South Salmara
Literacy Rate	Kamrup (M)	Dhubri
Population	Nagaon	Dima Hasao
Populati Density	Kamrup(M)1313	Dima Hasao - 44
Sex Ration	Baksa - 974	Dima Hasao - 932
Growth Rate	Dhubri -24.44%	Kokrajhar -5.21%
ST Population	Karbi Anglong	Hailakandi
SC Population	Nagaon	Dima Hasao
Urban Population	Kamrup (M)	Baksa
Rural Population	Nagaon	Kamrup (M)

Demographic Info. Of Major Cities/Towns

Rank	Name	Population	Literacy
1	Guwahati	9,68,549	91.22 %
2	Silchar	6,28,985	91.05 %
3	Dibrugarh	1,54,019	89.75 %
4	Jorhat	1,53,249	91.18 %
5	Nagaon	1,47,137	90.82 %
6	Tinsukia	1,25,637	90.42 %
7	Tezpur	1,00,477	89.12 %

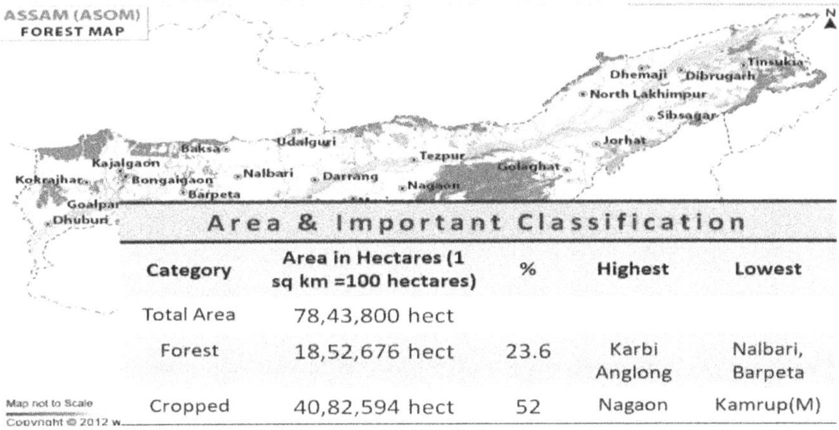

Area & Important Classification

Category	Area in Hectares (1 sq km =100 hectares)	%	Highest	Lowest
Total Area	78,43,800 hect			
Forest	18,52,676 hect	23.6	Karbi Anglong	Nalbari, Barpeta
Cropped	40,82,594 hect	52	Nagaon	Kamrup(M)

1.2: GE-2: Physiography, Drainage, Soils and Climate

➢ GE-2.1: Physiographic characteristics of Assam

PHYSIOGRAPHY OF ASSAM

Assam's physiography may be described in terms of physiographic elements like Plains, Hills, Foothills, Plateaus and River Valleys. Thus, the broad physiographic divisions of Assam can be described as:

- The Alluvial Plains
- The Plateau Region
- Tertiary Folded Hills of the NC Hills

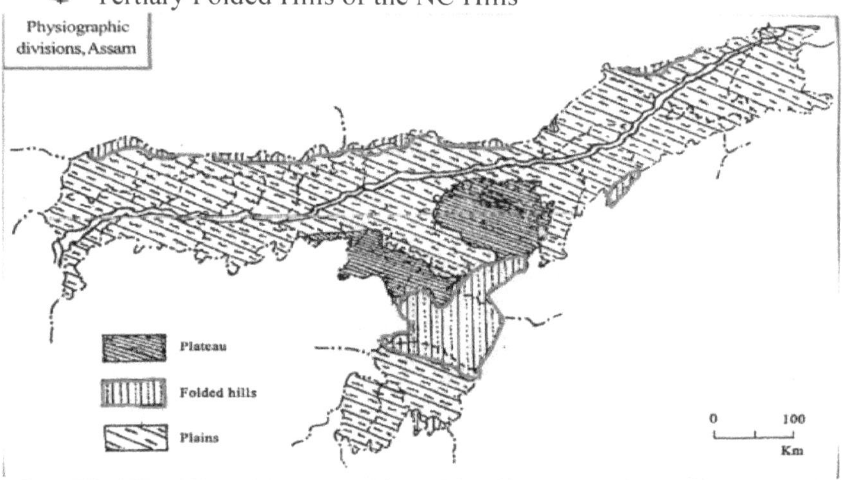

1. The Alluvial Plains:

There are 2 major Alluvial plains in Assam. Of the two, Brahmaputra plain is the larger and it is the largest plain in NE India and occupies an area of 58,315 sq. km.

a) The Brahmaputra Plain (Area: 58,315 sq. km)

The almond shaped Brahmaputra Valley is the result of depositional works of the river Brahmaputra and its tributaries. It is a flat plain with a length and breadth of 725 km and 80-100 km respectively. The Brahmaputra Valley covers a substantial part of the State and most of the important towns and cities of Assam are situated in this valley.

b) The Barak Plain (Area: 6,962 sq. km)

The Barak Valley is named after the river Barak. Like Brahmaputra, the river Barak has also created a fertile valley which is bordered by North

Cachar Hills, Manipur and Mizoram. The Barak Valley is a amazing plain interspersed with low hills and lakes.

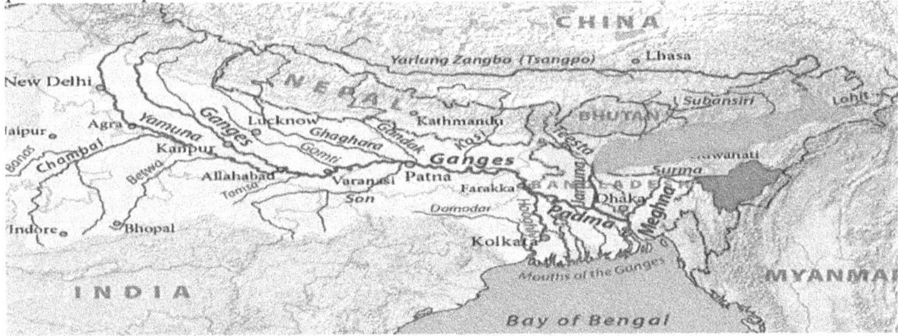

2. The Plateau Region:

The Karbi Plateau is the extended part of Meghalaya Plateau, which is an extension of the Chotanagpur Plateau.

a) The Central Karbi Plateau (Area: 7,400 sq. km)

It is the easternmost part of the plateau region. This part is separated from the Hamren division by the river Kapili & its tributaries & the river Dhansiri makes it isolated from the Naga Hills.

b) The Hamren Plateau (Area: 6,962 sq. km)

It is the continuous part of the **Jaintia Hills** in Meghalaya. The plateau has a general slope from south-west to south-east. The streams that flow in this plateau are the tributaries of Kapili & all of them flow south-west to north-east & join the Brahmaputra.

3. The Tertiary Folded Hills of NC Hills:

It is the southern extension or the off-shoots of Himalayas. The various ranges are found in the **NC Hills district**. The ranges in the district are known as Barail Ranges.

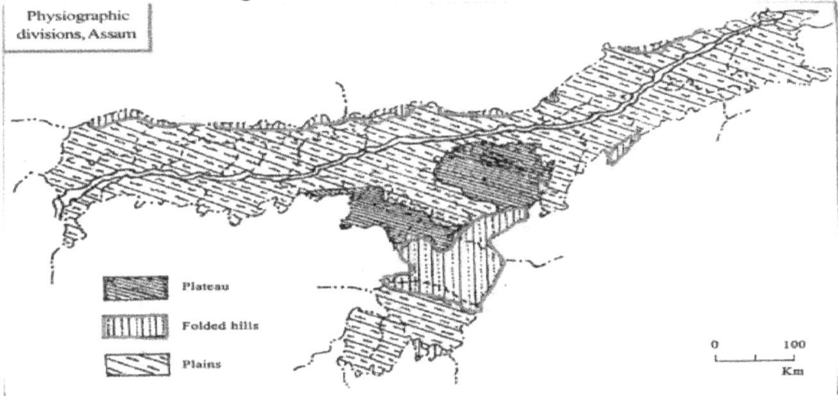

➤ GE-2.2: Assam's Drainage System - River System

River System of Assam

i) Brahmaputra River System

One of the largest river in the world, which flows through China, India & Bangladesh.

Length: **2900 km (India 916 km)**   Average Width: 5.46 km

15th Longest in the *World & 9th Largest* river in the World by Discharge

Originates: Kailash Manassarovar (elevation 5300 m)

Flows as Tsangpo (Yardlung Zangbo) in China

Flows Bangladesh as Jamuna (Brahmaputra in BANGLADESH)

Then it merges with Padma (Ganga in Bangladesh) & finally Meghna.

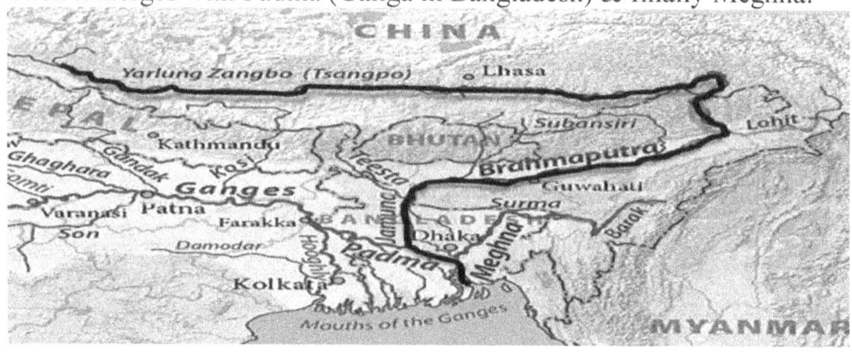

Left Bank Tributaries of the Brahmaputra River

Rivers	Length (km)
Buridihing	360
Desang	230
Dikhow	200
Jhanji	108
Bhogdoi	160
Dhansiri	352
Kopili	297
Krishna	81
Kulsi	93
Jinari	60

Right Bank Tributaries of the Brahmaputra River

Rivers	Length (km)
Subansiri	442
Ranganadi	150
Baroi	64
Bargang	42
Jia Bharali	247
Gabharu	61
Dhansiri	123
Noa-Nadi	75
Nanoi	105
Barnadi	112
Puthimari	190
Pagladiya	197
Manas-Aie-Beki	215
Champamati	135
Gaurang	98
Tipkai	108
Godadhar	50
Balsiri	110

ii) Barak River System

2nd Largest River in Assam as well as in North East

Length: 900 km   **Area:** 52,000 sq. km

Originates: Japvo Mountain of Manipur Hills (altitude 3015 m)

Barak river is divided in Haritikor (Bhanga, Near Badarpur) as Surma and Kushiyara.

Surma immediately enters into Bangladesh and Kushiyara makes a Indo-Bangla border & finally at Lakshmibazar it enters into Bangladesh.

Main Tributaries:

The Katakhal, Jatinga, Jiri, Chiri, Modhura, Longai, Sonai, Rukni and Singla

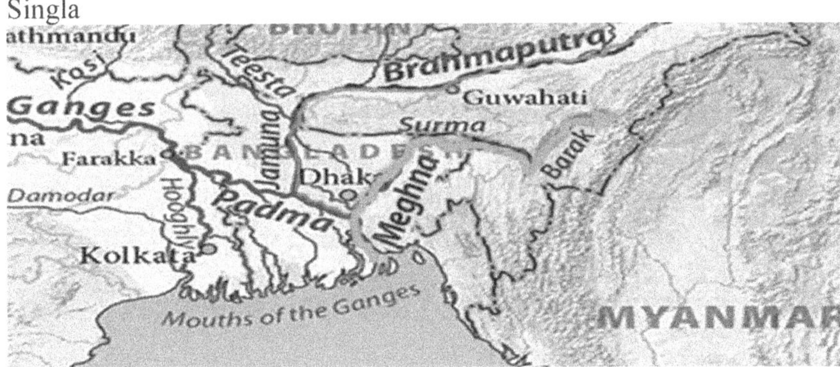

➢ **GE-2.3: Different Types of Soil & their Characteristics**

SOILS OF ASSAM

The soils of Assam are very rich in content of Nitrogen & organic matter. The Soil of Assam generally may be divided into four groups:

a) Alluvial Soils: The alluvial soils of Brahmaputra & Barak Valley are highly fertile & are very much suitable for raising of varieties of crops round the year such as Cereals, Pulses, Oilseeds, Plantation crops, etc.

This soils are further classified as: **Younger & Old Alluvium.**

The uses of alluvial soil are numerous and varied. **This type of soil is particularly suited for** rice cultivation, and is also used for growing crops such as jute, tea, and sugarcane. In addition, **alluvial soil is often used for horticulture and floriculture**, and is also used in the production of vegetables, fruits, and spices. Due to its high fertility, alluvial soil is an important resource for the agricultural sector in Assam.

The **formation of alluvial soil** is a **natural process** that occurs over time. As rivers and streams flow through an area, they carry sediment and debris with them. When the flow of water slows down, the sediment and debris settle to the bottom, forming layers of soil. Over time, these layers build up and become compressed, forming alluvial soil.

With its high fertility and wide range of uses, alluvial soil is a valuable resource for agriculture in Assam.

b) Piedmont Soils: These soils are concentrated to the Northern Narrow Zone & Piedmont Zone of the Himalayan Foothills. These soils comprise the **Bhabar soil & Tarai soil**, covering respectively Bbabar & Tarai belt of Brahmaputra.

c) Hill Soils: These are generally found in the Southern Hilly terrains of the state. The fertility of these soils defers greatly in different regions.

These soils are rich in Nitrogen & organic matters. Found in Assam Meghlaya Border, Karbi Plateau, Southern part of Barail Range.

In agriculture, hill farming is practiced using terrace farming techniques to prevent soil erosion and maximize land use. This involves building terraces on the steep slopes, which help to reduce soil erosion by slowing down the flow of water and allowing it to soak into the soil. Hill soil is also used in the construction of retaining walls, which help to prevent soil erosion and landslides.

Overall, hill soil has unique properties that make it useful in construction and agriculture. However, it is important to note that this type of soil is not suitable for intensive agriculture due to its shallow depth and rocky nature.

d) Lateritic Soils: Found almost Entire NC Hills (Dima Hasao), few patches of Hamren, Southern Border of Golaghat, Nothern part of barak Plains alongwith foothills of Barail range.

Despite its advantages, laterite soil mining can have a significant impact on the local ecosystem. The removal of soil can lead to erosion, loss of biodiversity, and soil compaction. Additionally, the mining process can release toxins and heavy metals into the environment, which can have long-term consequences on the health of local populations.

To mitigate these issues, responsible mining practices must be implemented. This includes minimizing the amount of soil removed, using sustainable mining techniques, and implementing reforestation programs to restore the natural ecosystem. With proper management, the use of laterite soil can continue to provide significant benefits to the construction industry while minimizing its impact on the environment.

> **GE-2.4: Climate details concentrating on Rainfall Pattern & Temperature**

CLIMATE, RAINFALL PATTERN & TEMPERATURE OF ASSAM

The Climate of Assam is typically Tropical Monsoon Rainfall type, with high levels of Humidity and heavy Rainfall.

A moderate climate all throughout the year, with warm summers and mild winters.

Climate variations can be seen regionally. While the plains of Assam have a tropical Climate with high Humidity, the Hills have sub-alpine type of climate.

There are **4 seasons in Assam**: Summer, Monsoon, Autumn & Winter

Summer: starts from March - extends till the ends of June. Average Temperature= 35-38 Degree Centigrade.

Average rainfall 70 inches in the West and 120 inches in the East.

In the afternoons, thunderstorms known as Bordoicila are very common.

Monsoon: Assam receives Typical Monsoon rains. The South-West monsoon rains starts from 3rd week of June & continue up to the middle of September. (Average **Rainfall 180 cm**)

Autumn: starts from September - continues till October. It is pleasant season with moderate temperature & rainfall. These are amongst the popular months for tourist rush.

Winter: This season is basically characterized by scanty rainfall & misty mornings & afternoons. It starts in November - continues till the moth of February. Average Temperature= 6 to 8 Degree Centigrade.

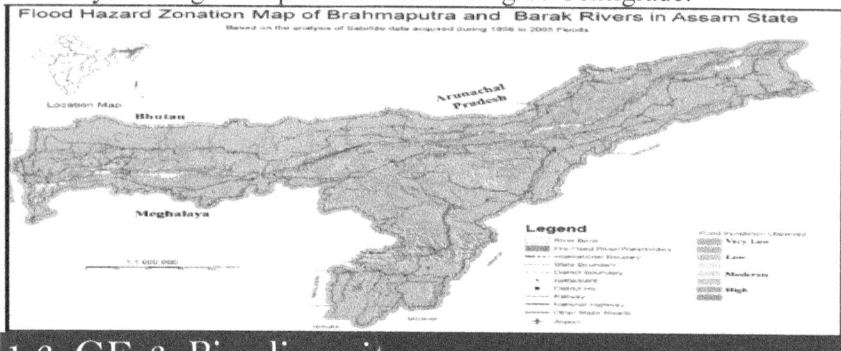

1.3: GE-3: Bio-diversity

> ## GE-3.1: Forests, Flora and Fauna (Plants & Animals)

FOREST COVER IN ASSAM

Total Forest Cover: 18,52,676 hectares (23.6%)

Highest Cover: Karbi Anglong Lowest Cover: Kamrup (M)

TYPES OF FORESTS

Tropical Wet Evergreen Forest	Tropical Semi Evergreen Forest
Tropical Moist Deciduous Forest	Sub-tropical Broad-leaf Hill Forest
Sub-tropical Pine Forest	Littoral and Swamp Forest
Grasslands and Savannahs	

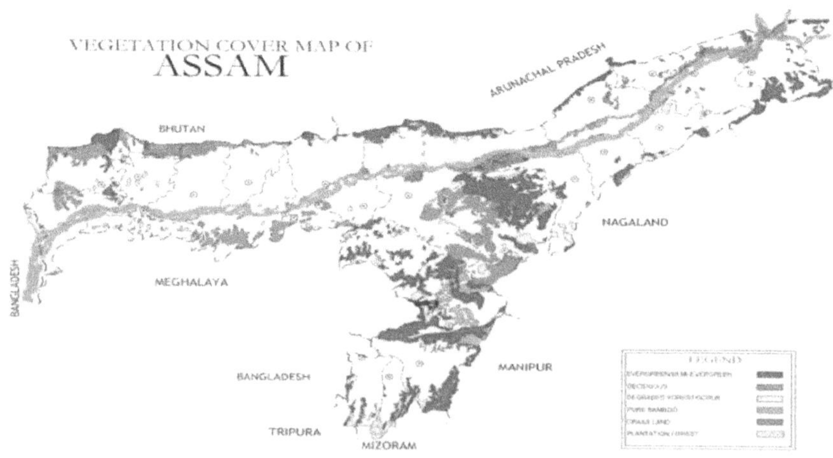

1. TROPICAL WET EVERGREEN FOREST

+ Found in the districts of Golaghat, Jorhat, Sivasagar, Tinsukia, Dibrugarh and in a narrow stretch in Lakhimpur & Dhemaji districts along Himalayan Foot Hills.

+ These Forests are also found in Lower Elevation in Borail Range & Sonai, Longai and Dohalia Reserve Forests in Cachar and Karimganj disticts.

+ Dihing Patkai WLS is mainly comprised of Tropical Evergreen Forests.

+ **Hollong**, the tallest tree of Assam & is also the "**State Tree**" is the most predominant constituent of these Forest.

+ The associated Species are – Sam, Nahar, Mekai, Borpat, Jutuli, etc.

2. TROPICAL SEMI EVERGREEN FOREST

Found in Hollangapar, Abhoypur, Dilli, Dhansiri, Mayong, Garbhanga, Rani, Kakoi, Naudar, Batasipur, Dohalia, Singla, Longai, Bhuban Pahar, Sonai, Barak and inner-line Reserve Forest along Northern & Southern part of the state.

Commonly found Trees are – Sam, Siris, Sau, Kakoi, Kodam, Khakan, Hingori, Kanchen, Ou-tenga, Pulsopa, Garoisopa, Teetachapa, Kolajamu, Bogijamu, etc.

3. TROPICAL MOIST DECIDOUS FOREST

It can further be described as Sal forest & they occupy considerable Forest Area in the Central and Lower parts of the state in the Districts of Nagaon, Morigaon, Kamrup, Parts of Nalbari & Barpeta, Darrang, Dhubri, Kokrajhar, Goalpara.

Commonly found Trees are – **Sal**, Ajar, Sam, Bor, Dimoru, Dhupbor, Bot, Gomari, Hilika, Bhomora, Bohera, Poma, etc.

These Forests support Rich Diversity of Shrubby ground Vegetation.

4. SUB-TROPICAL BROAD-LEAF HILL FOREST AND

5. SUB-TROPICAL PINE FOREST

These occur in the districts of **Karbi Anglong** and **Dima Hasao**.

Commonly found species are – **Ban-hanwalu**, etc,

Pure stands of **Khasi-pine** are found particularly in **Hamren** Region.

6. LITTORAL & SWAMP FOREST

It is also called Wetland forests. These forests have almost lost their identity because of biotic pressure on land.

Presently sedges & grasses form the largest component of vegetation.

Imp. Species include: Alocasia, Aplina, Amaranthus, Becopa, Blumea, Bombax Crotolaria species, etc.

7. GRASSLANDS AND SAVANNAHS

These are the major part of vegetation in:

Kaziranga, Dibru-Saikhowa, Manas National Park.

Pobitora, Orang, Sonai-Rupai, Laokhowa, Barnadi, Burachapori WLS

These grasslands support important wildlife population in Assam.

Commonly known species are Nol, Khagori, Kohuwa, Jhao, etc.

FLORA (PLANT SPECIES)

The Orchids of Assam: In Assam as many as **293 species** of **Orchids** are reported which represents **44.39%** of **North-East** species & **24.42%** of species occurring in **India.**

Altogether **38 naturally** growing species of **Bamboo** are recorded in Assam. Bamboo is cultivated widely in Assam and every household grows Bamboo in its House (Bari) land. Commonly cultivated species are Muli Bamboo, Jati Bamboo, Kako Bamboo, Bhaluka Bamboo, etc.

Fourteen **(14)** species of **Cane** grow in cane brakes in forests of Assam.

Assam is home **medicinal plants**. Altogether, **952 plants species** have been identified which have **uses in medical practices**. Asok, Bahok, Bel, Ban Halodhi, Dudhkuri, Mahabhringraj, Satmul, Thekera, Tulsi, Titaphool, etc. are some of the most commonly used plants in treatment of various aliments.

There are estimated **numerous Wetlands**, Ponds and Tanks such as Deepor Beel, Chandubi Beel, Ratabeel, Sohola, Tatalipather, Phokolai, Mer, Sonbeel, Jamjing, Sagunpara, Motapung, Sarlane, Sareswar, Roumari, Khalihamari, Goramga, Sapekhati, etc. They support as Rich variety of aquatic plants.

Mammal Species

- Several big animals includes:

1) Indian One Horned **Rhinoceros**: 2413 in Kaziranga (as per 2018)

2) **Asiatic Elephant**: Population 5620 (as per 2011)

3) **Royal Bengal Tiger**: Population 167 (as per 2014)

4) **Swamp Deer**: Population 1169 (as per 2011)

- **Other species** - Leopard, Asiatic Water Buffalo, Indian Bison (Gaur), Asiatic Wild Dog (Dhole), Himalayan Black Bear, Sloth Bear

- The spotted Deer, Barking Deer, Hog Deer, etc.
- Clouded Leopard (lotamakori Bagh), Marbled Cat, Golden Cat, Large Indian Civat, Small Indian Civat, Binturong (Bonmekuri), Mongoose (Neul), Clawless Otter (Ud)
- **Endangered** species - **Pygmy Hog** (Nol Gahori), Pangolin (Bonrau), Golden Cat, etc.

Primate Species (9 different Species Found)	
SPECIES	POPULATON
Rhesus Macaque	72,674
Assamese Macaque	30,866
Slow Loris (Lajuki Bandor)	431
Pig Tailed Macaque	649
Capped Langur	17,813
Golden Langur (Sunali)	2772
Hoolock Gibbon (Holuo)	1517
Stump Tailed Macaque	648
Spectacled Langur	132

REPTILES

Assam has a rich variety of reptiles – Gangetic Gharial, 19 species of Tortoises and 77 species of Snakes and Lizards.

- Reticulated Python, Indian Rock Python, Burmese Rock Python, Black Krait, Pit Viper, King Cobra, Indian Cobra, Monocled Kobra, etc.
- Assam roofed Turtle (Endemic)

- Indian Soft Shell Turtle
- Monitor Lizard (Bengal Monitor & the Water Monitor)
- Commercially important fish species includes – Rohu, Katla, Pabha, Pabha Chital, Magur, Singi, Sol, etc.

Note: The famous **Golden Mahsheer (Sil-goria)** is found in Assam particularly **Jia Bhorali River**.

BIRD SPECIES

Assam is one of the Endemic Bird areas in the World. With 950 bird species Assam is the home to 53.5% of Bird Species found in Indian Sub-continent.

- 17 species of Birds are Endemic to Assam. (i.e. only found in Assam)
- Grey-headed Fish Eagle (uh-hok), Pallo's Fish Eagle, Indian River Tern (gangsiloni), Red-headed Vulture (roja-sokun).
- Greater Adjutant Stork (Har-gila), Lesser Adjutant Stork (borto-kola), Open Bill Stork (samuk-vonga), Little Cermorant (Pani-kauri).
- Some common Birds – Purple Swamphen (kam-chorai), White Breasted Waterhen (Dauk), Indian Pond Heron (kona-musri), Kingfisher (Mach-ronga), Egret (Bogoli).
- **White Winged Wood Duck (Deo-hash)** = **State Bird** of Assam, Grey headed Goose (dhrito-raj), Spot-billed Duck (bormugi hash), Lesser Wistling Duck (Horali Hash), Ruddy Shell Duck (Chakoi-chakou), etc.

➢ **GE-3.2: Wildlife Species of Assam**

SOME IMPORTANT WILDLIFE SPECIES OF ASSAM

Wildlife Protection

In India Wildlife are protected under the **Wildlife (Protection) Act, 1972**.

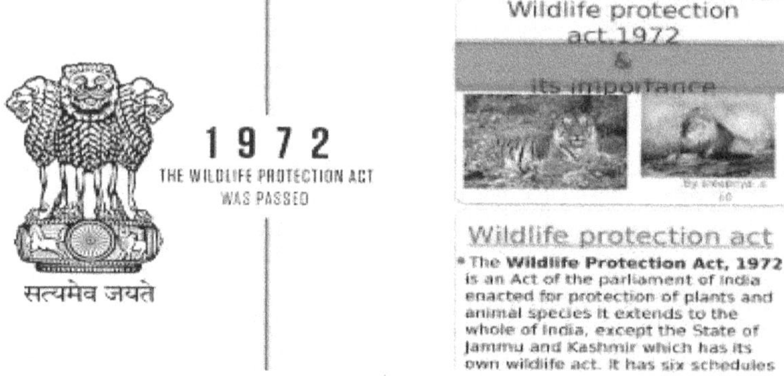

There are 6 schedules in this Act – of which

SCHEDULE – I: Animals have highest protection and they can not be hunted.

SCHEDULE – V: Animals may be hunted without permission (vermin's)

SCHEDULE – VI: This deals with Plants species.

International Union for Conservation of Nature (IUCN) is an international organization for wildlife conservation. It prepares a Red List of wild species which provides the conservation status of a particular Animal such as –

- Critically Endangered (CR)
- Endangered (EN)
- Vulnerable (VU)
- Near Threatened (NT)
- Least Concerned (LC)

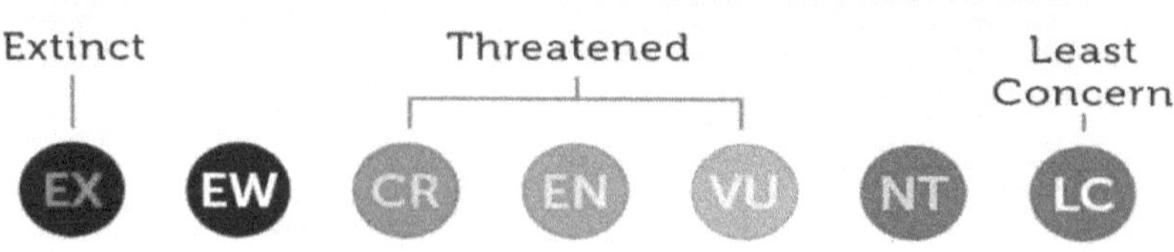

♣ Indian One Horned Rhinoceros

- One horned Rhinoceros native to the Indian Sub-continent.
- It is a thick Grey-brown skin and a horn.
- Its diet consists entirely grass. It inhabits the Alluvial Grasslands of the Terai and River Riverine Forests.
- Main threat – Indiscriminate Poaching for the Horn.
- **Found in** – Kaziranga, Manas, Orang, Pobitora WLS
- Also Found in –
  - o Dudhwa NP – Uttar Pradesh (Terai Region)
  - o Jaldapara NP – West Bengal
- IUCN Status: Vulnerable
- Population: 2413 in Assam (as per 2018 Census)

♣ Bengal Tiger (Dekiya-pothiya Bagh)

- Native to the Indian Sub-continent – India, Nepal, Bhutan, Bangladesh.
- Total Population in Assam is 167 & in India is 2226.
- Main threat – Poaching, Loss & Fragmentation of habitats.
- Found in – Four(4) Tiger Reserves of Assam
  - Kaziranga
  - Manas
  - Nameri
  - RG Orang (declared as Tiger Reserve in 2016) All are under Project Tiger (1973)
- IUCN Status: Endangered

⚡ Asiatic Elephant (Bonoriya Hati)

- Native to the South-east Asia.
- Total Population in Assam is 5281 (2nd Highest after Kerala)
- Main threat – Loss of Fragmentation of habitats & Leads frequent Human-Elephant Conflicts.
- Found in – Five(5) Elephant Reserves of Assam
  - Dihing-Patkai
  - Sonitpur
  - Kaziranga – Karbi Anglong
  - Dhonsiri-Lungding
  - Chirang-Ripu

All are under Project Elephant (1992)

- IUCN Status: Endangered

❏ Asiatic Wild Buffalo (Bonoriya Mo'h)

- Also called Water Buffalo. It is large Bovine native to **Indian Sub-continent** and **South-east Asia.**
- Inhabits the Grasslands, Swamps, River Valleys.
- **Global Population** – 3400 only and 90% found in Kaziranga alone.
- IUCN Status: Endangered

❏ Pangolin (Bon-rau)

- It is **nocturnal mammal** species. It is an Ant & Termite eater. It has large overlapping scales which acts as **Armour**.
- Found particularly in Karbi Hill Region.
- **Major Threat** – Due to hunting for its meat and for various body parts for traditional medicine.
- IUCN Status: Endangered

❑ Pygmy Hog (Nolgahori)

- Very small sized unique species of Wild Pig. It is **Endemic** Animal to Assam, i.e., found only in Assam.
- Significant population in **Manas** National Park. Recently, reproduction in Sona-Rupai.
- **Threat** – Due to habitat loss &human disturbance
- **IUCN** Status: **Critically Endangered**

Assam State Zoo is the only Zoo in the World to house Pygmy Hogs

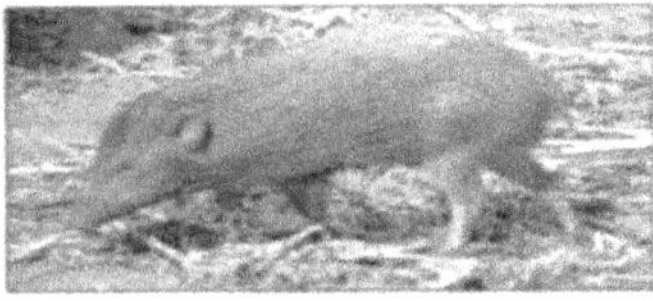

Currently there are two pairs of Pygmy Hog in Assam State Zoo

❑ Gangetic River Dolphin

- It is primarily found in Brahmaputra River System. It is a Fresh-water Mammal species.
- It is National Aquatic Animal & also **State Aquatic Animal** of **Assam**.
- It is also declared as Official City Mascot of **Guwahati**.
- **Threat** – Adversely affected by human use of the River system, Construction of Dams, Pollution
- IUCN Status: Endangered

❑ Slow Loris (Lajuki bandor)

- Official name is **Bengal Slow Loris**.
- It is the only Nocturnal Primate found in Assam.
- Total Population in Assam is 431.
- **They are solitary animal and canopy dwellers.**
- IUCN Status: Endangered

❑ **Golden Langur (Sonali)**

- It is an **Old World Monkey**. Found in Western Assam, India and Bhutan.
- Its habitat is bounded on the South by the Brahmaputra River, on the East by Manas River, on the West by Sonkosh River.
- **Chakrashila WLS** (Dhubri) is home of Golden Langur.
- **IUCN Status:** Endangered

❑ **Hoolock Gibbon (Holou)**

- Hoolock Gibbon is the only **ape** found in India and also found in Bangladesh and China.
- **Other Apes-** Gorilla & Chimpanzee found in **Africa**.
- Found in many **Protected Areas** of **Assam**.
- Its swings from one Tree to another with long arms.
- Found in – **Hollangapar Gibbon WLS** (Mariani, Jorhat) has significant population of Hoolock Gibbon.
- **IUCN Status:** Endangered-West, Vulnerable-Eastern
- Population: 1517 (in Assam)

❑ Swamp Deer (Dol-horina)

- It is different from all other Indian Deer species
- The Antlers of Swamp Deer carry more than **3 tines.**
- Known as Barasingha (12 tines) in North India.
- **Population** – Kaziranga NP has a significant population.
- **IUCN Status:** Vulnerable

❑ White Winged Wood Duck (Deo Hah)

- It is the official State Bird of Assam.
- This is one of largest species of duck. Commonly known as **Deohah of its very loud quack**
- Its current distribution is contracted in the lowlands of eastern parts of Assam. **Nameri** and **Dibru-Saikhowa** has a significant population.
- **IUCN Status:** Endangered

1.4: GE-4: Protected Areas

➢ GE-4.1: National Parks

VARIOUS PROTECTED AREAS OF ASSAM

National Parks	: 7*	Wildlife Sanctuaries:	17* (24)
Tiger Reserves	: 4	Elephants Reserves	: 5
Biosphere Reserves	: 2	Ramsar Sites	: 1
UNESCO Heritage Site	: 2	Important Bird Areas(IBA):	46
Zoological Garden(Zoo):	1	Botanical Garden	: 5

NOTE: Assam now has the 3rd most National Parks after the 12 in Madhya Pradesh and 9 in the Andaman and Nicobar Islands, forest officials said.

1. NATIONAL PARKS (TOTAL – 7)

1. **Kaziranga** – Estd in 1974 – Area: 858 sq. km – Golaghat, Nagaon, Biswanath
2. **Manas NP** – Established in 1990 – Area: 500 sq. km – Chirang and Baksa
3. **Nameri NP** – Established in 1998 – Area: 200 sq. km – Sonitpur
4. **Dibru-Saikhowa** – Estd. in 1999 – Area: 340 sq. km – Dibrugarh & Tinsukia
5. Rajiv Gandhi **Orang** – Estd. in 1999 – Area: 78 sq. km – Darrang & Sonitpur
6. **Raimona NP** – Established in 2021 – Area: 422 sq. km – Kokrajhar
7. **Dihing-Patkai** – Estd in 2021 – Area: 234.26 sq. km – Dibrugarh & Tinsukia

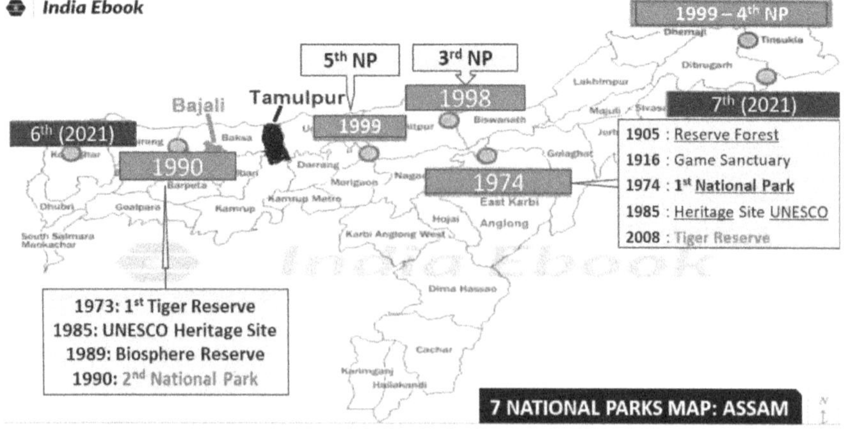

i) KAZIRANGA NATIONAL PARK

Kaziranga NP is world famous for great One-horned Rhinoceros is the oldest and largest National Park in Assam.

Kaziranga is unique mix of Grasslands, Wetlands & Forestlands.

It is located between Brahmaputra in the North and Karbi Hills in the South.

National Highway (**NH-37**) passes through Kaziranga NP.

Its original area was **430 sq. km** but after various additions, its total area is **858 sq. km.**

Kariranga NP spread over Nagaon, Golaghat and Biswanath (carved out from Sonitpur) districts.

Earnier Kaziranga NP was managed under One Adminisreative Division - Eastern Assam Wildlife Division with **Five (5)** Ranges:

a) Kaziranga (Kohora)   b) Eastern Range Agratoli

c) Western Range Bagori   d) Burapahar Range and

e) Northern Range, Biswanath

In **2018**, the Forest Department of Assam announced the bifurcation of Kaziranga National Park into Two (2) Divisions:

    i)   Assam Wildlife Division (Southern Division) and

    ii)   Biswanath Wildlife Division (Northern Division)

SOME IMPORTANT FACTS REGARDING KAZIRANGA NP

1) 1905: Proposed as Reserve Forest

2) 1916: Kaziranga Reserve Forest declared as Game Sanctuary

3) 1974: Declared as National Park

4) 1985: Declared as Natural - World Heritage Site by UNESCO for outstanding universal value.

5) 2008: Declared as Tiger Reserve under Project Tiger (1973)

Some Important Wild Species

Kaziranga NP is known as Land of **Big Five (5)** - One-horned Rhonoceroses, Royal Bengal Tiger, Asiatic Elephant, Asiatic Wild Buffalo, Swamp Deer.

Here, 80% of the World's Population of One-horned Rhinoceroses (2413 Rhinos as per Census).

Highest ecological Density of Royal Bengal Tiger (1 Tiger per 5 sq. km).

Significant Population of Asiatic Elephant.

World's largest Population of Asiatic Wild Buffalo.

Last surviving population of Swamp Deer (Dol-horina)

Kaziranga is also home to Nine (9) Primate species.

ii) MANAS NATIONAL PARK

SOME IMPORTANT FACTS REGARDING MANAS NP

Area: 500 sq km (**2nd Largest in Assam**)

- 1973: Declared as Tiger Reserve under Project Tiger (1973)
- 1985: Declared as UNESCO's World Heritage Site (Natural)
- 1989: Declared as Biosphere Reserve under Man & Biosphere Programme (MAP) of UNESCO.
- 1990: Declared as National Park

LOCATION & IMPORTANT WILD SPECIES (FAUNA)

Located in **Chirang** and **Baksa** Districts and at the base of **Foot-hills** of the **Bhutan-Himalayas**. The **Manas River** (Brahmaputra's Tributary) that transverses through the Park which also serves as an **International Border** between India and Bhutan.

MANAS

Animal Species (Fauna): Royal Bengal Tiger, Indian One-horned Rhinoceros, Clouded Leopard, Black Panther, Asian Golden Cat, Pygmy Hog (CR), Gaurs, Asian Water Buffalo, Barking Deer, Hog Deer (Sugori-pohu), Golden Langur (Sunali-bandar), Assamese Macaques, etc.

iii) NAMERI NATIONAL PARK

SOME IMPORTANT FACTS REGARDING NAMERI NP

Nameri NP is located in the Foot-hills of the Eastern Himalayas in the Sonitpur District of Assam near the bordering Arunachal Pradesh.

1979: It was notified as Reserved Forest

1988: Declared as National Park

1999: Declared as Tiger Reserve under Project Tiger (1973)

The river Jia Bhoroli (Kameng), a tributary of Brahmaputra passes through Nameri.

NAMERI

IMPORTANT WILD SPECIES (FAUNA)

Animal Species: Tiger, Leopard, Clouded Leopard, Gaur, Wild, Wild Pigs, Slow Loris, Palla's Fish-eagle, Lesser Adjutant Stork, White Winged Wood Duck (**State Bird of Assam**).

The most prized & most significant Wildlife in Nameri is the White Winged Wood Duck which has a flourishing population in Nameri officially in 1995.

In Nameri and its adjoining protected areas such as Sonai-Rupai Wildlife Sanctuary Critically **Endangered Pygmy Hog** is **re-introduced**.

Nameri NP is well known for the significant population of World Famous **Golden Mehseer** (Silghoria)

iv) DIBRU-SAIKHOWA NATIONAL PARK

SOME IMPORTANT FACTS REGARDING DIBRU-SAIKHOWA

Area: 340 sq km

1890: Declared as Dibru Reserved Forest

1997: Declared as Biosphere Reserve by Man & Biosphere Programme (MBP) of UNESCO.

1999: Declared as National Park

Feral horses are its Prime Attraction of Dibru- Saikhowa and its current population is more than 80. These horses have a World War-II connection.

Feral Horses are descended from domestic horses that strayed, escaped, or were deliberately relaeased into the wild & remained to survice and reproduce there.

LOCATION & IMPORTANT SPECIES (FAUNA)

Located in **Dibrugarh** and **Tinsukia** Districts & it is the Assam's eastern-most NP. It is an Island formed by Brahmaputra and Dibru River.

Animal Species: Tiger, Elephant, Leopard, Jungle Cat, Small, Indian Civat, Squirrels, Slow Loris, Assamese Macaque, Rhesus macaque, Crapped Langur, Hoolock Gibbon, Wild Pig, Sambar, Barking Deer, Water Buffalo, Gangetic Dolphin (City Muscot of Guwahati).

It is also an **IBA** (Important Bird Area) having more than 382 species of Birds. Some important Bird Species found - Greater Adjutant Stork, Lesser Adjutant Stork, Grey-headed Fishing Eagle, Open Bill Stork.

v) RAJIV GANDHI ORANG NP

SOME IMPORTANT FACTS REGARDING RG ORANG

Area: 78.80 sq. km (Assam's Smallest)

1915: Declared as Reserve (oldest)

1999: Declared as a National Park

2016: Declared as Tiger Reserve under
   Project Tiger (1973)

Orang is located in Sonitpur and Darrang district on the Northern Bank of Brahmaputra.

Important Species: One-horned Rhinoceros and Tiger

RG Orang is also paradise for Migratory Birds sauch as Spot-billed Pelican, Black-necked Stork (Toliya Sarang), Greater Adjutant Stork (hargila) etc.

vi) RAIMONA NATIONAL PARK

IMPORTANT FACTS OF RAIMONA

Located in Kokrajhar Districts.

Area: 422 sq. km

2021: Declared as National Park.

Raimona, on the other hand, will be administered by the Kachugaon Forest Division of Bodoland Territorial Council. The area was one of the oldest reserve forests of the State.

Raimona adjoins the **Buxa Tiger Reserve** in **West Bengal** to its west, **Phipsoo Wildlife Sanctuary** in **Bhutan** to its north and the first addition to Manas National Park to the east.

vii) DEHING PATKAI NP

SOME IMPORTANT FACTS REGARDING DEHING PATKAI

Dehina Patkai

Area: The 234.26-sq. km

2021 (June): Declared as National Park

Dihing Patkai straddling eastern Assam's Dibrugarh and Tinsukia districts is a major elephant habitat.

310 species of butterflies have been recorded there.

The park has **47 species** each of **Reptiles and Mammals**, including the Tiger and Clouded Leopard.

Dihing Patkai, in focus two year ago for illegal coal mining in the vicinity, encompasses the erstwhile Dehing Patkai Wildlife Sanctuary, the Jeypore Reserve Forest and the western block of the Upper Dihing Reserve Forest.

THE HINDU:
DEHING PATKAI IS THE ASSAM'S
7TH NP Ranking:

1. Madhya Pradesh – 12 National Parks
2. Andaman & Nicobar Is. – 9 National Parks
3. Assam – 7 National Parks

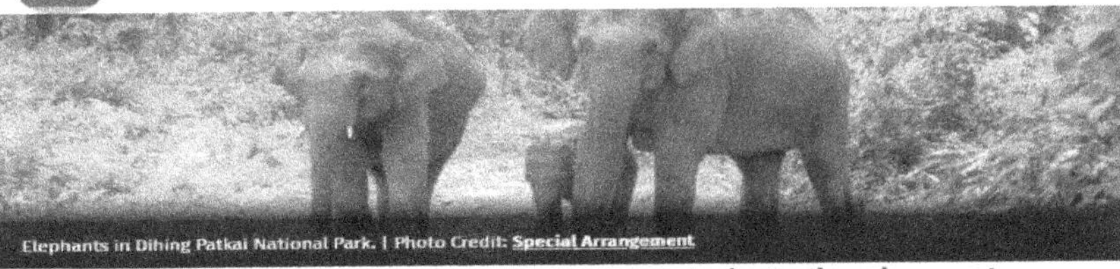

➢ GE-4.2: Wildlife Sanctuaries (WLS)

WLS covered Below=17 + 7 (NPs are also WLS), i.e., Total WLS=24

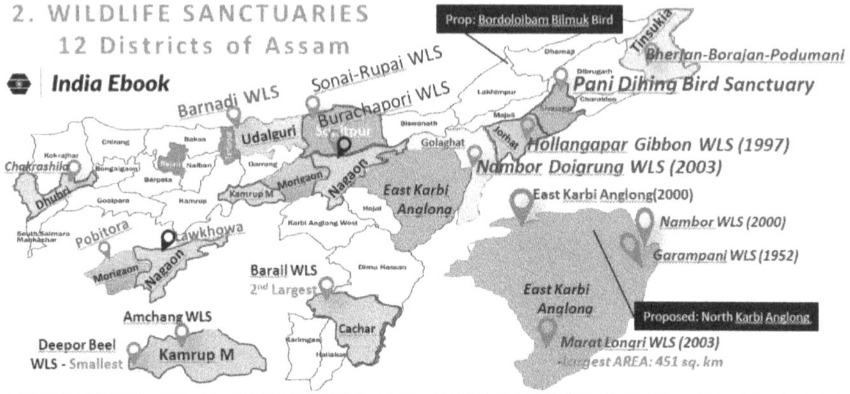

Wildlife Sanctuaries of Assam

SL	NAME	ESTD.	AREA	DISTRICT(S)
1	Garampani	1952	6.05	Karbi Anglong
2	Lawkhowa	1972	70.14	Nagaon
3	Barnadi	1980	26.22	Udalguri
4	Pobitora	1987	38.81	Morigaon
5	Chakrashila	1994	45.56	Dhubri
6	Burachapori	1995	44.06	Sonitpur
7	Pani Dihing Bird Sanctuary	1995	33.93	Sivasagar
8	Hollongapar Gibbon	1997	20.9	Jorhat
9	Sonai Rupai	1998	220	Sonitpur
10	Bherjan-Borajan-Padumani	1991	7.22	Tinsukia

Wildlife Sanctuaries of Assam

SL	NAME	ESTD.	AREA	DISTRICT(S)
11	East Karbi Anglong	2000	6221.81	Karbi Anglong
12	Nambor WLS	2000	37	Karbi Anglong
13	Marat Longri WLS **(Largest)**	2003	451	Karbi Anglong
14	Nambor Doigrung WLS	2003	97.15	Golaghat
15	Amchang WLS	2004	78.64	Kamrup(M)
16	Barail WLS (2nd Largest)	2004	326.25	Cachar
17	Deepar Beel WLS (Smallest) RAMSAR	**1989**	4.14	Kamrup(M)
P1	Bordoibam-Bilmukh Bird (Proposed)			Dhemaji, Lakimpur
P2	North Karbi Anglong WLS (Proposed)			Karbi Anglong

NOTE: Before June 2021, Dehing Patkai is WLS. Upto May 2021= 18 WLS, From **June 2021=17 WLS**

WILDLIFE SANCTUARIES

According to **Wildlife protection Act, 1972**, a sanctuary is an area which is of adequate ecological, faunal, floral, Geo-morphological, natural or zoological significance. The Sanctuary is declared for the purpose of protecting, propagating or developing wildlife or its environment.

Certain human activities like harvesting of timber, collecting minor forest products and private ownership rights are allowed inside sanctuaries.

Boundaries of sanctuaries are not well defined.

Wildlife Sanctuaries in Assam

At present there are **(17+7=24)** Wildlife Sanctuaries in Assam. The combined area of these sanctuaries is 1840 sq. km which covers 2.35% of total area of the state.

Largest Wildlife Sanctuary - Marat Longri WLS, Karbi Anglong (451 sq. km)

Smallest Wildlife Sanctuary - Deepor Beel WLS, Kamrup Metro (4.14 sq. km)

Number of Bird Sanctuary - 2 (Pani-Dihing and Deepor Beel)

District with highest number of **Wildlife Sanctuaries** - Karbi Anglong (4 WLS)

SOME IMPORTANT WILDLIFE SANCTUARIES

Garampani WLS (Karbi Anglong) - Famous for *Hotwater springs*. Homeland for a number of Primate Species.

Pobitora WLS (Morigaon) -Famous for *highest density of Indian One-horned Rhino.*

Chakrashila WLS (Dhubri) -Home of *Golden Langur* locally known as Sunali bandor.

Pani-Dihing WLS (Sivasagar) - It is a **Bird Sanctuary** bordered by Dishang and Brahmaputra River. It is famous for more than 70 species of migratory birds.

Hollongapar Gibbon WLS (Mariani, Jorhat) -It is the habitat of *Hollock Gibbon* which is locally known as Holou Bandor.

Amchang WLS (Kamrup Metro) -It is located in the outskirts of Guwahati City. It is facing threat to illegal encroachment. Eviction drive was done in 2018 directed by Gauhati High Court.

Deepor Beel WLS (Kamrup Metro) -Basically a Bird Sanctuary and Wetland located outskirts of Guwahati City. It is the only Ramsar Site in Assam.

TIGER RESERVES

Government of India has **'Project Tiger'** in **1973** for conserving the national animal - Bengal Tiger and 53 Tiger Reserves have been notified till date.

Project Tiger is administered by **National Tiger Conservation Authority (NTCA).**

There are **4 Tiger Reserves** in Assam:

Manas - 1973

Nameri - 1999

Kaziranga - 2008

RG Orang - 2016

ELEPHANT RESERVES

Government of India has **'Project Elephant'** in 1992 to protect Elephants and their habitats.

The are **5 Elephant Reserves** in Assam:

Dihing Patkai - Dibrugarh, Tinsukia

Kaziranga-Karbi Anglong - Sonitpur, Nagoan, Golaghat, Karbi Anglong

Dhansiri-Lungding - Karbi Anglong, Nagoan, Dima Hasao

Chirang-Ripu - Kokrajhar, Chirang, Baksa, Udalguri

Sonitpur – Sonitpur

➢ GE-4.3: BIOSPHERE RESERVES

Biosphere Reserves unique are natural and cultural landscape extending over large area of terrestrial or marine ecosystems. The concept of Biosphere id developed by UNESCO's Man and Biosphere (MAB) programme.

There are **18 Biosphere** reserves in India.

Out of which **2 Biosphere** Reserves in Assam:

Manas (1989)   Dibru-Saikhowa (1997)

WORLD HERITAGE SITES

The **United Nations Educational, Scientific and Cultural Organization (UNESCO)** designates World Heritage Sites of outstanding universal value to cultural or natural heritage which have been nominated by countries which are signatories to the **UNESCO** World Heritage Convention, established in **1972**.

As of 2022, there are **40 World Heritage Sites** located in India. Out of these, 32 are cultural, 7 are natural, and 1, the Khangchendzonga National Park, is of mixed type. India has the sixth largest number of sites in the world.

Out of which **2 Heritage Site** (natural) in Assam:

Kaziranga (1985)   Manas (1985)

RAMSAR SITES

Ramsar Convention is an international treaty under certain Wetlands of ecological importance are designated as ramsar Sites.

There are **80 (75 old+5 new) Ramsar Sites** in India (as of **2nd February 2024**) out of which there is **only 1 Ramsar site** in Assam.

Deepor Beel - It is declared in **2002**. It is located in the outskirt of Guwahati with an area of **4.14 sq. km**.

The national-level celebration of **World Wetlands Day** (2nd Feb), 2018 has been organised at Deepor Beel.

<u>**Tamil Nadu**</u> continues to have maximum number of Ramsar Sites **(16 sites)** followed by <u>**Uttar Pradesh (10 sites)**</u>.

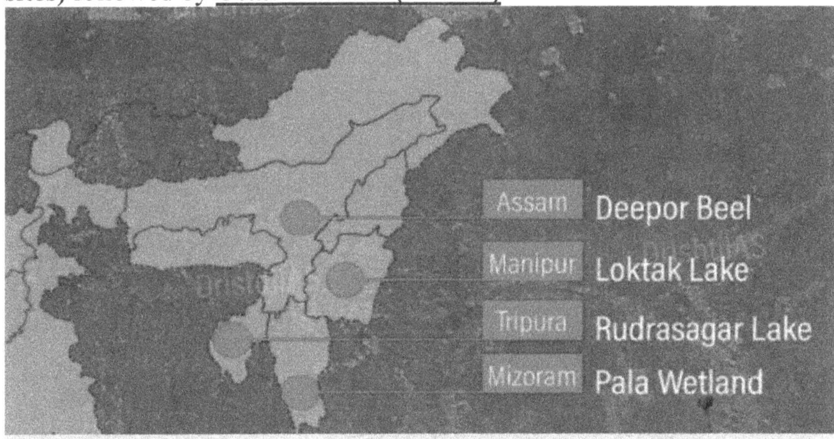

Ramsar sites in India(75 old)

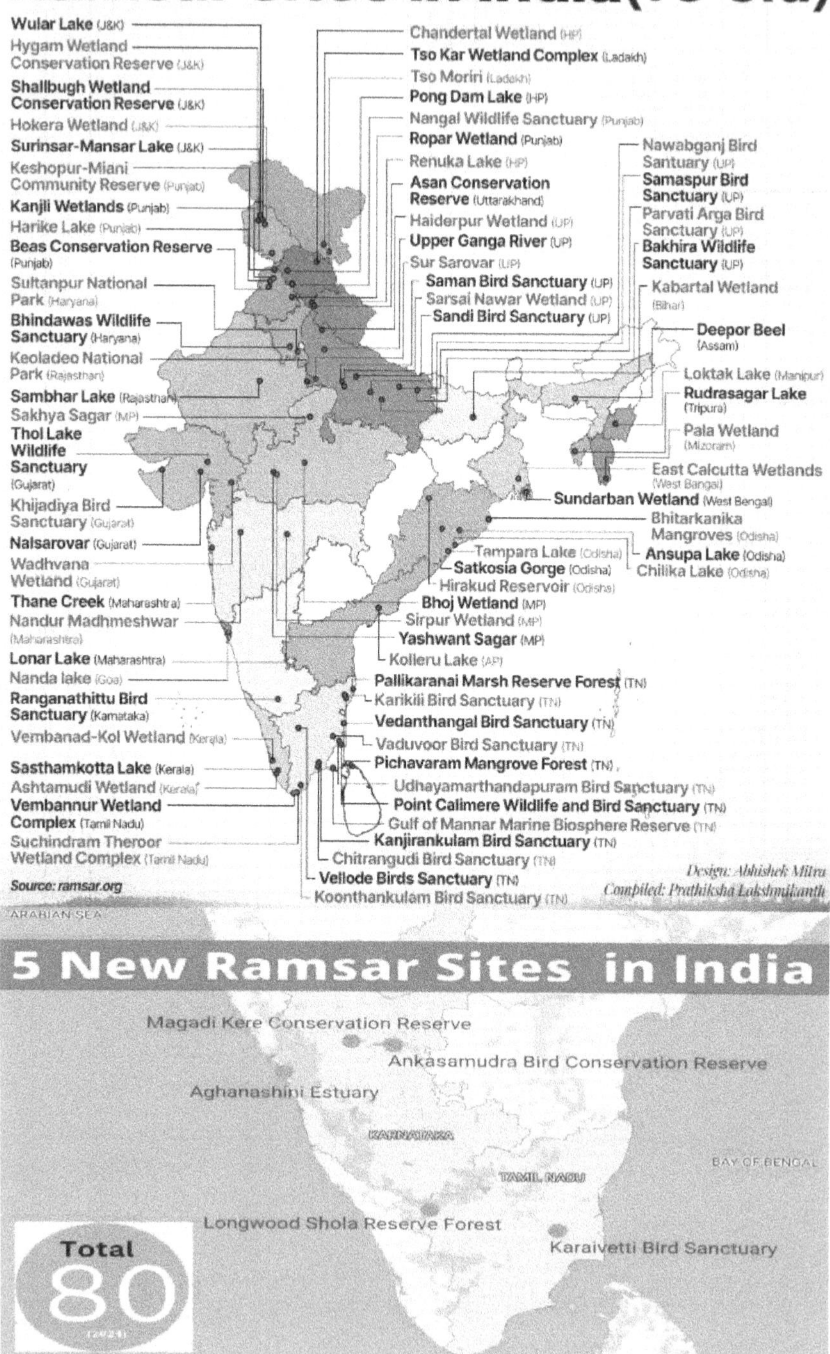

ZOOLOGICAL GARDEN (ZOO)

The Assam State Zoo is located in the **Hengrabari Reserve Forest** in **Guwahati**.

It is the largest Zoo in North East with an area of 1.75 sq. km.

It was established in the year 1957 and opened to public for the first time in the year 1958.

There is a **Rhino Breeding Centre** and a **Botanical Garden** in the State Zoo.

About 600 animals, birds and reptiles are kept.

BOTANICAL GARDEN

There are **5 Botanical Gardens** in Assam as per official records of Assam State Forest Department.

- Botanical Garden, Assam Sate Zoo, Guwahati
- Botanical Garden, Halflong
- North east Ecology Park, Regional Research Laboratory, Jorhat
- Institute of Rain & Moist Decidous Forest Research (Plantations), Jorhat
- Regional Research Centre (Ayurveda), Govt Ayurvedic College, Guwahati

NOTE: MCQs of Geography given in next Chapter:-2.5

2. ASSAM'S ECONOMY

GE-5: Agriculture
GE-6: Mineral and Power Resources
GE-7: Industry
GE-8: Transport and Communication   **GE-9: MCQs**

2.1: GE-5: Agriculture

➤ **Agriculture – Major Crops and Horticulture**

Agriculture of Assam at a Glance

☐ Around **75%** of the state's population depends on agriculture for their livelihoods as farmers or agricultural labourers or both.

☐ The share of Agriculture Sector in Gross State Domestic Product of Assam is **12.2%** in 2017-18.

☐ Total cropped area is **40825** sq km. (52%)

☐ Net area sown is **28273** sq.km.

Major Crops grown in Assam

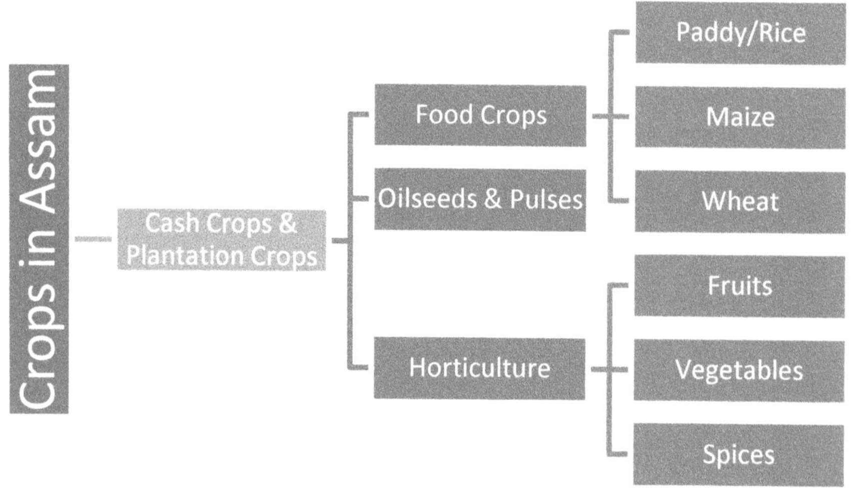

Rice or Paddy

☐ Rice or paddy is the main crop of Assam and also the staple diet.

☐ The total area under rice cultivation is 24.67 lakh hectares, which is 92.50% of the total area under food grains.

Rice Varieties

☐ **Winter Rice (Sali Dhan)** – It is the most important crop and it consists of 71% of rice area and 73% of the total rice production.

Growing season June to December. It is a long duration crop and grown transplanted. Sub classes are Sali and Lahi (fine grain).

Bao is another type of winter rice grown in deepwater.

☐ **Summer rice (Boro Dhan)** – Summer rice is traditionally grown in low-lying areas during November to May/June. Generally transplanted in fields with irrigation facilities and minimal tillage. High productivity compared to other two types.

☐ **Autumn Rice (Ahu Dhan)** – Grown under variable water depth. Very less productivity.

- Joha (Aromatic rice), Bora (Waxy rice), Komol or Chokowa (Soft rice) are some important local varieties of rice in Assam.

Wheat

☐ Mostly new alluvial soils are found suitable for growing wheat in Assam. Wheat has been successfully grown in the lower Brahmaputra valley comprising the districts of Dhubri, Goalpara, Kokrajhar, Bongaigaon, Barpeta , Nalbari and Kamrup.

☐ Wheat growing area occupies about 3 % of the total cropped area in the state.

Maiza

☐ It is another important Kharif crop. Mostly grown in hill areas like Karbi Anglong, Dima Hasao etc through Jhum cultivation. Also grown in plain areas.

Pulses

☐ Assam has around **4.70%** of the total food cropped area under Pulses in the country and contributes **only 0.5%** of the **national pulse production.**

☐ Among major varieties Black gram (Matimah) is predominant. Other varieties are Arhar, Gram(boot), Green Pea (Motormaah), etc.

☐ In earlier times, during the period of **Ahom rule**, Black gram and sticky rice were used as materials to build monuments, in place of cement due to its sticky nature.

☐ Pulses are mainly grown in alluvial flat lands near Brahmaputra particularly Goalpara, Barpeta and Kamrup.

☐ The production as well as the productivity of is far below due to the socio-economic and climatic condition.

Oilseeds

- Oil seeds contribute about **5 % of the total cropped area** in **Assam.**
- Rapeseed and Mustard are major oilseeds and accounts for **92% of total oil seeds** production in Assam
- Major mustard growing districts are Barpeta, Dhubri, Nalbari, Kamrup, Morigaon, Darrang, Sonitpur, Lakhimpur and Dhemaji.
- Mustards are mainly grown as rainfed crops in alluvial soils.
- Apart from these Sesamum(til), linseed(tisi), Castor(era) Coconut (narikal) are also grown.

Horticulture

- Major fruits are Bananas, Pineapple, Papaya, Jackfruit, Orange, lemons, etc.
- Banana is an important garden crop and several varieties are grown like Monohar, Chenichampa, Malbhog, Bhimkal, Jahaji, etc.
- Pineapple is an important fruit crop of North Cachar Hills.
- Turmeric, Ginger, Chillies- These are the major spices produced in Assam, mainly grown in hilly areas.
- Assam is an Agri Export Zone of Turmeric and Ginger.
- Ghost Chilli – It has high commercial demand. It is used as pepper spray.
- **DRDO** has developed a chilli grenade using **Ghost Chilli.**
- Areca Nut- It is traditionally grown in homelands of Assamese households. Betel leaf, Pepper, Mushroom, etc.

Non- food crops

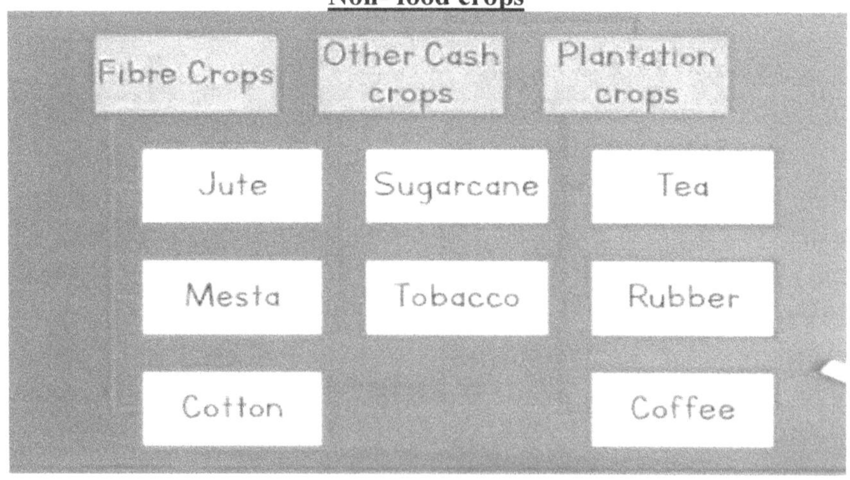

Assam also grows fibre crops mainly Jute, Cotton and Mesta.

Jute- It is the main fibre crop in Assam. It is grown in low lying areas during the monsoon.

Mainly grown in Dhubri, Goalpara, Barpeta, Nalbari, Darrang, Morigaon, Nagaon districts.

After cutting the trunks, they are kept under water to rot. Fibres are extracted from the barks.

Jute production has gradually declined over the years due to less demand. Total annual jute production is 8.6 lakh tonnes in 2015-16.

Mesta and Cotton

Mesta is another minor fibre crop, basically a rainfed crop. Can be grown in both high and low rainfall areas.

Cotton is another fibre crop. In hilly areas, cotton is cultivated in Jhums.

Seeds are sown and ripens in Nov-Dec.

The cotton of Assam is not good to spin to thread. It has very less demand.

Other Cash Crops

Sugarcane- It is a **traditional crop** in Assam and grown in highlands. It is planted between January- March. In Assam sugarcane is produced as a source of **jaggery and molasses.**

Tobacco- It is cultivated mostly for chewing and hookah. Districts of Goalpara and Cachar are important for its production. It is transplanted in November and harvested in Feb-March.

PLANTATION CROPS OF ASSAM

TEA

Tea is the major plantation crop in Assam. **Assam produces 51%** of total tea in India.

The indigenous tea of Assam was first brought to notice in **1823** by **Robert Bruce**. In **1838, Assam tea was sent for sale** in the **U.K.**

The climate considered most favourable to tea culture is characterised by small daily rise in temperature, generous rain throughout the year and absence of strong dry winds and freezing temperature.

◻ Tea is grown at **elevations** ranging from **45 to 60 meters** above sea level.

◻ Types- Both **Orthodox** and **CTC** (Crush-Tear-Curl) varieties of tea are produced in Assam.

◻ The **Assam orthodox Tea** has a registered Geographical Indication Tag (GI).

◻ In **Tocklai**, there is a **Tea Research Institute** which is the **world's oldest and largest research station** of its kind.

◻ In Guwahati, a **tea auction centre** is located (established 1970)

◻ There are as many as **85,344 tea gardens** in Assam with a cropped area of **3 lakh hectare.**

◻ Tea gardens are mainly concentrated in Upper Assam, Sonitpur, Nagaon and some parts of Barak Valley.

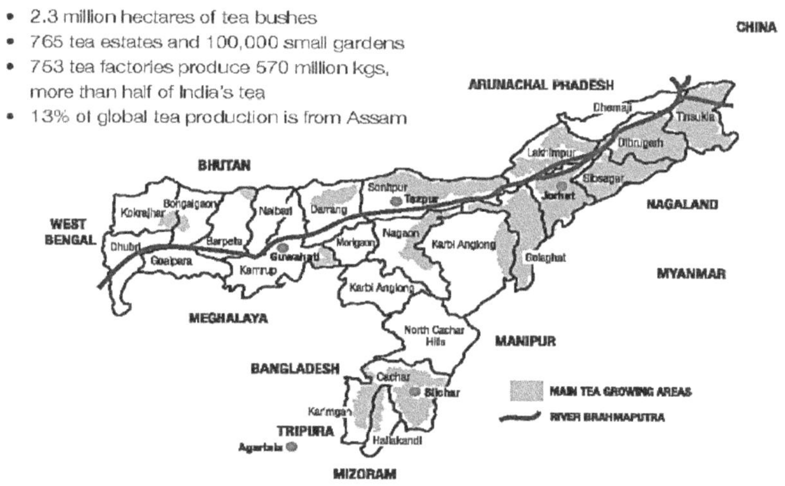

- 2.3 million hectares of tea bushes
- 765 tea estates and 100,000 small gardens
- 753 tea factories produce 570 million kgs, more than half of India's tea
- 13% of global tea production is from Assam

Rubber

◻ Rubber is another **plantation crop** in Assam. Rubber tree grows up to **30 m tall** and it starts yielding **latex at 6-7 years age.**

◻ Rubbers are used in many products from erasers to tubes, tyres and industrial products. Area under Rubber cultivation **57,646 hectares**.

Coffee

◻ Coffee is another plantation crop. Both **Arabica** & **Robusta** varieties are grown. Coffee was introduced in **North Cachar Hills** in **1954**.

☐ Coffee gardens are mostly located in **Dima Hasao and Karbi Anglong** in lower foothills. Harmati, Hamren, Chuti Nala, Mahur, Lasong Asalu, Gunjang are coffee gardens.

☐ Area under coffee cultivation- 1120 hectares.

Sericulture, Animal Husbandry & Fisheries

➤ Sericulture

☐ Sericulture is a traditional practice particularly in the rural economy of Assam.

☐ It is now an agro-based cottage industry of Assam

☐ Assam is placed **3rd** in **raw silk production** in India.

First - Karnataka and Second - Andhra Pradesh.

☐ The main centre of silk handloom and textile industry is **Sualkuchi** in Kamrup.

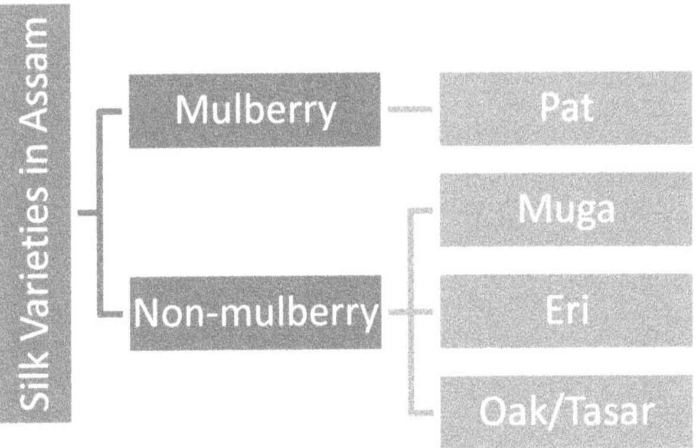

<u>Pat (Mulberry silk)</u>

☐ It is a brilliant white or off-white coloured silk thread and bulk of the commercial silk produced in the world comes from this Silk.

☐ It is derived from Mulberry Silkworms that feed on the leaves of <u>**Mulberry Plant**</u> locally called **Nuni**.

☐ Mulberry plant is cultivated widely in plains of Assam and neighbouring hilly areas.

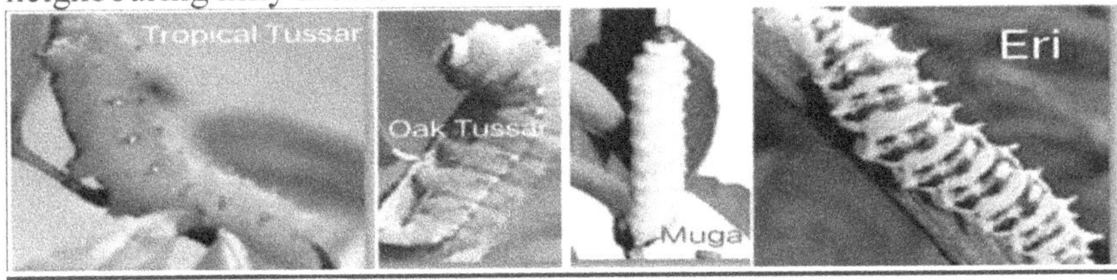

Muga Silk

It is a unique Golden Yellow silk thread and it has unique texture, lustre and durability.

Muga silk is obtained from Muga Silkworms which are basically wild. However, Muga silkworms are reared domestically and they fed mainly on Som and Soalu.

More than **97% of Muga Silk** in the world is produced in Assam

Muga silk worm rearing in Assam is suffering due to high climatic pollution, extreme temperature and continuous rearing under domestic nature.

Eri Silk

It is derived from Eri Silkworms. They feed on two major host plants-Castor and Kesseru. **65% of Eri silk** is produced in **Assam**.

Ericulture is a household activity. The silk is used **indigenously** for preparation of **Cheddars (wraps)** for own by local communities.

Oak /Tassar

Oak tasar silkworms are completely wild in nature. They feed on Oak plants. These silkworms are reared in wild combination in the Oak plantation available in North Cachar Hills, Karbi Anglong and Goalpara.

Animal Husbandry

Livestock in the state is highly livelihood oriented and is generally owned by small and marginal farmers and landless agricultural labourers.

Almost 90% of the rural households keep livestock of one species or another.

Livestock of Assam consists of cattle (63%), Goat (21%), buffaloes (5.8%), pig (8.62%) and sheep (0.66%).

Fisheries

Assam has a record of a total of **217 fish species**. Around 160 fish species i.e., more than 30% of the total freshwater fish varieties are found in Assam. **Catla, Rohu, Mrigal** are major carps in Assam.

☐ Eel fish and Prawns are also produced commercially.

☐ Botia, Chital, Chanda, Puntius are those varieties of fishes which are exported from Assam.

☐ The total contribution of the fishery sector to the State Domestic Product was 2.6% and total fish production – 2.49 metric tonnes (2015-16).

☐ Nagaon district has the highest area and quantity of fish production.

☐ There is also a fishery college in Roha, Nagaon.

☐ Dhubri, Cachar, Nagaon – these districts have the highest numbers of registered beel fisheries and river fisheries.

2.2: GE-6: Mineral and Power Resources

➢ **Minerals in Assam at a Glance**

☐ Assam is rich in mineral resources particularly in Crude oil, Natural Gas, Coal.

☐ Assam is poor in Ferrous and non-Ferrous metal ores.

☐ Assam is the Fourth largest producer of Crude Petroleum.

☐ Assam ranks Ninth in minerals production and it has contributed about 4% to the total value of mineral production in the country.

Minerals in Assam	Major Deposits	Coal
		Crude Oil
		Natural Gas
		Sulphur
	Minor Deposits	Granite
		Iron Ore
		Silimanite
		China Clay
		Fire Clay
		Quartz
		Fuller's Earth

Coal

☐ Coal in Assam was **first recorded** by **British Surveyor Lieutenant Wilcox in 1825** at **Borhat** near Disang river.

☐ In **1876, Mr. Mallet** examined the coal fields of Upper Assam into two fields- Makum and Jaipur.

☐ **First systematic coal mining** was done in **1882 at Ledo** by the erstwhile Assam Railways and Trading Company.

☐ After **independence**, the survey of the coal resources of assam was started by the **Central Fuel Research Institute at Dhanbad** in **1953**.

☐ There are **three major coalfields** in Assam

- o Makum Coalfields
- o Mikir Hills Coalfields
- o Dilli- Jeypore Coalfields

☐ Apart from these, Coking coal is found in **Singrimari coalfields** in Dhubri district.

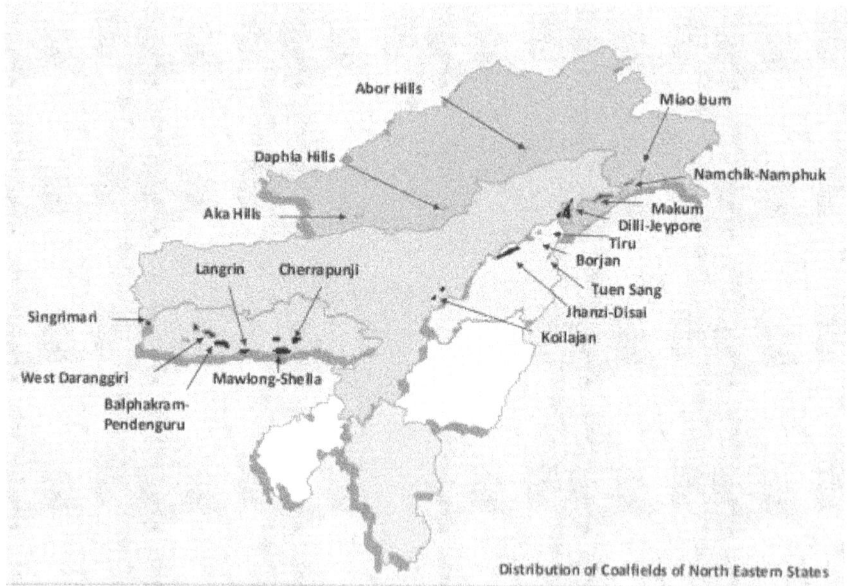

☐ **Makum Coalfields**- It is the oldest coalfield in Assam. It is located near Margherita in Tinsukia district.

☐ Important collieries are Ledo, Borgolai, Namdang, Tipong, Tirap, Tikak.

☐ **Dilli Jaypore** – Located at the Tirap foothills in Sibsagar and Dibrugarh districts.

◻ **Mikir Hills** - Located in Karbi Anglong district. Kailajan and Silbheta are important collieries.

◻ Mining cost is higher and coal quality is poor in comparison to other coalfields.

◻ Estimated coal reserve in Assam is 510MMT.

◻ In Assam, mainly tertiary coal is found. The coal of Assam has low moisture, high Sulphur, low ash and high volatile matter. Due to higher Sulphur content, the coke produced in Assam coal is unsuitable for metallurgical purposes and also for boilers.

◻ North Eastern Coalfields (Unit of Coal India Ltd.) looks after the coal mining in Assam.

◻ Both opencast and underground mining is done in Assam coalfields.

Crude Oil (Petroleum)

History of Crude oil in Assam

1828: 1st Discovery of Existence of Petroleum by Lieutenant Wilcox

1867: Successful Strike at oil at Makum

1889: 1st Well at Digboi Drilled

1901: Owned & operated by Assam Oil Company Ltd.

◻ Currently Crude Oil exploration is carried by ONGC and OIL India Limited.

◻ Refining is carried by **Indian Oil Corporation (3 refineries)** and **Numaligarh Refinery Limited -NRL (1 refinery).**

Oil Fields in Assam

◻ Two hydrocarbon basins – Upper Assam shelf and Assam-Arakan basin .

☐ 90% of the Upper Assam shelf and 10% of Assam – Arakan basin explored.

☐ Digboi oilfield- In the easternmost part of Assam , it was the first oil field in Asia. It was taken by OIL in 1981.

☐ Naharkatiya Oilfield- Located in Dibrugarh, it was discovered in 1953. It has five oil sand horizons.

☐ Moran oilfield- It is located in Dibrugarh and was discovered in 1956.

☐ Rudrasagar Oilfield- It is located in Sivasagar. Oil struck ONGC in 1960.

☐ Lakwa Oilfield – Located in Sivasagar and is managed by ONGC.

☐ Some more oilfields in Assam- Sonari, Amguri, Geleki, Dikom, Doomdooma, Kathaloni, Panidihing, Baghjan, Borhola, Namti, etc.

There is a good deal of debate among Marxist scholars on theoretical and methodological issues. Recently a group of Marxist historians, the '**Subaltern Studies**' group, has begun to study 'history from below'. They criticise the 'traditional' Marxist historians for ignoring the history of the masses, as if the 'subaltern' classes do not make history of their own, depending solely on the advanced classes or the elite for organisation and guidance.

Natural Gas

☐ In Assam, Natural gas is mostly found as associated gas with petroleum. Produced in the course of production of crude petroleum.

The Natural Gas production in Assam is 14% of the offshore production and 10% of total Natural gas production in India.

Petrochemicals industries like Namrup Fertilizer Plant, Assam Petrochemicals Limited, Brahmaputra Cracker and Polymer Limited use Natural Gas to produce various Petro- chemical   products.

Limestone

Limestone is an important mineral resource.

It is mainly used in manufacturing of Cement and flux material in metallurgical purpose (eg. Iron and steel production)

Limestone are mainly found in Karbi Anglong and Dima Hasao. Main deposits in Karbi Anglong are Silbheta, Koliajan, Sainilangso, Dillai Parbat.Deposits in North Cachar Hills are Panimur, Timbung, Umrangsu.

Annual Production – 442 Thousand MT.

Other Minerals

Iron Ore- In Assam low grade iron ore deposits are found in Goalpara district. Chanderdinga Hills has the highest deposits. Also found in Langapara, Kumri, etc. Small deposits are also found at Hahim, Kamrup.

Granite- Granite deposits mainly Pink Granite and Black Granite are found in Goalpara, Kamrup and Karbi Anglong.

Major deposits are- Mahamaya, Centre Bazar- Karbi Anglong, Agiya Hills, Dudhkuri Hills- Kamrup , Kakira, Khutamari – Goalpara.

Sillimanite- It is a refractory material. The important deposits are in Karbi Anglong district namely Chippilangso, Ingtigaon, Samelangso, Upper Chelabor and Amternag and also Nagaon district.

Clay – Various types of clay deposits occur in Assam. Fireclay is used in brick making and cement manufacture. Fireclay deposits are found in Tinsukia, Dibrugarh, Karbi- Anglong, Dima Hasao and Lakhimpur.

China clay – It is also known as Kaolin. It is mostly used in the manufacture of porcelain, files, paper, etc. Important deposits are in Upper Deopani, Sheelvata, Silonijan area of Karbi Anglong.

Fuller's Earth – A soft clay used in fire bricks and pottery. Important deposits are in Subankhata in Baksa on the bank of Pagladia river.

Quartz and Feldspar- Quartz is used in glass manufacturing. Small deposits are found in Hahim in Kamrup and Silbheta and Rangachali in Karbi Anglong.

◻ **Gypsum**- It is used in **plaster of paris(POP)**. Found in Karbi Anglong.

◻ **Sulphur**- It is not found in a free state. Tertiary coals in Assam contain high sulphur and it can be extracted from them.

◻ **Lithomarge, Ochre and Mica**- Lithomarge or white clay occurs at Nambar valley. The total reserve of Lithomarge is estimated at 35 lakh tones. Ochre occurs in the foothills of Kamrup. Mica occurs in Barigaon in Kamrup.

Power Resources

Power

◻ Earlier power distribution was operated under the **Assam State Electricity Board (ASEB)**.

◻ In 2004, ASEB was converted into three Public Sector companies.

◻ They are:

-The Assam Power Generation Corporation Limited (APGCL)

-The Assam Electricity Grid Corporation Limited (AEGCL)

-The Assam Power Distribution Company Limited (APDCL)

◻ The present installed capacity of APGCL is 364 MW.

There are **four running power generation projects** under **APGCL**

◻ **Lakwa Thermal Power Station (LTPS)** - Established in 1981, it is located in Maibella in Charaideo district. It produces power from Natural Gas. It has the highest power generation capacity – 127 MW

◻ **Namrup Thermal Power Station (LTPS)** - Established in 1965, located in Namrup, Dibrugarh. It produces power from Natural Gas and it has Gas Turbine and Waste Heat Recovery units. Power generation capacity at 99 MW.

◻ **Karbi Langpi Hydro Electric Project** - It is located in Lenegery, Karbi Anglong. It has two turbines and installed capacity is 100 MW.

☐ **Myntriang Small Hydro Electric Project** - It is located in Karbi Anglong. It has two turbines and installed capacity is 3 MW.

☐ There are **two thermal power stations** at Chandrapur, Kamrup and Amguri, Sivasagar. But they were shut down.

☐ APGCL has some other proposed projects-

PROJECT NAME	CAPACITY (MW)
Lower Kopili Hydro Electric Project	120
Borapani Small Hydro Electric Project, Karbi-Anglong	25
Margherita **Thermal** Power Project	1600

☐**Kopili Hydro Electric Project** - It is located on the Kopili river in Umrangso, Dima Hasao district and is operated by NEEPCO. The first and the largest Hydro Electric Project in Assam started in 1976. It has power stations – Khandong and Kopili and its present capacity is 275 MW.

☐ North Eastern Electric Power Corporation (**NEEPCO**) is a central PSU established in 1976 for hydel and thermal generation of power in North East Region. It operates the Ranganadi Project Arunachal Pradesh and Doyang Project Nagaland.

☐ **National Thermal Power Station** (earlier **Bongaigaon** Thermal Power Project) - A under construction Coal based power plant located at Salakati, Koikrajhar. First commissioned in 1981. However, due to technical problems it could not deliver the targeted power and it was shut down.

☐ **National Thermal Power Corporation (NTPC)** - It is setting up a new power plant at the same location. The total capacity is 750 MW and 500 MW has been commissioned by 2017. It will use Coal from the coalfields of Makum and Dilli-Jeypore.

2.3: GE-7: Industry

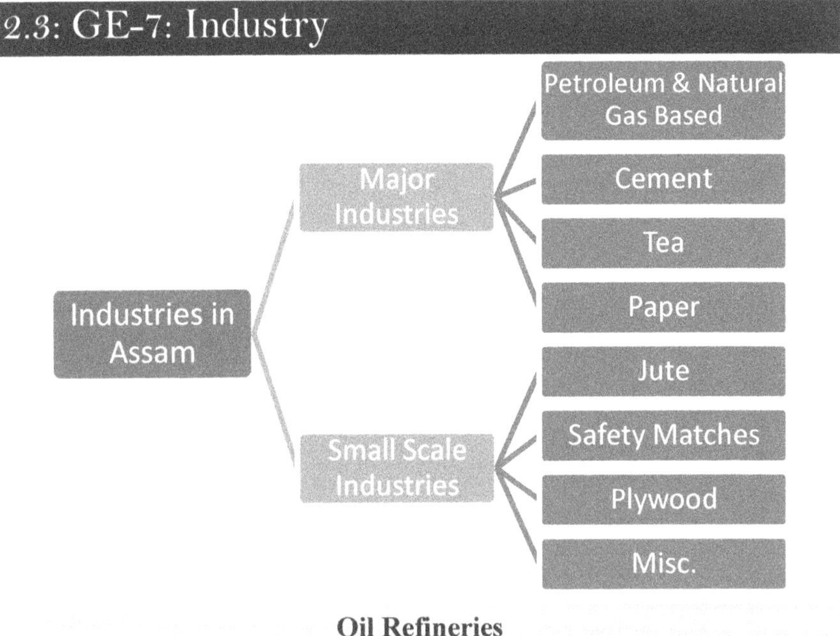

Oil Refineries

◻ **Digboi Refinery**- It was set up in **1901** by Assam Oil Company. It is the **first Oil Refinery in Asia** and has been termed as the **'Gangotri'** of the **Indian Hydrocarbon sector.**

- In **1981**, Digboi refinery was **taken over** by **Indian Oil Corporation**.

- The products are Motor Spirit, Superior Kerosene, Diesel, Furnace Oil, Bitumen, Petroleum Coke, etc.

- Some special products are Solar Oil, Jute Batching Oil and most importantly Paraffin Wax.

◻ **Guwahati Refinery-** It was set up in **1962** and it is the **first Public Sector Refinery of India** as well as the **first refinery of Indian Oil Corporation.** It was built with **assistance** with **Romania**.

- The Refinery refines the crude oil found at Naharkatia, Hoogrijan and Moran in Upper Assam which comes through **Oil India Limited** pipelines.

- The products are- LPG, Motor Spirit, Aviation Turbine Fuel, Kerosene Oil, High Speed Diesel, Light Diesel Oil and Raw Petroleum Coke.

◻ **Bongaigaon Refinery-** It was set up in 1979 as Bongaigaon Refinery & Petrochemicals Limited (BRPL). In 2009, it was merged with **Indian Oil Corporation**.

- It refines crude oil from Oil fields in Assam and Rawa Oil fields in Andhra Pradesh .
- Specialty products are Needle coke, Solvents(Petrosol and Bonmex – II), Naphtha, etc.
- The refinery has won several awards for its green initiatives- National Award for 'Prevention of Pollution', Indira Gandhi Paryavaran Puruskar

☐ **Numaligarh Refinery**- It was set up at **Numaligarh in Golaghat** in accordance with the **provisions made in the historic Assam Accord.**

- It was **commissioned in 1999** and owned and operated by Numaligarh Refinery Limited – **joint venture** between Bharat Petroleum Corporation, Oil India Limited and Govt. of Assam(12% share).
- It is the **largest refinery in Assam.**
- Specialty products are- Wax, Nitrogen, Mineral Turpentine Oil (MTO), Special Boiling Point Spirit (SBPS), Liquid Sulphur.

Natural Gas

☐ **Assam Gas Company** – It is a public sector undertaking of Assam Govt., set up in 1962 for distribution of Natural Gas.
- Its headquarter is in Duliajan.
- It has a network of underground distribution pipelines that supplies Natural Gas to the Tea estates, Domestic consumers and several big industrial consumers in Dibrugarh, Tinsukia, Sivasagar, Jorhat, Golaghat and Cachar.

☐ **Duliajan Numaligarh Pipeline Limited** - It is a joint venture between Assam Natural Gas Company Limited (AGCL), Numaligarh Refinery Limited (NRL) and Oil India Limited (OIL).
- It will be the first major cross-country natural gas pipeline in Assam.

Petro-Chemical Industry

☐ **Assam Petro Chemical Limited, Namrup** - Assam Petro-chemicals Limited is a Petrochemical complex set up in Namrup in 1971 for productive utilization of natural gas produced in Upper Assam Oil Fields.

- The first production started in 1976 with technology transfer from Japan.
- Main products are – Methanol and Formalin.

- It is a public sector company. The shareholders include Assam Industrial Development Corporation Ltd (AIDC), Assam Government and Public.

- It is the first company in the North Eastern region to have a public issue of shares.

☐ **Brahmaputra Valley Fertilizer Corporation (Namrup Fertilizer Plant) -** It was set up in 1962 and located on the Namrup (Dibrugarh) on the bank of Dilli river.

- Natural Gas, Sulphur, Phosphorus are basic raw materials.

- It is the **first fertilizer factory in India** which uses Natural Gas as basic raw materials for producing nitrogenous fertilizer.

- Initially the main products were Urea and Ammonium Phosphate.

- Currently there are a number of products- Pilled urea, Neem Coated Urea, Bio-fertilizer and Vermicompost.

☐ **Brahmaputra Cracker and Polymer Limited (BPCL) -** It is a Petrochemical Complex at Lepetkata in Dibrugarh commissioned in 2016.

- It was set up as a part of implementation of the famous Assam Accord signed on 15th August 1985.

- The main objective is to convert the Natural Gas produced during Crude Oil exploration into useful Polymers.

- BPCL procures Natural Gas from OIL and ONGC.

- The principal end products are High Density Polyethylene and Linear Low Density Polyethylene.

- Other products Poly-Propylene, Hydrogenated Pyrolysis Gasoline, Pyrolysis Fuel Oil.

☐ **Wax Plant, Numaligarh Refinery Limited -** The Wax Plant of Numaligarh Refinery Limited was commissioned in 2016.

- It is the largest wax producing unit of India with indigenous technology developed by Indian Institute of Petroleum - Dehradun, Engineers India Limited and NRL.

- Main products are Paraffin Wax (used in candles, PVC pipes etc) and Microcrystalline Wax (used in treys, rubbers, paint, etc).

- Apart from domestic supply, the produced wax has been exported to a number of countries viz., Mexico, Poland, Brazil, China, etc.

Tea Industry

☐ Tea was **first discovered** in Assam in **1823** by Robert Bruce.

☐ The **first Indian Tea** produced in **Assam** was **sent to the United Kingdom** for public sale in 1838.

1839: Assam Company started commercial Tea plantation & production	**1859: Jorhat Tea Company was formed**	**1911: Toklai Research Station to research on cultivation & manufacture of Tea**

Cement Industry

☐ Assam has a good quantity of Limestone. **Cement Manufacturing** constitutes the most important **use of limestone**.

☐ The <u>**Cement Corporation of India**</u> has set up the **Bokajan Cement Factory** in Bokajan, Karbi Anglong, Construction was started in **1971** and **production started in 1977.**

☐ It collects limestone from Limestone deposits in Karbi Anglong.

☐ The main product is Portland Cement.

☐ Apart from these, there are <u>**a number of private sector cement factories**</u> in Umrangso, Dima Hasao, Sonapur, Guwahati, etc.

<u>Other Industries</u>

Paper Industry

☐ Assam has rich bamboo resources for development of paper industry. The <u>**first Paper and Pulp Mill of Assam**</u>- **Ashok Paper Mills** was set up at **Jogighopa** in Bongaigaon in **1971.**

☐ The **Hindustan Paper Corporation** has set up the **second paper mill of Assam in 1981** at **Panchgram** in Hailakandi district. It also <u>**set up another paper mill in 1985**</u> at **Jagiroad** in Morigaon district.

☐ Currently all <u>**these three mills are shut down**</u> and efforts are underway to revive them. The **Kamrup Paper Mills Ltd.,** is the *only private sector small factory* located in **Amingaon** in the Kamrup district.

Sugar Industry

- The **first sugar mill of the state** is Assam Cooperative Mill was set up at <u>**Barua Bamun Gaon in Dergaon**</u> in **1955**.
- The **2nd sugar mill** was set up in **Chargola** in **Karimganj.**
- In **1986**, a sugar mill was established at **Kampur** in Nagaon with capacity 1250 tonnes. But at present the mills are in the closing stage.
- Apart from these medium scale mills, some small sugar mills were also set up at Biswanath Chariali and Manja and Hawaipur in Karbi Anglong.

Jute industry

- Assam produces a **good quantity of jute**.
- In **1971**, a full fledged large **Jute Mill** was established under the Cooperative sector in **Silghat** in Nagaon district.
- The Silghat Jute Mill is the first Cooperative jute mill in India.

Spinning Units

- In **1961**, a cotton spinning mill was set up at **Chariduar in Sonitpur** district. It was a <u>**private sector mill**</u> and the name was **"Assam Cotton Mills".**
- In **1963**, a spinning unit was set up at <u>**Chandrapur in Guwahati**</u> by <u>**Associated Industries Ltd**</u>. But it was **handed over to** the **National Textile Corporation.**
- Some other small mills and power looms are located in **Changsari, Dhamdhama, Badarpur,** etc.

Spun Silk Industry

- There is a spun mill at **Jagiroad** in Morigaon district set up in 1961.
- The mill produces yarn from Endi, Muga and Pat Silks.

Plywood Industry

- Timber is the most important raw material and suitable timbers are available in the forests of Assam.
- Assam has around <u>**50 plywood factories**</u> where plywood's produced are mainly used in making Tea Chests for packaging.
- The industry is now in declining trend due to absence of raw material.

Safety Matches Industry

- Simalu timber is the main raw material for safety matches.

☐ Due to its abundance of Simalu timber in Goalpara, Kamrup and Nagaon, the Assam match company (run by a Swedish company) set up a match factory at Dhubri in 1924 .

☐ The factory was able to produce 7% of the total requirement in India.

☐ Consequently a small match splint factory was set up at Bijni in 1963.

☐ Later both of these units were taken over by Western India Match Company.

Industrial Infrastructure and Trade Facilities

☐ At present, Assam Industrial Development Corporation (AIDC) has developed several Industrial estates, Industrial Growth Centres, Infrastructure Development Centres, Technology Parks in Assam.

☐ **Three** new Industrial Growth Centres (IGC) has been set up-

- **IGC Balipara (Sonitpur):** Industries are Patanjali Ayurveda Ltd. , Dabur India, Ltd.
- **IGC Matia (Goalpara):** Industries like Everyday India Ltd.
- **IGC Chaygaon–Patgaon-Jambar (Kamrup):** The **Bamboo Technology Park is located here.**

☐ **Export Promotion Industrial Park (EPIP)** – It is located at Amingaon (Kamrup) where a number of industrial units are producing export quality products. It is sponsored by the Ministry of Commerce, Govt of India.

☐ **AIDC** – It has also developed a number of Integrated Infrastructure Development Centres with assistance from the Ministry of Small and Medium Enterprises, Govt of India.

- These centres are located in – Demow, Dalgaon, Naltali, Malinibeel, Titabor, Silapathar, Nalbari, Moran, Pathsala.

☐ **Plastic Park**- It is being set up at Gelapukhuri, Tinsukia with assistance from the Ministry of Chemicals & Fertilizers, Govt of India.

- It will facilitate production of plastic items using the polymer products of BCPL, Lepetkata (Gas Cracker).

☐ **Mega Food Park** – It is being set up at Nathkuchi, Tihu in Nalbari with assistance from the Ministry of Food processing Industry.

☐ **Bamboo Technology Park** - It is located in Industrial Growth Centre, Chaygaon. It facilitates the production of various types of value added Bamboo products.

☐ **Tea Park** - It will be set up at Chaygaon, Kamrup.

☐ **Jute Park** - It will be set up at Dhing, Nagaon.

Trading facilities

☐ To facilitate foreign trade with neighbouring countries Bangladesh, Bhutan and Myanmar.

☐ **Five Border Trade Centres** are in Assam:

i) Border Trade Centre, Golakganj(Dhubri)- Indo Bangladesh Border.

ii) Border Trade Centre, Mankachar (Dhubri)- Indo Bangladesh Border

iii) Border Trade Centre, Sutarkandi(Karimganj)- Indo Bangladesh Border

iv) Trade Facilitation Centre, Jagun(Tinsukia) – Indo- Myanmar Border

v) Border Trade Centre, Darrang (Baksa)- Indo -Bhutan Border.

2.4: GE-8: Transport and Communication

Mode of Transport in Assam

- Road Transport
- Railways
- Inland Waterways
- Air Transport

➢ **Road Transport**

History of Road Transport

☐ During the reign of **Naranarayan**, The Gohain Kamal Ali was built from **Cooch Behar upto Lakhimpur**, which later became parts of **NH-31** and **NH-52**.

☐ The road on the South Bank of Brahmaputra from **Pancharatna (Goalpara)** to **Saikhowa (Tinsukia)** was built during World War II and known as Assam Trunk Road or the **AT Road** and now it is known as **NH 37**.

☐ The road on the North Bank of Brahmaputra from **Baihata Chariali** to **Murkongselek** in Dhemaji is known as North Trunk Road and now it is known as **NH 52**.

☐ Another road from **Srirampur** to **Baihata Chariali** is designated as **NH31**.

Road Transport

☐ At present the **total road network in Assam** is 58202 km.

☐ The road network in Assam as on 2017 is given below in the table-

CATEGORY OF ROADS	TOTAL LENGTH (IN KM)
National Highway (NH)	3900
State Highway	3134
Major District Road	4379
Rural Road	37030
Urban Road	1615

National Highways

☐ The National Highways are very important and comprise about 7% of the road network and carry about 40% of the total road traffic.

☐ Some major National Highways in Assam are given in the table below:

Highwaym(NH)	Route
31	Srirampur (West Bengal Border) – Baihata Chariali
52	Baihata Chariali – Jonai
37	Panchatantra (Goalpara) – Saikhowa
39	Numligarg – Nagaland Border

State Highways

☐ State Highways are important roads which link district headquarters and important cities and connect them with National Highways or highways of the neighbouring states.

☐ In Assam, the State highways are maintained by the **Public Works Department (PWD).**

☐ There are **53 State Highways** with a total length of 3134 km.

☐ Some Ahom age roads have also been designated as State Highway. **For example-** Dhudor Ali as **State Highway 1**.

Some Major State Highways

State Highway	Length (km)	District
SH-1	210	Golaghat (Kamargaon), Jorhat (Titabor), Sivasagar (Nazira), Dibrugarh (Joypur)

SH-2	161	Bongaigaon, Nalbari, Barpeta, Kamrup
SH-4	61	Darrang (Mangaldoi), Udalguri (Bhutan Border)
SH-10	103	Baksa, Nalbari, Udalguri, Kamrup, Darrang
SH-21	31	Lakhimpur, Jorhat (Kamalabari)
SH-25	8 (Shortest)	Tinsukia (Jugan) to Miao
SH-33	62	Jorhat, Golaghat (Nagaland Border)

Bridges over Brahmaputra

Brahmaputra river is known as life line of Assam state and separate the north east states with rest of India, There are 6 rail and road bridges have been constructed over the Brahmaputra in Assam and four new bridges are proposed.

☐ Dhola Sadiya Bridge, Dhola Sadiya – **9.15 km**

Dhola Sadiya Bridge or Bhupen Hazarika Bridge across the mighty Brahmaputra River (Lohit River, a major tributary of the Brahmaputra River) is the longest bridge in India and become operational in 2017.

The 9.15 kilometres long road bridge connect the states of Assam and Arunachal Pradesh. PM Narendra Modi inaugurates **India's longest road bridge** over Brahmaputra river on 26 May 2017.

☐ Bogibeel Bridge, Dibrugarh – 4.94 km Rail Cum Road Bridge

Bogibeel Bridge across the Brahmaputra river in Dibrugarh is be the longest road and rail bridge in India. The 4.94 kilometres long road cum rail bridge will connect Dhemaji district and Dibrugarh district of Assam. This is also **Asia's 2nd longest rail-cum-road bridge**, longest combined rail and road bridge in India and second longest bridge in Assam after Bhupen Hazarika Setu

☐ Saraighat Bridge, Saraighat, Guwahati

Saraighat Bridge in Guwahati is the first rail cum road bridge over mighty Brahmaputra river in Assam. The Saraighat Bridge over the river Brahmaputra links the North East region with the rest of the country.

☐ Kolia Bhomora Setu, Tezpur

Kolia Bhomora Setu is a 3.15km long road bridge over the Brahmaputra river near Tezpur, connecting Sonitpur with Nagaon. The bridge is one of the most important links between the North Eastern states and rest of India.

☐ Naranarayan Setu, Jogighopa

Naranarayan Setu is another important road cum rail bridge over the Brahmaputra river in Assam, connecting Jogighopa with Pancharatna. The 2.284 kilometres long double deck bridge is listed as one of the most impressive rail cum road bridges of India.

☐ New Saraighat Bridge, Guwahati

The 1.49 km long new Saraighat Bridge over the Brahmaputra river near old Saraighat rail cum road Bridge was inaugurated in year 2017.

This is the second bridge on Brahmaputra river at Saraighat.

☐ Proposed Bridges over Brahmaputra

There are three new bridges which have been proposed for construction by the Government over the River Brahmaputra and the project reports are under preparation.

National Highway	Location	Length (km)	Agency entrusted
127 B	Between Dhubri in Assam and Phulbari in Meghalaya	14	NHIDCL (National Highways and Infrastructure Development Corporation Ltd)
52 & 57	Between Gohpur on NH 52 and Numligarh in NH 37.	12	NHIDCL (National Highways and Infrastructure Development Corporation Ltd)
715	Between Kaupati and Rowta	12	PWD Assam

Assam state Transport Corporation (ASTC)

☐ On 16th January, 1948, a wing 'Road Transport, Assam' was set up under the Home Department of Assam Government. In 1950, it was reconstituted as a separate Transport Department of Government of Assam

☐ The Assam State Transportation Corporation was set up in 1970 uner Road Transport Corporation Act, 1950. It began with only two buses running between Nagaon and Guwahati for a distance of 123 kms.

Now there are 135 stations and three Inter-State Bus Terminals(Guwahati, Jorhat and Silchar) with a fleet of 1100 buses.

➢ RAILWAYS IN ASSAM

History of Rail Transport in Assam

- The first railway line in Assam was the Dibru Sadiya Line .
- The construction of the line was done in 1882-1884.
- The railway construction was done to evacuate tea, oil and timbers produced in the Upper Assam region and move them to the steamer port in Brahmaputra.
- In 1985, Jorhat Provincial Line was constructed to connect tea producing areas in Mariani with Nimati Ghat.
- In 1892, Assam Bengal Railway was incorporated. The headquarter of Assam Bengal Railways was at Chittagong(present – day Bangladesh)
- In 1942, the Assam Bengal Railway was combined with the Eastern Bengal Railway to form the Bengal and Assam Railway.
- In 1947, Bengal and Assam Railway was split into Assam Railway and East Indian Railway respectively.
- In 1952, two railway systems- Assam Railway and Oudh and Tirhut Railway was combined and North East Frontier Railway was formed.

Northeast Frontier Railway

- Northeast Frontier Railway is one of the railway zones in India with its headquarter in Maligaon, Guwahati.
- It is responsible for all rail operations in the entire Northeast and parts of West Bengal and Bihar.
- It has three divisions in Assam- Lumding, Rangiya and Tinsukia.
- Two other divisions- Katihar(Bihar) and Alipurduar(West Bengal).
- Major junctions are Tinsukia, Rangiya, Chaparmukh, Rangapara, North Kamakhya.
- Major routes or sections – New Jalpaiguri- New Bongaigaon
  - Rangia- Murkongselek
  - Guwahati- Lumding
  - Lumding-Dibrugarh
  - Lumding-Silchar
- In 1903, the hill section of the NFR was constructed linking Badarpur and Lumding . It was an iconic metre gauge railway through 37 tunnels in North Cachar Hills . This line was closed recently and replaced with a new broad gauge with 11 tunnels.

Key facts regarding Rail Transport in Assam

- The railways in Assam falls under North East Frontier Railways (NFR) Zone.
- Assam has a total railway route of length 2440.39 km., at present which is around 3.7% of the total Railway Route length of the country.
- Gauge Conversion of Lumding-Silchar-Jiribam(Manipur) and Rangiya – Murkongselek (Dhemaji) has been completed.
- Guwahati Railway Station has been made the first station in North East to run on 100% solar power.

Air Transport

- Assam is well connected with the rest of the country through Air transport.
- There are Six operational civil airports in the state.
- They are-

Name	Location
Lokapriya Gopinath Bordoloi International Airport	Guwahati
Rowriah	Jorhat
Mohanbari	Dibrugarh
Lilabari	Lakhimpur
Salonibari	Tezpur
Kumbhirgram	Silchar

- The Rupshi airport at Dhubri district of Assam is lying closed and non-functional for a long time.
- Lokpriya Gopinath Bordoloi International Airport is the only international airport in Assam. Direct flights up to Bhutan, London, USA, etc.
- Direct flights up to Singapore were introduced in September, 2018.

Inland Water Transport

- In 1839, a fleet of country boats for carrying goods between Assam and Bengal started by Assam Company Limited.
- In 1841, the first Steamboat 'The Assam' was launched by Assam Tea Company for navigation on the river Brahmaputra.
- In 1950, there was a set back river navigation due to heavy earthquake on the river Brahmaputra.

In 1968, the Directorate of Inland Water Transport, Assam started its function.

Present Scenario of Inland Water Transport

In 1988, the stretch of river Brahmaputra from Dhubri(Bangladesh Border) to Sadiya was declared as National Waterway -2.

The National Waterway-2 extends for a distance of 891 km and is fully operational with the following stretches – Dhubri(Bangladesh border) to Neemati, Dibrugarh to Neemati and Dibrugarh to Sadiya (Oriumghat)

Important terminals in NW-2 are- Dhubri, Jogighopa, Pandu, Tezpur, Biswanathghat, Silghat, Neemati(Jorhat), Dibrugarh, Sengajan, Panbari, Oriumghat and Sadiya.

Inland Waterways Authority of India is responsible to develop the waterway for navigation.

At Dhubri Terminal, Roll on Roll Off service is available.

At present the waterway is being used by vessels of Govt. of Assam, Security Forces, Tourism vessel and Private Operators, Oil Companies, cement manufacturers cargo services.

The ferry services operate under the Directorate of Inland Water Transport, Assam.

Communication

Important facts regarding Communication

The Assam Postal Circle has a network of 4012 Post Offices(2017).

Assam Telecom Circle of Bharat Sanchar Nigam Limited (BSNL) is the oldest telecom operator in Assam which was formed in 1987.

Private mobile service providers are also operating in Assam.

In 1948, the Guwahati Station of All India Radio was established.

At present there are **Six(6) All India Radio Stations** in Assam – Guwahati, Dibrugarh, Tezpur, Silchar, Diphu, Kokrajhar.

In 2009, Krishna Kanta Handique Open University started the first community radio service – Jnan Tranga in Assam.

In 2011, Guwahati University launched another community radio service – Radio Luit.

Television broadcasting started in Assam after Guwahati Doordarshan Kendra was set up in 1982.

2.5: MCQs – ASSAM'S GEOGRAPHY & ECONOMY (1-160)

GE 01- Which of the following states is not situated to the east of Assam?

a)   Manipur   b)   Nagaland

c)   Mizoram   d)   Arunachal Pradesh

Ans- c) Mizoram

GE 02- Area wise the rank of Assam among the north eastern states is-

a)   First   b)   Second

c)   Third   d)   Fourth

Ans- b) Second

GE 03- Which of the following north eastern states shares the longest boundary with Assam?

a)   Mizoram   b)   Nagaland

c)   Meghalaya   d)   Arunachal Pradesh

Ans- c) Meghalaya

GE 04- Which of the following north eastern states shares the shortest boundary with Assam?

a)   Mizoram   b)   Manipur

c)   Nagaland   d)   Tripura

Ans- d) Tripura

GE 05- Which of the following is adopted as the state tree of Assam by the Govt. of Assam?

a)   Sal   b)   Hollong

c)   Titachapa   d)   Teak(Segun)

Ans- b) Hollong

Explanation- Hoollong was adopted as the state tree of Assam by Govt. of Assam in 2003, It is the tallest tree found in the forests of Assam. Hollong is a medium hardwood, timber tree.

GE 06- Assam is located between which of the following longitudes?

a)   89'5 E & 96'1 E   b)   24'3 E & 27'58 E

c)   68'7E & 97'25 E   d)   None

Ans- a) 89'5 E & 96'1 E

GE 07- In which year the capital of Assam shifted from Shillong to Dispur?

a)   1971   b)   1972

c)   1973   d)   1974

Ans- b) 1972

Explanation- Meghalaya was created as a full-fledged state carving out of Assam in 1972 and Shillong became the joint capital of both Assam and Meghalaya.

Then the Government of Assam decided to shift the capital to Dispur, then first sitting of the budget session of the Assam Legislative Assembly was held at the temporary capital at Dispur on the 16th March, 1973.

GE 08- In which year Assamese was adopted as the official language of Assam?

a)   1947   b)   1960

c)   1971   d)   1985

Ans- b) 1960

Explanation: According to the Assam official Language Act, 1960, Assamese shall be used for all or any of the official purpose of the State of Assam.

•   As per Article 343 of the constitution, English may be also used for official purposes of the Secretariat and offices of the Heads of the Departments of State Government.

•   In 2014, Assamese was withdrawn from Barak Valley as the official language. Bengali is the official language in Barak Valley.

GE 09- Area wise the rank of Assam among the Indian States is-

a)   13   b)   15

c)   17   d)   20

Ans- c) 17

Explanation- The area of Assam is 78,434 sq. km. Its rank is 17th and covers 2.38% of the total area of the country.

GE 10- Which of the following is the first North Eastern state to carved out of Assam as a full-fledged state after Independence?

a)   Nagaland   b)   Mizoram

c)   Meghalaya   d)   Arunachal Pradesh

Ans- a) Nagaland

Explanation- After Independence of India in 1947, the Naga hills area remained a part of the province of Assam. In July 1960, Government of India recognized the formation of Nagaland as a full-fledged state within the Union of India.

GE11- Which river separates Karbi plateau with Naga plateau?

a) Dhansiri b) Subansiri
c) Jia Bharali d) Kopili

Ans- a) Dhansiri

GE 12- Which district of Assam has the highest number of Tea Garden?

a) Tinsukia b) Dibrugarh
c) Jorhat d) Nagaon

Ans- b) Dibrugarh

GE 13- Purnima Devi Barman from Assam is known for conservation of which species?

a) White winged wood duck b) Greater Adjutant Stork
c) One-Horned Rhino d) Feral Horses

Ans- b) Greater Adjutant Stork

GE 14- Marat Longri wildlife sanctuary is located in which of the following districts?

a) Karbi Anglong b) Udalguri
c) Dima Hasao d) Golaghat

Ans- a) Karbi Anglong

GE 15- Feral Horses are found in which of the following protected areas in Assam?

a) Nameri National Park
b) Dibru Saikhowa National Park
c) Manas National Park
d) Orang national Park

Ans- b) Dibru Saikhowa National Park

GE 16- Amchang WLS is located in which is located in Kamrup Metro is famous for __________

a) Birds b) Snakes
c) Gibbons d) Raptiles

Ans- a) Birds

GE 17- There are 3 Ramsar sites in Northeast, of which how many Ramsar sites in Assam-

a)   1   b)   2

c)   3   d)   None

Ans- a) 1

GE 18- Oak Tasar a wild silkworm is found in Dima Hasao districts of Assam is used to produce ____________ silk.

a)   Mulberry   b)   Non-mulberry

c)   Both   d)   None

Ans- b) Non-mulberry

GE 19- The total number of seats in legislative assembly in Assam is-

a)   126   b)   80

c)   33   d)   None

Ans- a) 126

GE 20- Which of the following States-pair is Bicamral?

a) Uttar Pradesh-Bihar   b) Maharashtra-Karnataka

c) Andra Pradesh-Telengana   d) All of these.

Ans- d) All of these

GE 21- Which of the following districts has the lowest literacy rate in Assam?

a)   Dhubri   b)   Dima Hasao

c)   Karbi Anglong   d)   Hailakandi

Ans- a) Dhubri

Explanation- As per census 2011, Dhubri has the lowest literacy rate of 59%.

• Kamrup has the highest literacy rate of 88.66%.

• Jorhat has the second highest literacy rate and highest urban literacy rate.

GE 22- Which one of the following districts of Assam has the highest sex ratio?

a)   Baksa   b)   Jorhat

c)   Karbi Anglong   d)   Nogaon

Ans- a) Baksa

Explanation- Baksa has the highest sex ratio- 974 per 1000 male (2011 census).

GE 23- Population wise the rank of Assam among the states of India is-

a)   10   b)   14

c)   24   d)   26

Ans- b) 14

Explanation- Population wise the rank of Assam is 14 among the states of India.

GE 24- The rank of Assam regarding the sex ratio among the states of India is-

a)   12   b)   13

c)   14   d)   15

Ans- d) 15

Explanation- As per 2011 census, the sex ratio of Assam is 958 per 1000 males.

•   The sex ratio of India is 940 per 1000 males.

GE 25- The percentage of population living in the urban areas in Assam according to 2011 census is-

a)   12   b)   14

c)   16   d)   20

Ans b) 14

Explanation- The exact percentage of population living in urban areas in Assam according to 2011 census is 14.09%.

•   Kamrup(M) has the highest urban population.

•   Nagaon has the highest rural population(24,57,906).

GE 26- Which of the following district has the lowest population density?

a)   Karbi Anglong   b)   Dima Hasao

c)   Hailakandi   d)   Dhemaji

Ans- b) Dima Hasao.

Explanation- Dima Hasao has the lowest population density of 44 people per sq. km. Kamrup(M) has the highest population density 1314 people per sq. km.

GE 27- The population density per sq. km in Assam according to 2011 census?

a)   398   b)   340

c)   368   d)   381

Ans- a) 398

Explanation- It was 340 per sq. km in 2001. Assam ranks 15th in terms of population density among Indian states.

GE 28- The maternal mortality rate(MMR) in Assam is-

a) 113   b) 227

c) 300   d) None

Ans-a) 113

Explanation- The MMR of Assam dipped to 113 per lakh live birth in 2016-18.

GE 29- Which of the following districts in Assam has the highest population growth rate?

a) Barpeta   b) Nagaon

c) Dhubri   d) Kamrup(M)

Ans-c) Dhubri

Explanation- The literacy rate in Dhubri is low and thus it results in high population growth. A kind of correlation can be seen in both the factors.

GE 30- The percentage of Scheduled Tribes (ST) population in Assam according to 2011 census is-

a) 7.15%   b) 12.45%

c) 14.06%   d) None

Ans- b) 12.45%

GE 31- Which of the following districts of Assam has the largest area?

a) Karbi Anglong   b) Sonitpur

c) Nagaon   d) Kokrajhar

Ans- a) Karbi Anglong.

Explanation- Current area -7399 sq. km

- Undivided area with Hamren- 10,434 sq. km.

GE 32- Which of the following districts of Assam doesn't come under the jurisdiction of BTC?

a) Kokrajhar   b) Bongaigaon

c) Udalguri   d) Chirang

Ans- b) Bongaigaon

Explanation- 5 districts come under Bodoland Territorial Council(BTC) i,e Kokrajhar, Udalguri, Chirang, Baksha & Tamulpur.

GE 33- Which of the following districts of Assam doesn't have any International boundary?

a)   Kokrajhar   b)   Baksha

c)   Cachar   d)   Dhemaji

Ans- d) Dhemaji

Explanation- Dhemaji doesn't have any International boundary. It shares a boundary with Arunachal Pradesh.

GE 34- Which of the following districts of Assam doesn't have any International boundary with Bangladesh?

a)   Cachar   b)   Hailakandi

c)   Karimganj   d)   Dhubri

Ans- b) Hailakandi

GE 35- When Majuli became the first island to be made a district in Assam?

a)   4th Sep, 2017   b)   6th Sep, 2017

c)   6th Sep, 2016   d)   8th Sep, 2016

Ans- c) 6th Sep, 2016

GE 36- The district headquarter of the newly formed Majuli district is

a)   Garmur   b)   Kamalabari

c)   Auniati   d)   Majuli

Ans- a) Garmur

GE 37- Which schedule of the constitution deals with the administration of **tribal areas** in Assam?

a)   Fifth   b)   Sixth

c)   Eleventh   d)   None

Ans- b) Sixth schedule

Explanation- Sixth schedule of the Indian constitution deals with administration of tribal areas in Assam, Meghalaya, Mizoram & Tripura.

GE 38- The total number of administrative districts in Assam is-

a)   23   b)   27

c)   34   d)   35

Ans- d) 35

GE 39- The total number of seats in legislative council in Assam is-

a)   126   b)   80

c)   33   d)   None

Ans- d) None

Explanation- Assam doesn't have any legislative council.

• It has a Legislative Assembly (Lower House) with 126 constituencies/seats.

GE 40- Which of the following Autonomous councils is **not** formed under **Sixth schedule** of the **Constitution**?

a) Bodoland Territorial Council

b) Mising Autonomous Council

c) Karbi Anglong Autonomous Council

d) Dima Hasao District Autonomous Council

Ans- b) Mising Autonomous Council

GE 41- Which of the following is a headstream of Brahmaputra river?

a) Dishang
b) Dihang

c) Dikhou
d) Kameng

Ans- b) Dihang

GE 42- Which of the following is the highest peak in the Karbi Plateau?

a) Dambuksu
b) Simhasan

c) Rengma
d) Barail

Ans- a) Dambaksu

Explanation- The highest peaks in Karbi Plateau are Dambaksu (1363 m) & Simhasan (1359 m)

GE 43- The origin of Barak river lies in-

a) Karbi Plateau
b) Barail Range

c) Jaintia Hills
d) Lushai Hills

Ans- b) Barail Range

Explanation- The origin of Barak river lies in Barail range near the Border of Nagaland and Manipur.

GE 44- The length of Brahmaputa within Assam is-

a) 920 km
b) 720 km

c) 2880 km
d) 640 km

Ans- d) 640 km

Explanation- The length of Brahmaputra within Assam is 640 km from Koba Chapori to Dhubri upto Bangladesh border.

• The length of Brahmaputra river in Assam is 640 km and 916 km in India.

- Total length of the river from head to mouth is 2880 km.

GE 45- Which of the following is the highest hill range in Assam?

a) Barail Hills b) Karbi Hills

c) Jaintia Hills d) Patkai Hills

Ans- a) Barail Hills

GE 46- Lohit river passes through which of the following districts?

a) Tinsukia b) Dibrugarh

c) Dhemaji d) Lakhimpur

Ans- a) Tinsukia

Explanation- Lohit river is one of the three headstreams of river Brahmaputra.

- The Dhola Sadiya Bridge is located over the Lohit river which connects Dhola with Sadiya.

GE 47- Which of the following is the westernmost tributary of Brahmaputra?

a) Dibru b) Manas

c) Sankosh d) Pagladiya

Ans- c) Sankosh

Explanation- Sankosh flows through Kokrajhar and Dhubri district.

- It also acts as a boundary between Assam and West Bengal.

GE 48- Which of the following is a north bank tributary of Assam?

a) Dikhrong b) Dibru

c) Disang d) Dikhou

Ans- a) Dikhrong

Explanation- Dikhrong river is north bank tributary of Brahmaputra in Lakhimpur district.

GE 49- which of the following rivers is known as Kameng river in Arunachal Pradesh?

a) Jia Bharali b) Jia Dhal

c) Subansiri d) Ranganadi

Ans- a) Jia Bharali

Explanation- It passes through Nameri National Park in Sonitpur district.

- It is famous for river rafting and **golden Mahseer (Sil Gharia) fish**.

GE 50- Which of the following is not a tributary of Barak Valley?

a)   Katakhal   b)   Dhaleswari
c)   Jinjiram   d)   Jiri
Ans- c) Jinjiram

Explanation- Jinjiram is a south bank tributary of Brahmaputra located in South Salmara district.

GE 51- Which of the following tree is predominant in the forests of Assam?

a)   Mango   b)   Sal
c)   Hollong   d)   Teak
Ans- b) Sal

Explanation- Sal tree is predominant in deciduous forests. Sal is the most important source of hardwood timber.

GE 52- Which of the following is the state bird of Assam?

a)   Greater Adjutant Stork (Hargila)
b)   White winged wood duck
c)   Himalayan Quail   d)   Sparrow
Ans- b) White winged wood Duck

GE 53- Tropical wet evergreen forests are predominantly found in which of the following protected areas?

a)   Kaziranga National Park   b)   Nameri National Park
c)   Pobitara Wildlife Sanctuary d)   Dihing Patkai WLS
Ans- d) Dihing Patkai Wildlife Sanctuary

Explanation- Dihing Patkai is a wildlife sanctuary and the only tropical wet evergreen forests in Assam.

•   It a part of tropical wet evergreen forests having three parts- Jaypore, Upper Dihing and Dirok.

•   Located in Dibrugarh and Tinsukia districts.

GE 54- Swamp Deer has a seizable population in which of the following protected areas in Assam?

a)   Kaziranga National Park   b)   Nameri National Park
c)   Pobitara Wildlife Sanctuary d) Garampani Wildlife Sanctuary
Ans- a) Kaziranga National Park

GE 55- Which of the following protected areas in Assam in known for Golden Langur?

a)   Nameri National Park   b)   Chakrashila wildlife sanctuary

c)   Pobitara wildlife sanctuary

d)   Garampani wildlife sanctuary

Ans- b) Chakrashila wildlife sanctuary

Explanation- It is located in Dhubri district.

•   Golden Langur is locally known as Xhunali Bandor.

GE 56- Marat Longri wildlife sanctuary is located in which of the following districts?

a)   Karbi Anglong   b)   Udalguri

c)   Dima Hasao   d)   Golaghat

Ans- a) Karbi Anglong

Explanation- It is one of the four wildlife sanctuaries in Karbi Anglong. It is the largest wildlife sanctuary in Assam.

GE 57- Feral Horses are found in which of the following protected areas in Assam?

a)   Nameri National Park   b)   Dibru Saikhowa National Park

c)   Manas National Park   d)   Orang national Park

Ans- b) Dibru Saikhowa National Park

Explanation- It is located in Tinsukia district.

GE 58- Lawkhowa wildlife sanctuary is located in which of the following districts in Assam?

a)   Karbi Anglong   b)   Nagaon

c)   Lakhimpur   d)   Sonitpur

Ans- b) Nagaon

Explanation- It is located in Nagaon district on the south bank of Brahmaputra.

•   To the north of it is Burachapori wildlife sanctuary.

GE 59- The total number of wildlife sanctuaries in Assam is-

a)   10   b)   16

c)   18   d)   20

Ans- c) 18

GE 60- Which of the following is the smallest national park in Assam?

a)   Nameri National Park

b)   Dibru Saikhowa National Park

c)   Manas National Park

d)   Orang National Park

Ans- d) Orang National Park

Explanation- It is located in Darrang and Sonitpur district on the northern bank of Brahmaputra with an area of 78.80 sq. km

GE 61- Which of the following is the oldest among the present wildlife sanctuary?

a) Garampani WLS   b) Pobitara WLS

c) Sonai Rupai WLS   d) Bornodi WLS

Ans- a) Garampani WLS

Explanation- Garampani WLS was notified in 1951 and is located in Karbi Anglong district.

GE 62- Which of the following is the state flower of Assam?

a) Lady's Slipper Orchid   b) Foxtail Orchid

c) Palash   d) Lotus

Ans- b) Foxtail Orchid

Explanation- Foxtail Orchid(Kopou Ful) is the state folwer of Assam.

• Lady's Slipper Orchid is the state flower of Arunachal Pradesh.

• Lotus is the national flower of India.

GE 63- In which year Kaziranga National Park became Tiger Reserve?

a) 1976   b) 2005

c) 2008   d) 2016

Ans- c) 2008

Explanation- In 2008, Kaziranga National Park had been notified as the third Tiger Reserve of Assam.

GE 64- Jatinga which is famous for mass suicide of migratory birds is located in which of the following districts?

a) Cachar   b) Dima Hasao

c) Karbi Anglong   d) Golaghat

Ans- b) Dima Hasao

Explanation- Jatinga village is located in the tiny hamlet near Haflong in the Dima Hasao district.

GE 65- The Biosphere Reverses in Assam are-

a) Kaziranga and Manas

b) Dibru Saikhowa and Manas

c) Kaziranga and Dibru Saikhowa

d) Kaziranga and Nameri

Ans- b) Dibru Saikhowa and Manas

Explanation- Biosphere reserves are recognized under the Man and Biosphere programme of UNESCO.

• At present there are 2 Biosphere reservers.

• Manas was notified in 1989 and Dibru Saikhowa was notified in 1997.

GE 66- Purnima Devi Barman from Assam in well known for the conservation effort of which of the following species?

a) One Horned Rhino b) Greater Adjutant Stork

c) Pygmy Hog d) Golden Langur

Ans- b) Greater Adjutant stork

Explanation- Assam's Purnima Barman and her Hargila Army is well known for the efforts in the conservation of Greater Adjutant Stork.

• She won the Whitey Award, a prestigious international nature conservation prize.

GE 67- Amchang WLS is located in which of the following districts in Assam?

a) Karbi Anglong b) Nagaon

c) Kamrup (M) d) Kamrup

Ans- c) Kamrup (M)

GE 68- The total number of Ramsar sites in Assam is-

a) 1 b) 2

c) 4 d) None

Ans- a) 1

Explanation- Deepor Beel is the only Ramsar site in Assam and is located in Kamrup (M).

GE 69- Which of the following is the oldest Tiger Reserve in Assam?

a) Nameri b) Kaziranga

c) Manas d) Orang National Park

Ans- c) Manas National Park

Explanation- Manas National Park is declared as a Tiger Reserve in the year 1973.

GE 70- Which of the following types of rice that has the highest production and also highest area under cultivation?

a) Winter rice b) Summer rice

c) Autumn rice d) Aromatic rice

Ans- a) Winter rice

GE 71- Which of the following cash crops is not produced in Assam?

a)   Rapseed   b)   Mesta

c)   Tobacco   d)   Soyabean

Ans- d) Soyabean

GE 72- In which year Tocklai Tea Research Institute was established?

a)   1911   b)   1920

c)   1931   d)   1938

Ans- a) 1911

GE 73- In which year the Tea Auction Centre in Guwahati was established?

a)   1950   b)   1960

c)   1970   d)   1980

Ans- c) 1970

Explanation- It was established in 1970, the Guwahati Tea Auction Centre (GTAC) is one of the busiest tea trading facilities in the world.

•   It has been the largest volume of CTC tea auctions in the world.

GE 74- Assam is not a traditional growing area of-

a)   Paddy   b)   Tobacco

c)   Maize   d)   Rubber

Ans- d) Rubber

Explanation- Assam is not a traditional Rubber growing area.

•   Rubber is introduced in North Cachar Hills in 1950's

GE 75- Which of the following types of rice has the highest productivity in Assam?

a)   Summer rice   b)   Winter rice

c)   Autumn rice   d)   None

Ans- a) Summer rice

Explanation- Summer rice, locally known as Boro Dhan has a highest productivity

•   In 2016-17, the yield was 2773 kg per hectare.

GE 76- The average **rainfall** in Assam is-

a)   1000mm   b)   1500mm

c)   1700mm   d)   2300mm

Ans- d) 2300 mm

Explanation- The average rainfall in Assam is 2300mm

Winter: 48mm, Summer-550mm, Monsoon: 1500mm(60-65% of the total rainfall), Post Monsoon: 160mm

GE 77- Red laterite soil are found in which of the following areas in Assam?

a)   BTAD area(Bhutan-Himalayan Foothills)

b)   Karbi Hills and Dima Hasao

c)   Majuli Island

d)   Brahmaputra flood plains of eastern Assam

Ans- b) Karbi Hills and Dima Hasao

Explanation- Red Laterite soils found in the high hills of Karbi Anglong and Dima Hasao and also in southern parts of Kamrup and Goalpara.

GE 78- Which of the following types of Silkworm is basically wild nature?

a)   Eri   b)   Pat

c)   Muga   d)   None

Ans- c) Muga

Explanation- Muga is basically wild in nature. But it is domestically reared in Assam.

•   Muga silkworms feeds on Som leaves.

GE 79- Which of the following districts in Assam produces the highest quantity of fish?

a)   Barpeta   b)   Sonitpur

c)   Nagaon   d)   Cachar

Ans- c) Nagaon

Explanation- Nagaon has the highest production of fish and also highest area under fisheries.

GE 80- The rank of Assam in terms of crude oil production is-

a) 1st b)   3rd

c) 4th d)   6th

Ans- c) 4th

Explanation- 4th largest producer of crude oil(petroleum).

• Assam is a leading producer of crude petroleum with 4.2 million MT.

• 24% of onshore crude production.

• 12% of total crude production in India.

GE 81- Which of the following year tea was discovered in Assam?

a)	1823	b)	1826

c)	1838	d)	1867

Ans- a) 1823

Explanation- The indigenous tea of Assam was discovered in 1823.

•	Mr. Robert Bruce, a British official discovered tea plants growing wild in upper Assam.

In 1838, Assam tea was sent for sale in U.K

GE 82- In which year crude oil was drilled in Assam for the first time?

a)	1824	b)	1889

c)	1901	d)	1911

Ans- b) 1889

Explanation- The existence of petroleum in this area was first discovered in the year 1828 by Lieutenant Wilcox. The first successful strike at oil took place in Makum near Margherita on 26th March, 1867.

•	The first well at Digboi was drilled in 1889.

GE 83- Coal was discovered in Assam in which of the following year-

a)	1901	b)	1867

c)	1825	d)	1889

Ans- c) 1825

Explanation- First systematic coal mining was done in 1882 at Ledo by AR&T Co. (Assam Railways and Trading Company).

GE 84- Which of the following is the largest coal field in Assam?

a)	Makum	b)	Dilli Jaypore

c)	Mikir Hills	d)	Singri Mari Hills

Ans- a) Makum coal fields.

Explanation- It is the oldest and the largest coal field in Assam located in Tinsukia district.

GE 85- Which of the following minerals is not found in Assam?

a)	Copper	b)	Granite

c)	Sulphur	d)	Gypsum

Ans- a) Copper

GE 86- Which of the following products in Assam gas/have a Geographical Indication Tag?

a)   Muga Silk   b)   Assam Orthodox Tea

c)   Both a and b   d)   None

Ans- c) Both a and b

GE 87- Which of the following characteristics is true regarding the coals found in Assam?

a)   High ash content   b)   High Sulphur

c)   High Moisture   d)   Low Volatile Matter

Ans- b) High Sulphur content

GE 88- In which of the following areas in Assam iron ore deposits are found?

a)   Subankhata   b)   Silbheta

c)   Chanderdinga Hills   d)   Hahim

Ans- c) Chanderdinga Hills

Explanation- In Assam low grade iron ore deposits are found in Goalpara district.

GE 89- Oak Tasar a wild silkworm is found in which of the following districts in Assam?

a)   Barpeta   b)   Sonitpur

c)   Kokhrajhar   d)   Dima Hasao

Ans- d) Dima Hasao

Explanation- Oak Tasar is found in Dima Hasao and Karbi Anglong districts which are completely wild in nature.

•   The silkworm feeds on Oak plant's leaf.

GE 90- With which countries Assam shares its borders?

a)   China & Nepal   b)   Bangladesh & Bhutan

c)   Bhutan & Bhutan   d)   Bangladesh & China

Ans- b) Bangladesh & Bhutan

GE 91- Which of the following is the largest coalfield in Assam?

a)   Dilli-Jaipur   b)   Makum

c)   Longloi   d)   Digboi

Ans- b) Makum

GE 92- Chand Dubi Lake was formed due to earthquake in which year?

a)   1867   b)   1833

c)   1897   d)   1887

Ans- c) 1897

GE 93- The pre monsoon condition is in Assam is locally known as-

a)   Mango shower   b)   Bordoichila

c)   Cherry blossom shower d)   Coffee shower

Ans- b) Bordoichila

GE 94- When Assam attained it's statehood?

a)   26th Jan, 1963   b)   26th Jan, 1950

c)   26th Jan, 1958   d)   26th Jan, 1961

Ans- b) 26th Jan, 1950

GE 95- Assam is located about _ meter above the sea level?

a)   76   b)   80

c)   79   d)   75

Ans- c) 79

GE 96- Name the world's biggest river island?

a)   Umananda   b)   Dharmadam Island?

c)   Little Andaman Island   d)   Majuli

Ans- d) Majuli

Explanation- Majuli is the world's biggest river Island and Umananda is the world's smallest river Island.

GE 97- Which of the following state is in north east of Assam?

a)   Manipur   b)   Arunachal Pradesh

c)   Nagaland   d)   Tripura

Ans- b) Arunachal Pradesh

Explanation- Arunachal Pradesh is situated is in the most east part of India.

GE 98- In which district Bornadi wildlife sanctuary is located?

a)   Jorhat   b)   Sibsagar

c)   Udalguri   d)   Tinsukia

Ans- c) Udalguri

GE 99- Which of the following countries is to the south of Assam?

a)   Bangladesh   b)   Bhutan

c)   Myanmar   d)   None of these

Ans- a) Bangladesh

GE 100- Area wise the rank of Assam among north eastern state is-

a)   1st   b)   2nd

c)   3rd   d)   4th

Ans- b) 2nd

Explanation- Area wise Arunachal Pradesh is the largest state and Assam is the 2nd largest state in Assam in north east.

GE 101- Which of the following is the most natural common calamities of Assam?

a) Cyclone b) Drought
c) Earthquake d) Flood

Ans- d) Flood

GE 102- Where is the oldest oil refinery located in India?

a) Jamnagar, Gujrat b) Digboi, Assam
c) Haldia, near Kolkata d) Noonmati, Assam

Ans- b) Digboi, Assam

GE 103- Which of the following geographical lines passes through the state of Assam?

a) Tropic of Cancer b) Equator
c) Tropic of Capricorn d) None of the above

Ans- d) None of the above

GE 104- Which of the following is a headstream of Brahmaputra river?

a) Dikhou b) Kameng
c) Dihang d) Dishang

Ans- c) Dihang

GE 105- What is the total area of Assam under the forest?

a) 29% b) 34%
c) 45% d) 19%

Ans- b) 34%

GE 106- Which of the following does not share border with Assam?

a) Sikkim b) Nagaland
c) Arunachal Pradesh d) Mizoram

Ans- a) Sikkim

GE 107- Which of the following state shahs boundaries with the maximum number of other states in India?

a) Gujarat b) Maharashtra
c) Rajasthan d) Assam

Ans- d) Assam

GE 108- Which town is also known as Manchester of Assam?

a)	Jorhat	b)	Sualkuchi
c)	Nagaon	d)	Dibrugarh

Ans- b) Sualkuchi

GE 109- When was Assam Zoo established?

a)	1947	b)	1957
c)	1967	d)	1977

Ans- b) 1957

GE 110- Which one of the following north eastern state share the shortest boundary with Assam?

a)	Nagaland	b)	Mizoram
c)	Tripura	d)	Manipur

Ans- c) Tripura

GE 111- The largest city in the north east of India is-

a)	Guwahati	b)	Agartala
c)	Dimapur	d)	Shillong

Ans- a) Guwahati

GE 112- Which forest is single handedly planted by Jadav Payeng?

a)	Barnadi Forest	b)	Molai Forest
c)	Barail Forest	d)	Dihing Forest

Ans- b) Molai Forest

GE 113- Which of the following is a north bank tributary of Assam?

a)	Dikrong	b)	Dikhou
c)	Disang	d)	Dibru

Ans- a) Dikrong

GE 114- The Bhupen Hazarika Setu(Dhola-Sadiya bridge) is constructed over which river?

a)	Barak	b)	Brahmaputra
c)	Lohit	d)	Dihang

Ans- c) Lohit

GE 115- Which of the following product/products in Assam has/have Geographical Indication (GI) Tag?

a)	Muga Silk	b)	Burmese Grapes
c)	Gamocha	d)	Both [a] and [c]

Ans- d) Both [a] and [c]

GE 116- Where is Momai Kata Garh?

a)	Sivasagar	b)	Kamrup
c)	Morigaon	d)	Sonitpur

Ans- b) Kamrup

GE 117- Where is Chinnamara Tea Estate?

a)	Sivasagar	b)	Jorhat
c)	Tinsukia	d)	Lakhimpur

Ans- b) Jorhat

GE 118- The length of the Bogibeel bridge is-

a)	4900m	b)	4940m
c)	4840m	d)	4880m

Ans- b) 4940m

GE 119- Padum Pukhuri which is a beautiful lake with an island is located in_

a)	Tezpur	b)	Bongaigaon
c)	Jorhat	d)	Sivasagar

Ans- a) Tezpur

GE 120- Assam is having international boundary in the north side by which of the following countries?

a)	Bhutan	b)	China
c)	Myanmar	d)	Bangladesh

Ans- a) Bhutan

GE 121- Assam is belonged to which seismic plate?

a)	Alps-Himalayan plate	b)	Alps-Alpine plate
c)	Alps-Satpura plate	d)	None of the above

Ans- a) Alps-Himalayan plate

GE 122- What is the state aquatic animal of Assam?

a)	Olive ridley turtle	b)	Rohu fish
c)	River dolphin(Sihu)	d)	Crocodile

Ans- c) River dolphin(Sihu)

GE 123- What is the new name of North Cachar Hill district?

a)	Kamrup	b)	Dibrugarh
c)	Karbi Anglong	d)	Dima Hasao

Ans- d) Dima Hasao

GE 124- What is the khasi name of Shillong?

a)	Yeddo	b)	Peddoo

c)   Nangpo   d)   None of these

Ans- a) Yeddo

GE 125- What is the other name of Barak valley?

a)   Assam valley   b)   Surma valley

c)   Shylet valley   d)   None of these

Ans- b) Surma valley

GE 126- The Barail wildlife sanctuary is located in-

a)   Cachar and Dima Hasao

b)   Karbi Anglong and Dima Hasao

c)   Dibrugarh and Tinsukia

d)   Sivasagar and Dibrugarh

Ans- a) Cachar and Dima Hasao

GE 127- What is the highest peak of Assam?

a)   Laikei   b)   Dumbukocho

c)   Mahadeo   d)   None of the above

Ans- a) Laikei

GE 128- Name the state in the north east which shares the longest boundary with Assam

a)   Arunachal Pradesh   b)   Nagaland

c)   Meghalaya   d)   Manipur

Ans- c) Meghalaya

GE 129- Which hill ranges separates Brahmaputra valley from Barak valley?

a)   Barail ranges   b)   Patkai ranges

c)   Burah paper ranges   d)   Dibru ranges

Ans- a) Barail ranges

GE 130- In which month monsoon starts in Assam?

a)   March   b)   April

c)   May   d)   June

Ans- d) June

GE 131- Tipaimukh Dam is a proposed embankment on_

a)   Brahmaputra   b)   Barak

c)   Lohit   d)   Kapili

Ans- b) Barak

GE 132- Which hill station is regarded as the 'Scotland of Assam'?

a)   Tezpur   b)   Maibong
c)   Haflong   d)   Diphu
Ans- c) Haflong

GE 133- Tamranga lake is situated of which of the following district of Assam?

a)   Barpeta   b)   Sonitpur
c)   Bangaigaon   d)   Dhubri
Ans- c) Bangaigaon

GE 134- Which among the following shelters the largest congregation of birds in the winter?

a)   Urpad Beel   b)   Deepor Beel
c)   Tamranga beel   d)   Kamuri Beel
Ans- b) Deepor Beel

GE 135- Assam's soil is suitable for which food grains?

a)   Rice and Tea   b)   Apple and Grapes
c)   Coconut and spices   d)   Wheat and Pulses
Ans- a) Rice and Tea

GE 136- Which districts of Assam are famous for limestone?

a)   Dibrugarh and Sivasagar
b)   Nalbari and Barpeta
c)   Karbi Anglong and Dima Hasao
d)   Tinsukia and Dibrugarh
Ans- c) Karbi Anglong and Dima Hasao

GE 137- Hoollongapar Ginbbon Sanctuary is located in which district of Assam?

a)   Karbi Anglong   b)   Dima Hasao
c)   Jorhat   d)   Golaghat
Ans- c) Jorhat

GE 138- Deepor Beel is located in which district of Assam?

a)   Kamrup   b)   Nagaon
c)   Barpeta   d)   Dhubri
Ans- a) Kamrup

GE 139- Jaysagar Pukhuri is belonged to which district of Assam?

a)   Dibrugarh   b)   Jorhat
c)   Sivasagar   d)   Nagaon

Ans- c) Sivasagar

GE 140- Chapanala is a-

a)   Name of a river   b)   Name of a waterfall

c)   Name of a peak   d)   Name of a park

Ans- b) Name of waterfall

GE 141- When was the Jute Mill established at Silghat?

a)   1950   b)   1960

c)   1970   d)   1975

Ans- c) 1970

GE 142- Assam is the only state in India which produces the product. Name the product-

a)   Tea   b)   Muga

c)   Oil   d)   Banana

Ans- b) Muga

GE 143- When was the Railway Lines first set up in Assam?

a)   1870   b)   1875

c)   1882   d)   1884

Ans-c) 1882

Explanation- In Dibrugarh-Makum-Lekhapani route the first Railway lines set up was made.

GE 144- Who discovered tea plant in Assam?

a)   David Scott   b)   Captain Wells

c)   CA Bruce   d)   None of these

Ans- c) CA Bruce

GE 145- Who was the first tea planter of Assam?

a)   Maniram Dewan   b)   Piyoli Barua

c)   Jagannath Barua   d)   Maniklal Barua

Ans- a) Maniram Dewan

GE 146- Name the place in Assam which has the distinction of the production of materials made from cane and bamboo.

a)   Kacharighat of Golaghat

b)   Mugakuchi village of Nalbari

c)   Dabaka of Nagaon

d)   None of these

Ans- b) Mugakuchi village of Nalbari

GE 147- Name the place where there is the production of cloths made from Eri, Muga, Silk.

a) Sarthebari b) Umrangsao

c) Hojai d) Sualkuchi

Ans- a) Sarthebari

GE 148- Name the oil refinery which established as per the Assam Accord.

a) Digboi b) Noonmati

c) Numaligarh d) Bongaigaon

Ans- c) Numaligarh

GE 149- When was the Noonmati/Guwahati Oil Refinery set up?

a) 1961 b) 1962

c) 1963 d) 1964

Ans- b) 1st Jan, 1962

GE 149A- Numaligar Refinery Limited (NRL) which was **<u>incorporated</u>** in **<u>1993</u>** and **Commissioned in 1999** is a subsidiary of-

a) Oil India Limited (OIL)

b) Hindustan Petroleum

c) Bharat Petroleum Corporation Limited(BPCL)

d) Indian Oil Corporation Limited(IOCL)

Ans- c) Bharat Petroleum Corporation Limited(BPCL)

GE 150- What is the length of the historic Gohain Kamal Ali road?

a) 460 km b) 560 km

c) 660 km d) 760 km

Ans- b) 560 km

GE 151- When was the Assam Co-operative APEX bank established?

a) 1940 b) 1942

c) 1944 d) 1948

Ans- d) 1948

GE 152- When was the Financial Corporation established?

a) 1952 b) 1953

c) 1954 d) 1955

Ans- c) 1954

GE 153- Assam Gramin Vikas bank was set up in-

a) 2005 b) 2006

c)   2007   d)   2008

Ans- b) 2006

GE 154- Where is the headquarter of Oil India Limited?

a)   Guwahati   b)   Nalbari

c)   Bongaigaon   d)   Duliajan

Ans- d) Duliajan

GE 155- The first sugar mill was established at_ in Assam.

a)   Golaghat   b)   Sivasagar

c)   Jorhat   d)   Dibrugarh

Ans- a) Golaghat

GE 156- Where was the first paper mill set up?

a)   Jogiroad   b)   Badarpur

c)   Jogigopha   d)   None of these

Ans- c) Jogigopha

GE 157- Which is the cash-crop of Assam?

a)   Banana   b)   Tea

c)   Vegetable   d)   Sugar

Ans- b) Tea

GE 158- When was Assam Telecom Circle, Bharat Sanchar Nigam Limited (BSNL) formed?

a)   1984   b)   1985

c)   1986   d)   1987

Ans- d) 1987

GE 159 ___________ is the largest agro-based industry of Assam?

a)   Rubber   b)   Silk

c)   Tea   d)   None of these

Ans- c) tea

GE 160- Border Trade Centre is located at____

a)   Dalgaon   b)   Raniganj (Dhubri)

c)   Amingaon   d)   Sutarkhandi (Karimganj)

Ans- d) Sutarkhandi (Karimganj)

3. ASSAM'S POLITY

AP-1: ASSAM'S LEGISLATURE
AP-1: ASSAM'S EXECUTIVE
AP-2: JUDICIARY
AP-2: APEX BODIES

3.1: AP-1: ASSAM'S LEGISLATURE

AP-1.1: Assam Legislative Assembly (Assam Secretariat)

• The state legislature of Assam is unicameral. It consists of only Lower House. (i.e., The Assam Legislative Assembly)

• There is *no Legislative Council* in Assam.

Note-1: In India, out of **28 states** only <u>**6 states are Bicameral**</u>. These are- **Uttar Pradesh - Bihar**

Maharashtra - Karnataka

Andra Pradesh - Telengana

Note-2: In India, 3 UTs have their Legislative Assemblies:- Delhi, Puducherry, Jammu & Kashmir (Jammu & Kashmir- Still no election conducted after re-organisation in 2019)

Note-3: Unicameral- Only Legislative Assembly

Bicameral- Both Legislative Assembly & Legislative Council

At present Assam Legislative Assembly has 126 seats. Out of which Reserved seats are:-

• Schedule Tribe (ST)= 16

• Schedule Caste (SC)= 8

All **126 members** are directly elected on the basis of Adult Franchise. (Voters are above 18 years of age)

Note: The term of Assembly is 5 years & Legislative Assembly is dissolved like Lok Sabh.

Present Speaker of Assam Legislative Assembly: **Shri Biswajit Daimary** (15th Legislative Assembly)

AP-1.2: State List (List-I) & Concurrent List (List-II)

➢ **STATE LIST**

The **7th schedule** of the constitution of India provides 3 lists-

LIST-I : Union List

LIST-II : State List

LIST- III: Concurrent List

- In **List-II**, there are **61 items** (42nd amendment) {initially 66 items} on which State Legislature can make laws.
- Some important in state list are:-

Animal Husbandry , Betting & Gambling, Fisheries, Irrigation & canal, Intoxicating Liquors, Land Revenue, Libraries Museums, Local Government, Market & Fairs, Public Order, Police, Prisons, Public Health& Sanitation, Pension(State), Public Service(State), Taxes On Vehicles, Theatres Cinema Sports, water Supply.

➢ **CONCURRENT LIST**

- The **7th schedule** of the constitution of India also provides a concurrent list which includes *52 items* (initially *47 items*) on which both central & state legislature can make laws.
- Through the 42nd Amendment Act Of 1976 five (5) items were transferred from State to Concurrent List. These are:-

o Education
o Forests
o Weights & Measures
o Protection of Wild Animals & Birds
o Administration of Justice

AP-1.3: Historical Perspective of Assam Legislative Assembly

- The 1st Legislative Assembly of Assam was formed in 1937 as per the GOI Act, 1935 with 108 elected members.
- The **1st sitting** was on April 7, 1937 at **Shillong**.
- **1st Speaker**- Late Babu Basanta Kumar Das.
- After Independence, the 1st Election to Assam LA was held on 27th March, 1952. (Officially known as 1951 Assam Legislative Assembly Election)
- The **1st Legislative Assembly** after *Independence* was 1952-1956.
  The Speaker was = **Kuladhar Chaliha.**
- In 1973, the Capital was shifted from Shillong to Guwahati.
- The 1st Sitting of Assam LA at Dispur was held on 16th March, 1973.

Assembly	Member Strength
1952-57 (First)	108
1957-62 (Second)	105
1962-72 (Third)	114

1972-78 (Fourth)   126

Ap-1.4: President Rule in Assam (4 Times)

PRESIDENT RULE IN ASSAM- 4 TIMES

(i)   1979-1980: Due to Assam Agitation

(ii)   1981-1982: Due to Assam Agitation

(iii)   1982-1983: Due to Assam Agitation

(iv)   1990-1991: Due to ULFA (United Liberal Front of Assam) Movements

3.2: AP-1: ASSAM'S EXECUTIVE

AP-1.5: Governor and Powers of Governor

Governor

• Article 153 of the constitution of India provides that there shall be a Governor in each state. However, the same person can be appointed as a Governor for two or more states.

• The Governor is appointed by the President of India &the Governor holds office during the pleasure of the President. He shall hold the Office for 5 years.

• **Qualification of a Governor-**

o   Citizen of India.

o   Minimum age of 35 years.

o   He should not be a member of Union or State Legislature.

Powers of Governor:

As per **Article 163**, the Governor acts on the aid and advice of Council of Ministers.

The Governor appoints the Council of Ministers of the State and summons or dissolves the Assembly.

A bill is sent to the Governor after it passed by State Legislature. Governor can give his assent or withhold his assent or return the bill or Reserve the bill for President's consideration.

He can issue Ordinances under **Article 213** [President can under *Article 123*] when State Legislature is not in session.

He has power to grant pardon, respite, remission or commute sentences of offences against a law related to the matters in the State List. However, **Governor** has **no power to Pardon Death Sentences**.

The Governor sees that the Annual Financial Statement (State Budget) is laid before the State Legislature.

Money bills can be introduced in the States Legislature only with his prior recommendation.

He appoints Advocate General and the members of State Public Service Commission and constitute a State Finance Commission in every 5 years.

Note: Though **State PSC's** members are appointed by the Governor but they can only be removed by the President of India.

AP-1.6: Special Discretionary Powers of Governor of Assam

☐ He can determine the amount payable by the Government of Assam to an Autonomous Tribal District Council as Royalty accruing from licenses for mineral exploration.

☐ He can make provisions for administration of tribal areas in Assam under **6th schedule**.

Autonomous Councils under the 6th Schedule of the Constitution of India (**Three (3) in Assam**)

- ➢ North Cachar Hills District
- ➢ Karbi Anglong District
- ➢ Bodoland Territorial Areas District

AP-1.7: Governor of Assam

☐ In British India, Sir Nicolas Dodd Beatson Bell became the first Governor of Assam-1921.

☐ After Independence, Sir Md. Saleh Akbar Hyderi became the 1st Governor of Assam.

Shri Jagdish Mukhi (2017-2023).

AP-1.8: CM & Council of Ministers

* The Chief Minister is the Real Executive Authority of a State.
* Article 164 says that the Chief Minister shall be appointed by the Governor.
* A Council of Ministers shall be appointed by the Governor on the advice of the C.M. The Council of Ministers is collectively responsible to the Legislative Assembly.
* **1st CM/Premier** of Assam (in Independent India) = **Gopinath Bordoloi**

AP-1.9: Premier/CM of Assam

Premier (Chief Minister) Before Independence

NAME of Premier	FROM	TO
Sir Syed Muhammad Saadulla, Premier	Apr 1, 1937	Sept 19, 1938
Gopinath Bordoloi, Premier	Sep 19, 1938	Nov 17,1939
Sir Syed Muhammad Saadulla, Premier	Nov 17, 1939	Dec24, 1941
Sir Syed Muhammad Saadulla, Premier	Aug 25, 1942	Feb 11,1946

CM after Independence (Name)	FROM	TO
Gopinath Bordoloi	Feb 11,1946	Aug 6, 1950
Bishnu Ram Mehdi	Aug 9, 1950	Dec 27, 1957
B.P Chaliha	Dec 28, 1957	Nov 6, 1970
Mohendra Mohan Choudhury	Nov 11, 1970	Jan 30, 1972
Shri Sarat Chandra Sinha	Jan 31, 1972	Mar 12, 1978
Shri Gulap Borbora	Mar 12, 1978	Sept 4, 1979
Shri Jogendranath Hazarika	Sept 9, 1979	Dec 11, 1979
Syed Anwara Taimur	Dec 6, 1980	June 30, 1981
CM after Independence (Name)	FROM	TO
Keshab Chandra Gogoi	Jan 13, 1982	Mar 19, 1982
Shri Hiteswar Saikia	Feb 27, 1983	Dec 23, 1985
Shri Prafulla Kumar Mahanta	Dec 24, 1985	Nov 27, 1990
Shri Hiteswar Saikia	June 30, 1991	Apr 22,1996
Dr. Bhumidhar Barman [only 22 days]	Apr 22,1996	May 14, 1996
Shri Prafulla Kumar Mahanta	May 15, 1996	May 17, 2001
Shri Tarun Gogoi [3 terms]	May 17, 2001	May 24, 2016
Shri Sarbananda Sanawal	May 24,2016	2021

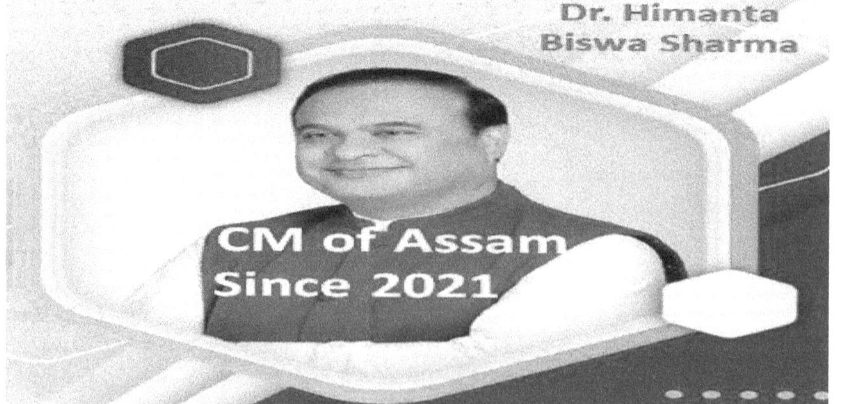

AP-1.10: Assam State Secretary and Departments of Assam

Assam State Secretary

• State Secretariat includes the departments of Assam Government and the office of the Ministers.

• All these departments function under the Chief Secretary to the Govt. of Assam.

• At district level, each district is administered by a Deputy Commissioner (D.C).

Each Sub-division is administrated by Sub Divisional Officer (SDO).

Each Revenue Circle is administrated by Circle Officer.

• Each Revenue circle comprises of Mouzas. Mouzas are placed under Mouzadar.

Departments of Assam Govt.

Admin Reforms & Training, Agriculture, Animal Husbandry & Veterinary, Assam Accord, Border Protection And Development, Chief Electoral Officer, CM's Secretariat, Chief Secretary's Office, Co-Operation Department, Cultural Affairs, Elementary Education, Hill Areas Department, Home And Political, Horticulture Department, Information Technology, Information & Public Relations, Industries & Commerce, Irrigation, Judicial Department, Labour & Employment, Legislative, Mines & Minerals Dept., Public Works Building & NH, Public Works Roads, Printing & Stationary Dept., Revenue & Disaster, Science & Technology, Secondary Education Department, Secretariat Administration, Social Welfare, Soil Conservation, Sports & Youth Welfare, Transport, Excise, Tea Tribe, Guwahati Development Board

AP-1.11: Local Self Government - Panchayati Raj, Urban Bodies

➢ **Local Self Governments**

Panchayati Raj [**73rd** Amendment, 11th Schedule 1992]

Assam has a **3 Tier** structure of Panchayati Raj Institutions to which elections are held in every (5) years.

1. **Zilla Praishad (ZP)-** District level President, Vice President, Memebers= Directly elected Auto Member: Presidents of GP, MLA, MP.

2.   **Anchalik Panchayat (AP)-** Block level President, Vice President, Members= Directly elected Auto Member: Presidents of GP, MLA, MP.

3.   **Gaon Panchayat (GP)-** Village level President, Vice President, Members= Directly elected

History

The 1st Panchayati Raj Act in Assam was "Assam Rural Panchayati Raj Act, 1948". This Act was amended and replaced by-

- ➤ Assam Panchayati Act, 1959
- ➤ Assam Panchayati Raj Act, 1972
- ➤ Assam Panchayati Raj Act, 1986
- ➤ Assam Panchayati Raj Act, 1994 (Enected as per the provision of 73rd Amendment Act, 1992)

Elections to the Panchayats are held in every 5 years by the State Election Commission.

1st Election was held in Oct, 1996. Last one 2018

- ➢ **Urban Local Bodies (ULBs)**

ULBs are small local bodies that administers or governs a city or a town or urban areas of specified population.

Three (3) types of ULBs in Assam-

- ➤ Municipal Corporation - 1
- ➤ Municipal Board – 34
- ➤ Town Committees- 66

Municipal Board & Town Committees were constituted under Municipal Act, 1956.

Guwahati Municipal Corporation (GMC) was constituted in 1974 under Guwahati municipal Corporation Act, 1969.

GMC is the **only Municipal Corporation** in Assam and also in North East.

AP-1.12: Autonomous Councils & Development Councils

Autonomous Councils

6th schedule of Constitution of India

The 6th schedule (Article 244 & 275) of the Constitution of India make special provisions for the administration of Tribal areas in **Four** States: Assam, Meghalaya, Mizoram and Tripura

Some key provisions under 6th schedule.

1. Autonomous Districts & Autonomous Regions: It designates some tribal areas as Autonomous Districts. If there are different scheduled tribes in a district, then the Governor may divide the Areas into Autonomous Regions.

2. District Councils & Region Councils: There shall be a district Council in each Autonomous District & Regional Council for Autonomous Regions.

3. Powers of the District Councils and Regional Councils: They have the powers to make laws on some subjects like Industries, Agriculture, Education, Fisheries, Minor Irrigation, Public Health, Trade & commerce etc.

4. Administration of Justice: The district & Regional Councils have Judicial powers to for trial of offences (Both Civil an Criminal) in their Jurisdiction.

The Council can also establish Primary Schools, provide license for Mineral extraction.

Act of The State Legislature is not applicable to an Autonomous District or Regions unless it is directed or approved by the District council or Autonomous Regions.

Autonomous Councils Of Assam

(i) Bodoland Territorial Council (BTC):

It was constituted in 2003 after the Bodo accord [Memorandum of Settlement], 2003.

It has jurisdiction in ~~Five~~ **Four** districts:

Kokrajhar

Chirang

Baksa

~~Tamulpur~~   **(As Tamulpur merged with Baksa)**

Udalguri

40 members are eleted and 6 are nominated by Governor of Assam from unrepresented (non-tribal) communities to the General Council. Executive Council consists of 14 members. CG& SG allocates fund to BTC every year.

(ii) Karbi Anglong Autonomous Council (KAAC):-

KAAC was formed on 17th November, 1951 and the Karbi Anglong Autonomous Council

(KAAC) constituted on 23rd june, 1952.

Jurisdiction over 2 districts- Karbi Anglong & West Karbi Anglong.

In KAAC, there are 30 members of which 26 are 4 are Nominant.

The Executive Committee headed by a Chief Executive Member and 14 executive members.

The Chief Executive Member (CEM) is elected by the General Council and other Executive Members are nominated by the CEM and the Governor of Assam formally appoints them.

(iii) Dima Hasao District Autonomous Council:

North Cachar Hills Districts Council in Assam was set up on 29th April, 1952. The district was renamed as "Dima Hasao" in 2010.

There are 30 members in the Council of which 28 elected and 2 are nominated.

The Executive Committee headed by the Chief Executed Member (CEM) and 14 executive members and it exercises the functions of Dima Hasao Districts Autonomous Council.

Autonomous Councils Under State Govt. Acts:

Autonomous councils are constituted under State Government Acts for Social, Economic, Educational, Ethnic and Cultural Advancement of the Scheduled Tribes. There are 6 autonomous Councils-

Rabha Hasang Autonomous Council- Goalpara

Mising Autonomous Council- Dhemaji

Tiwa Autonomous Council- Morigaon

Deori Autonomous Council- Lakhimpur

Thengal Kachari Autonomous Council- Titabor

Sonowal Kachari Autonomous Council- Dibrugarh

Development Councils

Assam Govt. has also created 33 Development councils for the Socio-Economic, Educational, Cultural development of different backward communities such as.

Modok Development Council, Tai Ahom Development Council etc.

Each of the Development Councils has their Council body with minimum 15 and maximum 25 members and these are created by separate Gazette Notification.

Moran D.C, Mottok D.C, Maimal D.C, Moria D.C, Gorkha D.C, Chutia D.C, Adivasi D.C, Nath Jogi D.C, Kuch Rajbanshi, Bishnupriya Manipuri, Tai Ahom D.C, Mech Kachari, Manipuri Jati D.C, Singpha (Man Tai) Dev. Council, Amri Karbi, Sarania Kacharia Dev. Council, Barak Velley, Hill Tribes Dev. Council, Tea & ex Tea, SC Dev Council, Chaodong D.C, Kumar D.C, Hojong D.C, Sut D.C, Goria D.C, Barman Kachari D.C, D.C of Karbi people oat KA, Hindi speaking D.C, Bengali Speaking D.C, Jolha D.C, Brahmin D.C, Kalita D.C

3.3: AP-2: JUDICIARY

AP-2.1: Judiciary in India

AP-2.2: High Courts in India

High Courts in India

• The Judiciary in the State consists of a High Court (H.C) and system of sub-ordinate courts below it.

• The H.C is at the Apex of the Judiciary in the State.

• **Article 214** of the Constitution of India provides for 1 H.C for each state.

But under **Article 231**, there can be common H.C for two or more States established by Parliament.

• At present there are **25 H.Cs** for 28 States and 8 Union Territories in India.

AP-2.3: Gauhati High Court

Gauhati High Court (Estd. 1948)

• It is the H.C for 4 States: Assam, Nagaland, Mizoram and Arunachal Pradesh.

• Seat = Guwahati (Principal Bench) {Benches at Kohima, AIzawl & Itanagar}

• Originally known as Assam H.C till 1971.

• Sanctioned strength of Judges: 23+1=24 and 6 additional judges.

• Current Chief Justice = Mr. Justice R.M. Chhaya

History of Gauhati High Court

• The High Court of Assam was established on 5th April, 1948.

• **1st** Chief Justice was = **Sir R.F Lodge** and the initial sitting was in **Shillong**.

• **Shifted to Guwahati** on 14th August, 1948.

• Renamed as Gauhati High Court in 1971.

• It was established as a common H.C for 7 sisters- Assam, Meghalaya, Mizoram, Tripura, Manipur, Nagaland, Arunachal Pradesh.

• Separate H.Cs for Meghalaya, Manipur & Tripura were established in 2013.

AP-2.4: Sub-ordinate Courts of Assam

• There are 33 Sub-Ordinate Courts in Assam for 35 districts.

Note- ☐ Newly formed Bajali have Sub-Ordinate Courts But, Tamulpur have not District Court.

☐ There is one Court in Karbi Anglong & West Karbi Anglong.

AP-2.5: Articles related to High court

ARTICLE	SUBJECT MATTER
214	High Courts for States
215	High Courts to be Courts of Record
216	**Constitution of High Courts**
217	**Appointment & Conditions of the Office of a Judge of a High Court**
218	Application of certain Provisions relating to Supreme Court to High Courts
219	**Oath or affirmation by Judges of H.Cs**
220	Restriction of Practice after being a Permanent Judge
221	Salaries etc. of Judges
222	Transfer of a Judge from one HC to another
223	**Appointment of acting Chief Justice**
224	Appointment of Additional & Acting Judges
224-A	**Appointment of Retired Judges at Sitting of H.Cs**
225	Jurisdiction of Exiting H.Cs
226	**Power of HCs to issue certain WRITS**
227	Power of Superintendence over all Courts by HCs.
228	Transfer of certain cases to HCs.
229	Officers & Servants & Expenses of HCs
230	**Extension of Jurisdiction of HCs to UTs.**
231	Establishment of a Common HCs for 2 or more States

AP-2.6: Articles related on Sub-ordinate Court

ARTICLE	SUBJECT MATTER
233	Appointment of District Judges
233-A	Validation of Appointments of and Judgement etc. delivered by certain District Judge
234	Recruitment of Persons other than District Judges to the Judicial Service
235	Control over Sub-Ordinate Courts
236	Interpretation
237	Application of the provisions of this chapter to certain class or classes.

3.4: AP-2: APEX BODIES

> ### AP-2.7: Assam Public Service Commission (APSC)

• It is the State Public Service Commission of Assam.

• It is a constitutional Body as per the provisions in Article 315-323. Chapter II, Part XIV of the Constitution of India.

• At present total **members are 7**- one chairman and 6 members (fixed in 2015).

• It conducts examinations and recommends candidates for direct recruitment into different services under Assam Govt. & departmental examinations.

• It advices Government on different matters related to the service rules, promotions, recruitments etc. of different services.

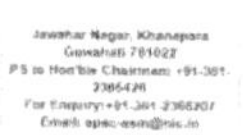

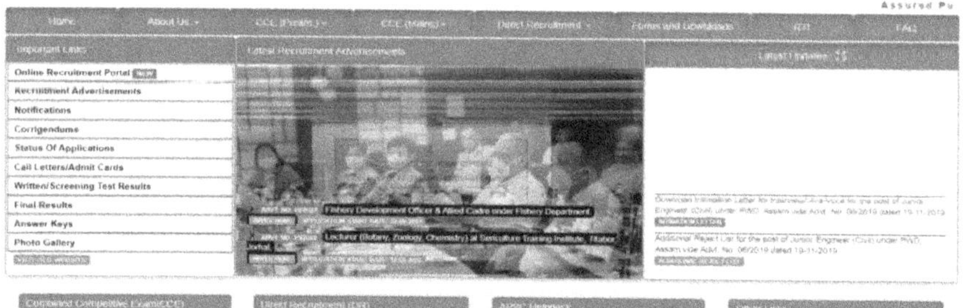

Historical Perspective of APSC

APSC was set up before Independence i.e., **1st April, 1937** as per the provisions of GOI Act, 1935.

Mr. James Hazelett (ICS) was the **first Chairman of APSC**.

After Independence, new regulations of APSC were formed under Constitution of India on 1st Sep, 1951.

First Non-Official Chairman of APSC was Kameswar Deka(1951-52).

Current Chairman of APSC= **Dr. Ajanta Nath**.

> ### AP-2.8: Assam Lokayukta

• The institution of Lokayukta/ Upa Lukayuktas are Established in a to investigate complaints and grievances against public functionaries including Ministers and other elected authorities.

• In Assam, there is a Assam Lokayukta and Upa. Lukayuktas Act, 1985.

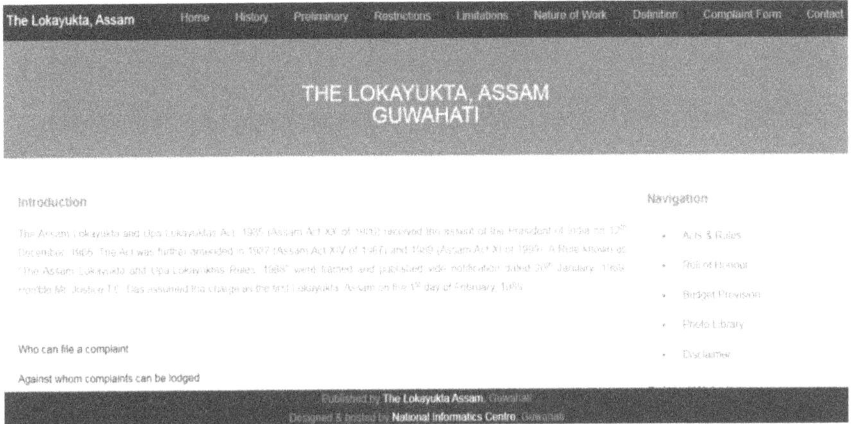

• Honourable Mr. T.C Das (Justice) assumed the charge as the first Lukayukta of Assam on 1st Feb, 1989.

> **AP-2.9: State Finance commission**

• **Article 243** of the constitution provides that the Governor of a State shall constitute a Finance Commission in every 5 years to review financial position of the local bodies- Panchayats and Municipalities and make recommendations on the following:-

• Distribution of Taxes, Duties etc. between the State Govt. and the Panchayats/Municipalities.

• Determination of Taxes, Duties etc. which can be levied by the Local Bodies.

• Determination of Grants-in-aid to the Local Bodies from the Consolidated Fund of State.

State Finance Commission of Assam

1st Finance Commission 1996-2001
(Chairman Shri MM Taimer)
2nd Finance Commission 2001-2006
3rd Finance Commission 2006-2011
4th Finance Commission 2011-2016
5th Finance Commission 2016-2021

➤ AP-2.10: State Human Rights Commission (SHRC)

The State Government constitutes a State Human Rights Commission under the Protection of Human Rights Act, 1993 to address the public grievances relating to Human Rights Violation.

SHRC consists of-

A Chairperson who has been a Chief Justice of High Court.

One member who is or has been a judge of a high Court or a District Judge in the State.

One member to be appointed amongst persons having knowledge or Practical experience in the matter relating to Human Rights.

Assam Human Rights Commission

1st constituted on 19 March 1996.

Its main function is to inquire Suo-moto or on a petition regarding complaint of violation of Human Rights.

It can also intervene in any proceeding involving any allegation of violation of Human Rights.

Present Chairperson

➤ AP-2.11: Assam State Commission for Protection of Child Rights

It has been constituted under the Commission for Protection of Child Rights Act, 2005.

It examines and review the safeguards provided by any law for the Protection of Child Rights and recommend measures for their effective implementation.

Inquiry into complaints and take Suo-Moto notice of matters relating to deprivation & violation of Child Rights.

Present Chairperson= Mrs. Runumi Gogoi.

AP-2.12: State Symbols

State Animal	: One Horned Rhino
State Bird	: White- Winged Wood Duck
State Tree	: Hallong
State Flower	: Foxtail Orchid
State Aquatic Animal	: Gangetic River Dolphin

Official State Anthem : "O Mur Apnar Desh" Composed by Laxminath Bezbarua [1st published in 1909 and was adopted in 2013.]

Kopu Fool: It is adopted State Flower of Assam in 2003. It is a exotic blooming Orchid. It is famous for it's use as an hair adornment by Assamese women during Bihu dance.

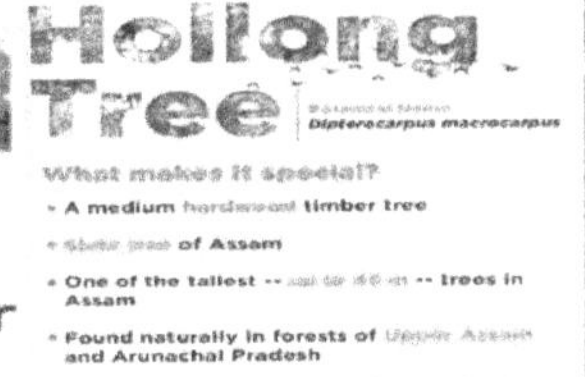

Hallong: It is adopted as the State Tree of Assam in 2003. Hollong is a medium hardwood, timber tree. It grows naturally in the forests of Upper Assam & Arunachal Pradesh. Hollong is a sacred tree for Moran Community of Assam. Today Hollong is used in plywood industries.

3.5: MCQs – ASSAM'S POLITY (161-250)

AP 161- Which one of the following writs literally means "To have the Body"?

a)   Habeus Corpus   b)   Certiorari
c)   Quo Warranto   d)   Prohibition
Ans- a) Habeus Corpus

AP 162- Which one of the following writs literally means "We Command"?

a)   Mandamus   b)   Certiorari
c)   Quo Warranto   d)   Prohibition
Ans- a) Habeus Corpus

AP 163- Which one of the following writs literally means "By what Authority or Warrant"?

a)   Habeus Corpus   b)   Certiorari
c)   Quo Warranto   d)   Prohibition
Ans- c) Quo Warranto

AP 164- Which one of the following writs is used in case of Breach of Fundamental Rights?

a)   Habeus Corpus   b)   Mandamus
c)   Quo Warranto   d)   Prohibition
Ans- b) Mandamus

AP 165- If no decision has been finalised by the court, which of the following writs issed?

a)   Habeus Corpus   b)   Mandamus
c)   Quo Warranto   d)   Prohibition
Ans- d) Prohibition

AP 166- Which one of the following writs issued by superior court for re-examination of an action of a lower court?

a)   Habeus Corpus   b)   Certiorari
c)   Quo Warranto   d)   Prohibition
Ans- a) Habeus Corpus

AP 167- Who was the first woman justice of the Guwahati High Court?

a)   Rupam Kurmi   b)   Renupama Rajkhowa
c)   Mira Sharma   d)   Anima Hazarika
Ans- c) Mira Sharma

AP 168- Who was the **first Premier** of Assam?

a)   Tarunram Phukan   b)   Bishnuram Mehdi

c)   Gopinath Bordoloi   d)   Sir Syed Muhammad Saadulla

Ans- d) Sir Syed Muhammad Saadulla

AP 169- Article _____, there can be common H.C for two or more States established by Parliament.

a)   231   b)   232   c)   233   d)   235

Ans- a) 231

AP 170- At present there are _____ **High Courts** for 28 States and 8 Union Territories in India.

a)   25   b)   35   c)   28   d)   21

Ans- a) 25

AP 171- How many members of the Legislative Assembly should be present to hold the session of the house?

a)   One fifth   b)   One third

c)   One tenth   d)   One fourth

Ans- c) One tenth

AP 172- Who was the first Assamese elected to the post of president of Indian National Congress?

a)   Gopinath Bordoloi   b)   Maniram Dewan

c)   Golap Borbora   d)   Deba Kanta Baruah

Ans- d) Deba Kanta Baruah

AP 173- Which Assamese was nominated to the Drafting Committee of Constituent Assembly of India?

a)   Gopinath Bordoloi   b)   Manik Chandra baruah

c)   Syed Md. Sadulla   d)   Tarunram Phukan

Ans- c) Syed Md. Sadulla

AP 174- Who was the Assamese represented Congress party in the Round Table Conference held in London?

a)   Gopinath Bordoloi   b)   Manik Chandra Baruah

c)   Syed Md. Sadulla   d)   Chandradhar Baruah

Ans- d) Chandradhar Baruah

AP 175- Write the name of the first Assamese lawyer who became the Justice of High Court.

a)   Mira Sharma   b) Holiram Deka

c)   Gauri Sankar Bhattacharya d) Parvati Prasad Goswami

Ans- b) Holiram Deka

AP 176- Write the name of the first Assamese lawyer who became the Justice of Supreme Court.

a)   Hoilram Deka   b)   Gauri Sankar Bhattacharya
c)   Syed Md. Sadulla   d)   Parvati Prasad Goswami

Ans- d) Parvati Prasad Goswami

AP 177- Write the name of the first Governor of Independent Assam.

a)   Tarunram Phukan   b)   Loknath Mishra
c)   Vishma narayan Singh   d)   Sir Md. Saleh Akbar Hydari

Ans- d) Sir Md. Saleh Akbar Hydari

AP 178- In which year President rule was imposed for the first time in Assam?

a)   1982 AD   b)   1974 AD
c)   1979 AD   d)   1981 AD

Ans- c) 1979 AD

AP 179- In which year President rule was imposed in Assam due to United Liberal Front of Assam (**ULFA**) Movements?

a)   1979-1980 AD   b)   1981-1982 AD
c)   1982-1983 AD   d)   1990-1991 AD

Ans- d) 1990-1991 AD

AP 180- Who was the chief minister of Assam elected for the third time at a stretch?

a)   Prafulla Kr. Mahanta   b)   Hiteswar Saikia
c)   Tarun Gogoi   d)   Gopinath Bordoloi

Ans- c) Tarun Gogoi

AP 181- Which of the following minister was not elected for two times as the Chief Minister of Assam?

a)   Prafulla Kr. Mahanta   b)   Hiteswar Saikia
c)   Bishnuram Mehdi   d)   Keshab Ch. Gogoi

Ans- d) Keshab Ch. Gogoi

AP 182- What is the name of the first woman minister representing Tea Tribes of Assam?

a)   Rupam Kurmi   b)   Lakhmi Orang
c)   Damayanti Munda   d)   Jaimati Gowala

Ans- a) Rupam Kurmi

AP 183- What is the maximum limit of members of a Gaon Panchayat?

a)   10   b)   12
c)   15   d)   20

Ans- a) 10

AP 184- In which year Guwahati High Court was established?

a)   1947 AD   b)   1948 AD
c)   1955 AD   d)   1960 AD

Ans- b) 1948 AD

AP 185- Who appoints the Vice-Chancellor of state universities?

a)   Governor   b)   Chief Minister
c)   Chief Justice of High Court
d)   President of India

Ans- a) Governor

AP 186- Who is the first Assamese woman became the minister in the Union Government?

a)   Renuka Devi Barkakati b)   Anowara Taimur
c)   Bijaya Chakrabarty   d)   Rekhu Rani das Bodo

Ans- a) Renuka Devi Barkakati

AP 187- Who is the first woman Deputy Speaker of Assam Legislative Assembly?

a)   Renupama Rajkhowa   b)   Rupam Kurmi
c)   Pranati Phukan   d)   Banale Khangmen

Ans- d) Banale Khangmen

AP 188- Who was the first woman justice of the Guwahati High Court?

a)   Rupam Kurmi   b)   Renupama Rajkhowa
c)   Mira Sharma   d)   Anima Hazarika

Ans- c) Mira Sharma

AP 189- Who was the first Chief Minister of Independent Assam?

a)   Tarunram Phukan   b)   Bishnuram Mehdi
c)   Gopinath Bordoloi   d)   Bimala Prasad Chaliha

Ans- c) Gopinath Bordoloi

AP 190- Who was the first Assamese Governor of any other state except Assam?

a)   Gopinath Bordoloi   b)   Bishnuram Medhi
c)   Mahendra Mohan Chowdhury
d)   Debananda Konwar

Ans- b) Bishnuram Medhi

AP 191- Who was the first Assamese elected as the president of Indian?

a)   Gopinath Bordoloi   b)   Deva Kanta Baruah

c)   Debananda Konwar   d)   Fakaruddin Ali Ahmed

Ans- d) Fakaruddin Ali Ahmed

AP 192- Who was the first woman Chief Minister of Assam?

a)   Hemaprava Saikia   b)   Banale Khangmen

c)   Anowara Taimur   d)   Renuka Devi Barkakti

Ans- c) Anowara Taimur

AP 193- How many Parliamentary Constituencies are there in Assam to the Lok Sabha?

a)   25   b)   20

c)   26   d)   14

Ans- d) 14

AP 194- How many Rajya Sabha seats are there in Assam?

a)   5   b)   7

c)   10   d)   13

Ans- b) 7

AP 195- What is name of the recognized regional party in Assam?

a)   DMK   b)   TDP

c)   AGP   d)   NC

Ans- c) AGP

AP 196- Which one of the following writs literally means "What is your authority"?

a)   Habeus Corpus   b)   Certiorari

c)   Quo Warranto   d)   Prohibition

Ans- c) Quo Warranto

AP 197- Who is the administrative head of the Guwahati Municipal Corporation?

a)   Mayor   b)   Commissioner

c)   Chief Planning Officer   d)   Deputy Commissioner

Ans- b) Commissioner

AP 198- The total number of Legislative Constituency in Assam is-

a)   125   b)   126

c)   127   d)   128

Ans- b) 126

AP 199- What is the tenure of a Governor of a State?

a)   4 years   b)   5 years

c)   6 years   d)   7 years

Ans- b) 5 years

AP 200- What is the tenure of the state minister?

a)   4 years   b)   Max 5 years

c)   Only 5 years   d)   6 years

Ans- b) Max 5 years

AP 201- Who presided over in the meeting of State Cabinet?

a)   Chief Minister   b)   Governor

c)   Senior Most Minister   d)   Speaker of Assembly

Ans- Chief Minister

AP 202- According to which article of the Indian Constitution, the Governor of a state appoints the Chief Minister?

a)   Article 164   b)   Article 165

c)   Article 155   d)   Article 163

Ans- a) Article 164

AP 203- Who appoints the members of Assam Public Service Commission?

a)   The Chief Minister   b)   The President of India

c)   Chief Secretary   d)   The Governor

Ans- d) The Governor

AP 204- Who appoints the Chairman of Assam Public Service Commission?

a)   The Chief Minister   b)   The President of India

c)   Chief Secretary   d)   The Governor

Ans- d) The Governor

AP 205- Who is called the opposition leader of State Assembly?

a)   The leader of the largest opposition party

b)   The leader chosen by the Speaker

c)   The leader elected by the members   d) The senior most MLA

Ans- a) The leader of the largest opposition party

AP 206- What is the highest body of the local self Govt. of rural areas?

a)   Anchalik Panchayat   b)   Mahkuma Parishad

c)   District Council   d)   Gaon Panchayat

Ans- c) District Council

AP 207- How many types of members are there in an Anchalik Panchayat?

a)   Two types of members b)   Three types of members

c)   Four types of members d)   Five types of members

Ans- b) Three types of members

AP 208- What is the full form of BDO?

a)   Bodo Development Office b) Block Development Officer

c)   Bodo District Office   d) None of the above

Ans- b) Block Development Officer

AP 209- Which Governor of Assam initiated commendable effort to introduce a medal at the name of Lachit Barphukan in the Indian Army?

a)   Lok Nath Mishra   b)   Devi Das Thakur

c)   S.K Sinha   d)   Vishma Narayan Singh

Ans- c) S.K Sinha

AP 210- Which citizen of the state takes the responsibility of the care-taker Governor in absence of the Governor?

a)   Chief Secretary   b)   Chief Minister

c)   Chief Justice of the concerning High Court

d)   The President of India

Ans- c) Chief Justice of the concerning High Court

AP 211- When was Guwahati Municipal Corporation constituted?

a)   1970   b)   1974

c)   1976   d)   1980

Ans- b) 1974

AP 212- Who is the chancellor of state universities?

a)   Governor   b)   Chief Minister

c)   Chief Justice of High Court d)   President of India

Ans- a) Governor

AP 213- Write the name of the first Assamese lawyer who became the Justice of Gauhati High Court and Supreme Court?

a)   Mira Sharma - Parvati Prasad Goswami respectively

b)   Holiram Deka - Parvati Prasad Goswami respectively

c)   Gauri Sankar Bhattacharya - Holiram Deka respectively

d)   Parvati Prasad Goswami - Holiram Deka respectively

Ans- b) Holiram Deka - Parvati Prasad Goswami respectively

AP 214- What is the lowest body of the local self Govt. of rural areas?

a)   Anchalik Panchayat   b)   Mahkuma Parishad

c)   District Council   d)   Gaon Panchayat
Ans- d) Gaon Panchayat

AP 215- What is the highest body of the local self Govt. of rural areas?
a)   Anchalik Panchayat   b)   Mahkuma Parishad
c)   Zila Parisad   d)   Gaon Panchayat
Ans- c) Zila Parisad

AP 216- Anowara Taimur was the first woman ______ of Assam?
a)   Deputy Speaker   b)   Chief Justice
c)   Chief Minister   d)   Governor
Ans- c) Chief Minister

AP 217- Which Chief Minster of Assam had the lowest tenure of 22 days only?
a)   Tarun Gogoi   b)   Dr. Bhumidhar Barman
c)   Sarbananda Sonowal   d)   Anowara Taimur
Ans- c) Chief Minister

AP 218- How many Members are there in the Lower House from Assam?
a)   25   b)   20   c)   26   d)   14
Ans- d) 14

AP 219- How many Members are there in the Upper House from Assam?
a)   14   b)   0
c)   7   d)   10
Ans- c) 7

AP 220- How many MLAs are there in the Assam Legislative Assembly?
a)   14   b)   0
c)   7   d)   126
Ans- d) 126

AP 221- How many Member of Legislative Councils (MLCs) are there in Assam?
a)   14   b)   0
c)   Not Applicable   d)   126
Ans- c) Not Application

AP 222- When was Assam Legislatiove Council Abolished?
a)   1957   b)   1937
c)   1947   d)   2001
Ans- c) 1947

AP 223- When was Assam Legislatiove Council formed?
a) 1957   b) 1937   c) 1913   d) 2001
Ans- c) 1913

AP 224- In List-II, there are 61 items {initially 66 items} on which State Legislature can make laws. By which Amendment Act such change made?

a)   41st Amendment Act   b)   42nd Amendment Act
c)   43rd Amendment Act   d)   None
Ans- b) 42nd Amendment Act

AP 225- The 7th schedule of the constitution of India also provides a concurrent list which includes 52 items(initially 47 items) on which both central & state legislature can make laws. By which Amendment Act such change made?

a)   41st Amendment Act   b)   42nd Amendment Act
c)   43rd Amendment Act   d)   None
Ans- c) 42nd Amendment Act

AP 226- Through the 42nd Amendment Act Of 1976, which of the following items were transferred from State to Concurrent List. These are:-

1. Education
2. Forests
3. Weights & Measures
4. Protection of Wild Animals & Birds
5. Administration of Justice
Select the Correct items above, from the options below:
a)   1, 2 & 3   b)   1, 2, 3 & 4
c)   1, 3 & 5   d)   1, 2, 3, 4 & 5
Ans- d) 1, 2, 3, 4 & 5

AP 227- Who was the Chief Mnister of Assam when the 5 year Plans were first introduced?

a)   Gopinth bordoloi   b)   Bishnuram Medhi
c)   Sarat Chandra Singh   d)   Bimala Prasad Chaliha
Ans- b) Bishnuram Medhi

AP 228- When was Assam seperated from the Bengal Presidency?
a) 1854   b) 1874   c) 1905   d) 1910
Ans- b) 1874

AP 229- Which article of the constitution of Indian has special provision with respect to the state of Assam?

a)   Article 371   b)   Article 371-B
c)   Article 126-A   d)   Article 226
Ans- b) Article 371-B

AP 230- Assam Language Bill was passed in the year______
a) 1940   b) 1950   c) 1960   d) 1970
Ans- c) 1960

AP 231- Which State was separated from Assam in 1963?
a)   Nagaland   b)   NEFA
c)   Mizoram   d)   Meghalaya
Ans- a) Nagaland

AP 232- Which State was separated from Assam in 1972?
a)   Nagaland   b)   NEFA
c)   Manipur   d)   Sikkim
Ans- c) Manipur

AP 233- Which State was separated from Assam in 1972?
a)   Nagaland   b)   NEFA
c)   Sikkim   d)   Meghalaya
Ans- d) Meghalaya

AP 234- Which State was separated from Assam in 1972?
a) Nagaland   b) NEFA   c) Sikkim   d) Tripura
Ans- d) Tripura

AP 235- In the 1978 election, Golap Barbora was the first Non-congress CM of Assam, he was CM of which Political Party?
a)   Janata Party   b)   BSP
c)   AGP   d)   Gana Sakthi
Ans- a) Janata Party

AP 236- The historic Assam Accord was signed on
a)   15th Aug 1985   b)   26th Jan 1986
c)   15th Aug 1986   d)   None
Ans- a) 15th Aug 1985

AP 237- When the Assam Gana Parisad (AGP) was came to power in Assam?
a) 1980   b) 1983   c) 1985   d) 1989
Ans- c) 1985

AP 238- Who was the first CM of Assam from the Regional Political Party AGP?
a)   Anowara Taimur   b)   Fakur Uddin Ali Ahmed
c)   Dr. Bhumidhar Barman d)   Prafulla Kumar Mohanta
Ans- d) Prafulla Kumar Mohanta

AP 239- When the Assam Gana Parisad (AGP) was formed?
a) 1980   b) 1983   c) 1985   d) 1989
Ans- c) 1985

AP 240- A Committee to implement Clause VI of the Assam Accord is being led by
a)   Justice BK Sharma   b)   Justice Ranjan Gogoi
c)   Justice PK Goswami   d)   None
Ans- a) Justice BK Sharma

AP 241- Which of the following cultural institutions was born out of the Assam Accord?
a)   Rock Garden   b)   Assam State Museum
c)   Rabindra Bhavan   d)   Shankardeva Kalakhestra
Ans- d) Shankardeva Kalakhestra

AP 242- Who was the Prime Minister of India during the signing of Assam Accord?
a)   Indira Gandhi   b)   Devegoda
c)   Rajiv Gandhi   d)   Morarjee Desai
Ans- c) Rajiv Gandhi

AP 243- How many Autonomous Councils are there in Assam under 6th Schedule of Indian Constitution?
a) 1   b) 3   c) 5   d) 6
Ans- c) 5

AP 244- How many Autonomous Councils are there in Assam under the Assam State Act?
a) 1   b) 3   c) 5   d) 6
Ans- d) 6

AP 245- When the 2-Tier Panchayati Raj System was adopted in Assam?
a) 1948   b) 1950   c) 1958   d) None
Ans- a) 1948

AP 246- When the 3-Tier Panchayati Raj System was adopted in Assam?
a) 1948   b) 1950   c) 1986   d) None
Ans- c) 1986

AP 247- Which of the following Article is related to Panchayati Raj System?
a) Article 243   b) Article 241   c) Article 245   d) None
Ans- c) Article 243

AP 248- Subject on which Centre and State both can make laws are mentioned in
a)   Union List   b)   State List
c)   Concurrent List   d)   None
Ans- c) Concurrent

AP 249- Relation of Centre and State lies in which of the following Schedules
a) 5th b) 7th c) 11th d) 12th
Ans- b) 7th

AP 250- Which of the following Schedule is related to Panchayat and Municipality?
a) 5th b) 7th c) 11th d) 12th
Ans- b) 7th

4. ASSAM'S HISTORY

ANCIENT HISTORY OF ASSAM (AH-1.1 to AH-1.4)

- ➢ AH-1.1: Mythological Period & Kamrup
- ➢ AH-1.2: Varman Dynasty (355 to 650 AD)
- ➢ AH-1.3: Salastambha Dynasty
- ➢ AH-1.4: Pala Dynasty

MEDIEVAL HISTORY OF ASSAM (AH-2.1 to AH-2. 9)

- AH-2.1: Muslim Invasions
- AH-2.2: Kamata Kingdom
- AH-2.3: Khen Dynasty
- AH-2.4: Bhuyans
- AH-2.5: Chutiya Kingdom
- AH-2.6: Kachari Kingdom
- AH-2.7: Koch Kingdom
- AH-2.8: Jaintia Kingdom
- AH-2.9: **Ahom** Kingdom
- AH-2.10: Archaeological Ruins & Places Of Importance

MODERN HISTORY OF ASSAM (AH-3.1 to AH-3.)

- o AH-3.1: British Rule & Freedom Struggle
- o AH-3.2: Bodo Accord
- o AH-3.3: Language Movement in Assam
- o AH-3.4: Assam Agitation   **AH-3.5 MCQs**

4.1: AH–1.1: Mythological Period & Kamrup

Introduction

• Ancient Assam was initially known as **Pragjyotishpur** & later as **Kamrup.**

• According to the Ramayana, this city was founded by **Amurtaraja-** Son of **Kusha** & Grandson of **Viswamitra Muni**.

• According to Kalika Purana (10th Century), <u>Lord Brahma first</u> created Stars here & the city is known as Pragjyotishpur.

• It is also believed Pragjyotisha is derived from the term Prag-Jotish means The Eastern Lights as it was a **ancient centre of Astronomy**.

• Origin of the name Kamrup: When Sati died, Lord Siva wandered carrying her dead body in grief. Meanwhile Kamdev made him fall in love again but angry Siva burnt Kamdev into ashes and later Kamdev recovered his original form in this land-hence the place is known as Kamrupa.

- As per **Yogini Tantra**, Kamrup had **four (4) parts**:-
    - Kampith (Karatoya-Sankosh)
    - Ratnapith (Sankosh-Rupahi)
    - Suvarnapith (Rupahi-Bharali)
    - Saumarpith (Bharali-Dikhrang)

The above **division** is also mentioned in **Hara Gauri Sambad**.

- The **first historic reference to Kamrup** is made in Allahabad Pillar inscription of Samudragupta of the 4th Century A.D.

The Ruler of Kamrup In The Mythological Period:

- The **earliest** mentioned ruler of Kamrup - **Mahiranga Danav**.
- The **Mairong Hill**, named after him is located near present day Guwahati.
- Mahiranga is succeeded by Hatakasura, Sambar Asur and Ratna Asur.
- They were followed by Ghatak.
- **Ghatak** was slained by **Narakasura**, who was one of the most powerful & prominent ruler. He made **Pragjyotishpur** the Capital City.
- **Narakasura** formed a new dynasty known as **Bhouma or Varaha Dynasty.**

Note: The epithets (suffix) **Danava**, **Asura** indicates that they were **Non-Aryans.**

- There is a legend that Narakasur was born of Prithivi(Earth) by Vishnu in his Varaha(Boar) Avtar and brought-up by Janaka- The King of Videha/North Bihar.
- **Narakasur** built the **Kamakhya Temple** and the stairs upto temple at Nilachal Hills.
- It is believed that Naraka was very religious and prosperous in his early days. But later he came under the **influence of Banasura**- The king of Sonitpur & grew irreligiously.
- Legend goes that **Narakasur proposed Goddess Kamakhya** to marry him. Then the Goddess Kamakhya accepted the proposal on a condition- Narakasur would construct a temple, a tank and a road from the foothills to the top of the Nilachal Hill in one night.

All these were nearly completed but the Goddess played a trick- made a cock to crow before the usual hour to indicate dawn and Narakasura's effort went in vein.

• When the news of his atrocities reached Sri Krishna, he came to Pragjyotisha with his army, **defeated & killed Narakasur** in a battle and placed Narakasur's son **Bhagadatta on the throne of Pragjyotisha.** Note: Search "Ashwaklanta Temple".

• Bhagadatta is mentioned in the epic Mahabharat as Sailyalaya(dwelling among the mountains) and refers to his troops as consisting of the Kiratas, Chinese and Dwellers of Sea coast.

• Bhagadatta had fought along with the **Kauravas** against the pandavas in the Battle of Kurukshetra & got killed.

• Bhagadatta's daughter Bhanumati married to Durjyodhana.

• Bhagadatta was succeeded by Vajradatta & Vajrapani. Narakasur descendents generations ruled for 19 (nineteen) generations. Last kings were- Subahu and Suparna.

Other Rulers in Mythological Period:

• The **Kalika Purana** & other Puranas contains the account of King Bana or Banasur of Sonitpur. [Bana- **Contemporary** to Narakasur]

• Legend goes that Bana defeated by Sri Krishna in the famous **Hari-Hor Yudha** after the **secret marriage of Aniruddha** with Bana's daughter **Usha**.

• The **Bhagavata** and the **Vishnu Purana** narrate the story of another ruler Bhismak who ruled **Sadiya region.** His capital was **Kundil Nagar.** He had a beautiful and accomplished daughter named **Rukmini** and Lord Krishna had married her.

• Another Sudra King named Debesvar also ruled Kamrupa.

• Nagokhya ruled at Pratapgarh in Biswanath.

• Dharma pal founded another kingdom in kamrupa. Succeeded by Padma Narayan, Chandra Narayan and Ram Chandra.

• Ram Chandra was another famous King & his capital was Majuli. His son was **Arimatta** & capital was **Baidyanath.** There were very legends about Arimatta. Jungalbolohu was a son of Arimatta & a famous ruler. Jungalbolohu Garh is still in existence in Raha, Nogaon.

Note: Aritmatta's head like a fish head.

4.2: AH-1.2: Varman Dynasty (355 to 650 AD)

• The real political history of Ancient Assam begins with the Varman Dynasty.

• The **inscription of Bhaskara Varman**, **Badaganga epigraph of Bhuti Varman**, **Banabhatta's Harsha-Charita** and the **account of Chinese Pilgrim Huen Tsang** furnish considerable materials relating to the history of the Varmanas.

• The **first ruler** of Varman Dynasty is Pushya Varman (355-380 AD).

• Pushya Varman assumed the title **Maharaja-dhiraja** which indicates his **independent status** and he was **contemporary of Samudragupta.**

• Pushya Varman was succeeded by Samudra Varman, BalaVarman, Kalyan Varman, Ganapati Varman and Mahendra Varman.

• During the reign of Kalyan Varman, the Davaka region or Kapili valley (Comprising the present district of Nogaon, Karbi Anglong and North Cacher) was included into the empire of Kamrupa. He also sent a **Diplomatic Mission to China in 428 A.D.**

• Mahendra Varman expanded his empire to South-East Bengal upto the sea. He is the **first king of Assam** to perform **Ashwamedha Yajna (twice).** His grandson Bhuti Varman conquered Pundra Vardhana (North-Bengal).

• **Bhuti Varman** was succeeded by Susthita Varman. He suffered a defeat at the hands of Mahasena Gupta and lost the possession of Pundra Vardhana.

• **Susthita Varman** was succeeded by his son Bhaskar Varman (600-650A.D), the most powerful king of Varman Dynasty.

• Bhaskar Varman made alliance with famous king **Harsha Vardhan**.

• He recovered Pundra Vardhana (North Bengal) and also brought **Gauda** with with its **capital Karna Suvarna** under his control.

• He had also brought Sylhet and Tripura including South-East Bengal under his control.

• After the death of **Harsha Vardhan in 648 A.D**, Bhaskar Varman became the most powerful ruler of **Eastern India upto Nalanda** (in Bihar now).

• During **Bhaskar Varman** reign the great Chinese pilgrim **Huen Tsang visited Kamrupa in 643 A.D.** A lot of authentic description about

Kamrupa is obtained from the accounts of his travel. Huen Tsang also speaks highly about the noble qualities of Bhaskara.

• Because of his depth knowledge, **Bhaskar Varman** was also called **Second Brihaspati**. He made Kamrupa a noted center of learning attracting students from outside.

• Bhaskar Varman remained unmarried and therefore also known as Kumar Bhaskar Varman.

• With his death in 650 A.D Varman Dynasty came to an end.

RECAP (Important Kings of Varman Dynasty)

1. Pushya Varman	: Founder of Varman Dynasty
2. Kalyan Varman	: Sent Diplomatic Mission to China in 428 AD
3. Mahendra Varman	: 1st King of Assam, performed **Ashwamedha Yajna (twice)**
4. Bhaskar Varman	: Allaiance with Harsha, **Huen Tsang visited Kamrupa in 643 AD.**

4.3: AH-1.3: Salastambha Dynasty

• After the death of **Bhaskar Varman**, a *Non-Aryan* chief Salastambha occupied the throne which is mentioned in Bargaon Grant of Ratnapala. Hara Gauri Samvada mentions about **Salastambha Dynasty**.

• Salastambha's reign was about **655 to 675 A.D**. The names of only 15 descendents of Salastambha have so far been found.

• During the rule of this Dynasty, the **capital city** was located at **Haruppeswara** which is the present day **Tezpur**.

• The 6th king of this Dynasty, Sri Harsha or Harshadeva (C. 725-750 A.D) was the most famous. He conquered Gauda, Odra, Kaling, Kosala.

• After conquering Kalinga and Kosala, harshadeva led on expedition to the south but he was defeated and finally was overthrown and killed by Yaso varman of Kanauj.

• During the reign of Harshadeva, **Kamrup reached the Zenith of military glory**.

• According to Hayunthal epigraph, Harshadeva was succeeded by his son **Bala Varman II** (C.750-765 A.D).

• Pralambha, the great grandson of Harshadeva was contemporary of Gopala, the **1st king of Pala Dynasty of Gauda**.

• Pralambha's son Harjara Varman was another famous ruler.

- **Harjana Varman** was the **1st ruler of Salastambha Dynasty** to perform his **coronation ceremony to Vedic rites**. He assumed the high sounding title Moharojadhiraja Parameswara Paramabhatta-raka.
- He made **two (2) inscriptions**- the Hayunthal Copper Plates found at Nogaon and the Tezpur Rock Epigraph.
- He also built a lofty **Siva temple** and rows of stately buildings in the capital city at Haruppeswara along with the existence of a **big tank** called **Hajarapukhuri** (Tezpur).
- Tyaga Singha was the **last king** of Salastambha Dynasty.

4.4: AH-1.4: Pala Dynasty

- **Tyaga Singha** possibly died childless. Therefore, after his death to avoid any rebellion the officers chosen Brahmapala to the throne. He was also known as **Jitari**. Brahmapala's reign may be placed between 990 – 1010 A.D.
- The title **"Pala"** is an abbreviation of *Sanskrit* term **"Palaka"** which means protector i.e., a ruler or Administrator.
- He was succeeded by *his son* Ratnapala (1010-1040 A.D) - a powerful king. He shifted the capital city of his kingdom of Pragjyotishpur, strongly fortified and named it as Durjaya or Sri Durjaya.
- Ratnapala appears to have encouraged trade and commerce as well as learning and education.
- Ratnapala's son died at early and succeeded by his grandson Indrapala.
- Indrapala (1040-1065 A.D) defeated **Kalyan Chandra- the Ruler of Bengal.**
- Gopala, Dharmapala are the other important rulers of this dynasty.
- **Three (3) inscriptions** belonging to Dharmapala's **reign** are found. He was a great patron of religion and learning and himself a poet.
- The **first 8 verses** of the Pushpabhadra grant were **composed by him**.
- Towards the end of his reign, Dharmapala was conducting his administration from his capital at Kamrupanagar which is an extension of the old city of Pragjyotishpur to North Guwahati.
- He was succeeded by Jayapala.
- During Jayapala's reign, Kamrupa was **attacked by Mayana** who was the general of Bengal Pala king Ramapala.
- Jayapala lost his possession in North Bengal.

• After defeating Jayapala, the Bengal king placed Tishayadeva (Tingyadeva) as his feudal king in the part and Pala dynasty came to an end.

• Soon the Feudal king Tingyadeva rebeiled, the Pala king Kumar Pal sent Vaidyadeva.

• Vaidyadeva conquered Kamrupa and declared his independence in 1138 A.D. He assumed the title Maharajadhiraja Parameswara Paramabhattaroka.

• Later Vaidyadeva was killed in the hands of Rayarideva king of Kamrupa.

• Rayarideva was succeeded by Udayakarna and Vallabhadeva.

• Vallabhadeva was defeated by Lakshmanasena.

• His successor **Viswasundardeva** recovered his kingdom and established his **independent status**. Viswasundardeva was also popularly known as **Prithu or Barthu**. He was very powerful king.

• There are many considerable archeological evidence particularly rock epigraph, cppper plate inscription and land grants regarding the ancient period up to 12th century.

4.5: AH–2.1: Muslim Invasions

• After **fall of Pala Dynasty**, **Rayarideva** established himself an independent king of Kamrupa. **His son Prithu** was a very powerful king.

• In 1205 A.D, during the reign of Prithu, **Muhhammad-bin-Bakhtiyar** attacked Kamrupa (**1st Muslim** Invasion). **Prithu** defeated entire army. This is recorded in Kanai Barasi Bowa Inscription.

• **Minhaj-i-Siraj Juzjani** also provided a brief account of this invasion in his **book** Tabaqat-i-Nasiri.

• In 1227 A.D **Sultan Ghiyasuddin-Iwas Khilji** invaded Kamrupa. But he was **also defeated by Prithu**. That was **2nd invasion**.

• In 1228 A.D, **Nasiruddin** – the **son** of Sultan **Iltutmish** invaded Kamrupa. This time **Prithu was defeated & killed** in the hands of Nasiruddin. Following that **Nasiruddin placed** Sandhya as a tributary king of Kamrupa. But later Sandhya threw off his allegiance.

• During the reign of Sandhya, another **Muslim invasion** took place in 1256-57 AD which was led by **Ikhtiyaruddin Yuzbeg Tughril Khan**. He was successful and erected a Mosque. But later **Sandhya defeated Tughril Khan.**

4.6: AH-2.2: Kamata Kingdom

- After defeating Tughril Khan, <u>**Sandhya shifted**</u> his **capital to Kamalpur** in Koch Bihar and assumed the title Kamateswara. After that the kingdom came to be known as Kamata or Kamrup-Kamata.
- **Sandhya** had given his **daughter in marriage** to Chutia king Ratnadhvaja.
- Singha-dhaja was the **last king** of this line [**Descendents of Prithu**].
- After his death his minister Mainak Chandra occupied the throne and assumed the name **Pratap-dhaja**. His daughters, **Rajani & Bhajani** was given in **marriage** to the Ahom King Sukhangpha. He ruled from 1305-1325 A.D.
- After **Pratapdhaja** his nephew Dharma-narayan occupied the throne & shifted the **capital to Dimla** in Rangpore and assumed the title Gaudeswara.
- Later he was challenged by <u>**Pratapdhaja's son Durlabhanarayan**</u>.
- Finally in 1330 A.D the **Kamrup-Kamata** kingdom was <u>**divided**</u> as:
  - ➤ Durlabh-narayan taking Northern & Eastern part along with a city of Kamatapur.
  - ➤ Dharma-narayan retained the rest which included **Rangpore & Mymensingh.**
- **Durlabh-narayan** was a <u>**great patron of learning**</u>. His court was adorned by-
  - ☐ Harihar Bipra   ☐ Ram saraswati &   ☐ Hem Saraswati
- **Dharma-narayan** was succeeded by his son Tamradhvaja.
- **Durlabh-narayan** was succeeded by his son Indra-narayan (1350-1365 A.D) who assumed the title "**Pancha Gaudeswara**".
- The history of the Kamata Kingdom after Indra-narayan is uncertain.
- According to some Historians <u>**Indra-narayan**</u> was killed at the hands of Arimatta. Arimatta established his *capital near Betna*. Arimatta ruled probably during the period 1365-85 A.D.
- He was succeeded by Gajorka, Sutaranka and Mriganka successively. Their rule can be placed between 1385-1440 A.D.
- The Ahom king **Sudangpha** (1397-1407 A.D) invaded the <u>**Kamata Kingdom when Gajanka**</u> was ruling over it and the latter sued for peace by offering his daughter to the Ahom king.
- Mriganka was the <u>**last King of Arimatta's line**</u> & he died childless.

4.7: AH-2.3: Khen Dynasty

- **After Mriganka**, the throne was occupied by Niladhvaj Khan (Century 1440- 1460 A.D)
- He assumed the **title** of **Kamateswar** and rebuilt the city of **Kamatapur**. This came to be known as Khan or Khen Dynasty.
- Niladhvaj and his successors ruled over the **Singimari region**, upto the bank of the Brahmaputra opposite **Hajo**.
- Succeeded by Chakradhvaj **and** Nilambar who occupied north eastern part of Bengal. He was overthrown by the **Bengal Sultan Alauddin Hussain Shah** in **1498 A.D.**

4.8: AH-2.4: Bhuyans

- **Bhuyans** were <u>petty chiefs</u> who held a vast territory toward the west of the Kacharis on the south bank and west of the Chutiyas on the north bank of the river Brahmaputra.
- The term **'Bhuyan'** has nothing to do with the caste. It meant the <u>**"Lord of the Land"**</u>. It is also believed the word **Bhuyan thus originated** from the word **"Bhuma"**.
- After the fall of the Ancient Kamrup, Bhuyans became powerful in Medieval Assam.
- <u>**Origins of Bhuyans:**</u> According to the Guru Charita and the Sankar Charita after the war between Kamateswara Durlabhnarayan and Gaudeswara Dharmanarayan has **executed a treaty.**
- As per the treaty, **Dharmanarayan** sent seven **(7)** families of **Brahmins** and seven **(7)** families of **Kayasthas** to <u>Durlabhnarayan</u>, who settled them on the frontier as the wardens.
- Chandibar, the **forefather of Srimanta Sankardeva** later became their <u>**leader (Siromoni)**</u>. They are called **Pumwa Bhuyans**.
- Chandibar finally settled at **Bardowa at Nagaon** where his great grandson <u>**Srimanta Shakardeva was born**</u>.
- The **other belief** says Bara-Bhuyans are connected with Samudra, Santanu and Samanta **descendents** of Dharmapala and Arimatta.
- **Santanu's descendents** were **Bor(elder)-** Bor Barobhuyans and **Samanta's descendents** were **Soru (yonger)** were Soru Barobhuyans.
- <u>**Two (2) branches of Bhuyans:**</u> One is connected with **Chandibar Pumwa Bhuyans** and other with **Arimatta** (Native Bhuyans).

Rule of Bhuyans

• Each Bhuyan chief was independent of the others, but they **got united** whenever they **were threatened by a common enemy**.

• A powerful prince might bring of them under his control, but they regained their independence under weak prince.

• Gadadhar Bhuyan, **son of Chandibar attacked** Chutiyas and Khomtis.

• The **Bhuyans resisted** the invasion by **Sultan Allauddin Hussain Shah**. (in 1498 A.D).

• Each Bhuyan chief has their **own courts** known as **"Karkhana"**.

Fall of Bhuyans:

• After the 15th century, with the rise of Ahom and Koch Kingdom, the glory of the Bhuyans started declining.

• Koch king Biswasingha defeated the Bhuyan chiefs of lower Assam.

• In 1535 A.D, Ahom king the Dihingia Raja defeated the Baro-Bhuyans and ransacked the territory and made them feudatory chiefs.

• During the reign of Pratap Singha, Bhuyans led by Uday Bhuyan declared independence. Uday Bhuyan was killed and Bhuyans were shifted to south bank of Brahmaputra.

4.9: AH-2.5: Chutiya Kingdom

• This kingdom was the **largest kingdom in Assam** after the fall of Kamrupa and **before the rise of Ahom** kingdom.

• It was **established** by Birpal in 1187 A.D. He claimed himself to be a **descent** from the **legendary Bhismark.**

• **Birpal's son** Gaurinarayan (Ratnadhwajapal) was the most powerful king. He defeated many other powerful King. He defeated many other Chutiya groups and attached the territories into his kingdom. He built **capital at Ratnapur (Majuli).**

• **Ratnadhwajapal made alliance** with **Gaudaraj Biswarup Sen** and sent his son to Gauda for education who met with ultimately death.

• The place where the **dead body** (Solsa) of the son received and cremated by **Ratnadhwajapal** later came to known as **"Sa Diya"**.

• According to **Mythology**, this place was known as **Bidarva** and the **capital** was **Kundil Nagar.**

• After Ratnadhwajapal, nine (9) Chutiya kings ruled according to **Deodhai Assam Buranji.**

Chutiya–Ahom Conflicts:

- During the Ahom King Sutupha, the **conflict** between **Chutiya & Ahom** started.
- In 1376, Sutupha was killed by the Chutiya king during a friendly encounter.
- Ahom king TaoKhamathi invaded and occupied Chutiya kingdom to take revenge.
- However, TaoKhamathi abandoned the mission in between and Chutiyas are occupied the territory.
- In 1513, Dhirnarayan or Dharmadhajpal attacked Ahom kingdom during the reign of Suhungmung but got defeated.
- In 1520, the Chutiyas invaded Ahom territory twice. They were successful in defeating the Ahoms in the Battle of Dihing.
- Dhirnarayan's daughter **Sadhani** was married to **Nitai** who did not belong to the royal family.
- After Dhirnarayan, **Nitai occupied the throne** and took the name **Nitipal.**

Fall of Chutiya Kingdom:

- Due to incapable rulership of nitipal, a number of internal disturbances gradually weakened the kingdom.
- Taking that advantage of weakening Chutiya kingdom, **Suhungmung conquered Sadiya in 1524 and Nitipal was killed.**
- **His wife** Sati Sadhani preferred death to dishonor and **committed suicide** from the top of **Chandragiri Hills** near Sadiya.

NB: In respect of her sacrifice, every year **21st April** is recommended as Sati Sadhani Divas.

- Following that, Ahom get set up colonies in the Sadiya territories and a number of Brahmins, blacksmiths and artisans were deported from **Sadiya to Charaideo** in Ahom Kingdom.
- Suhungmung also appointed a frontier officer **"Sadiyakhowa Gohain"** to look after the annexed territory.
- The **Ahom-Chutiya conflict continued till** 1673 A.D when the Chutiyas were finally absorbed into the Ahom kingdom.

4.10: AH-2.6: Kachari Kingdom

• Kacharis were **ancient inhabitants** of Assam.

• They belong to the broadly constituted **Bodo group** of **Tibeto-Burman** races. They were also called **Kirat** in **ancient texts**. [Mahabharat]

• As tradition states, there were **two factions of Kacharis.**

• The **founder of one faction** is said to be one Mainak who founded a powerful kachari Kingdom at Sadiya and his son-in-law Mukuta ruled after him.

• They lived originally in a land called Kumkuli (Kamrup). From there they were driven out and got to place called Kundilo(Kundil or Sadiya).

• The Kachari kingdom of Sadiya as per Chronicle, bounded by Sadiya on the east, the river Dikhou on the west, the south bank of the river Dihing on the north and Kenduguri on the south.

• According to **the another legend**, the **earliest Kachari king** was one Birahas or Barahi. They were known as **Barahi Kacharis**.

• They claimed to be **descendents of Ghatotkoch**, son of Bhim. Mother of Ghatotkoch was **Hirimba.**

• The **capital** of Kachari kingdom was **Hirimbapur** was named after her, which **later renamed as Dimapur.**

• Maha Manikya was famous king of the **Barahi Kacharis** & ruled about the **middle of the 14th century at Dimapur.**

• During the reign of Maha-Manikya- a Barahi king.

  Sri Madhav Kandali composed the assamese version of Ramayana.

Kachari-Ahom conflicts:

• In 13th century, before the rise of the Ahom kingdom, the Kachari kingdom was extended from **Dikhou river** in the east upto the **Kolong river** in the west.

• Suteupha, son of Syu-ka-pha occupied some territory of Kachari kingdom to the east of Dikhou river.

• In **1490** A.D, Ahom king Suhanpha **attacked Kachari kingdom** but got defeated and **Kacharis re-occupied** their lost territories.

• Following that Ahom king Suhungmung attacked Kachari kingdom.

• Ahom army led by **Konseng Barpeta Gohain** who occupied a large territory under Kacharis & pushed the boundary upto Dhansiri River.

• In **1526**, *Kacharis attacked Ahom kingdom* but that attempt was failed.

• Ahom occupied **Kachari capital Dimapur** and placed one "Detsung" as a feudal king.

• Later he revolted and in **1536 A.D**, Ahoms again invaded Kachari kingdom and Detsung was slained(killed).

• Ahom king Suhungmung chose **Madam Konwar**, son of Detsung to the throne. He took the name Nirbhay-narayan.

• Suhungmung annexed the entire territory into Ahom kingdom and appointed on administrator **"Morongi-khowa Gohain"**.

• The Kacharis were driver out and they established a **new capital at Maibong.**

• Nirbhay-narayan was succeeded by- Durlav-narayan & Megh-narayan.

Kachari-Koch conflicts:

• In 1562 A.D, Koch army commander chilarai invaded Ahom kingdom and subsequently Kochari kingdom.

• Durlav-narayan was defeated & became a feudal king of Koch kingdom.

• In 1568 A.D, following the defeat of Chilarai at the hands of Sultan Sulaiman, Durlav-narayan declared independence.

• After Durlav-narayan's reign upto the beginning of 17th century, no reliable information has been found regarding kacahris.

Kacharis after 17th century:

• In the beginning of the 17th century, Kachari king Jashnarayan became powerful.

• He defeated **jayantia king Dhanmanik** and annexed his territory and also married two Jayantia Princess.

• In **1606 A.D** during the reign of Ahom king Pratap Singha, again a **battle** was fought between **Ahoms & Kacharis**. Although in the initial phase, Kacharis got defeated later they won.

• During the battle, Ahom king established several new villages in the Ahom Kachari border which later came to known as **"Na-gaon"**.

• Following the victory Jashnarayan took the name Pratap-narayan.

• He was succeeded by his son Naranarayan and brother Bhimbal-narayan.

• **Bhimbal-narayan** was a powerful king and he later made **alliance with Pratap Singha.**

• Till his death in 1637 A.D, there was no major conflict between Ahoms & Kacharis.

• After the **death of Bhimbal-narayan in1637 A.D**, his son Indrabal-narayan ruled till 1644 A.D.

• Succeeded by Birdarpa-narayan who almost independently ruled kachari kingdom.

• During that time, Ahom kings always considered to be feudal kings and led to frequent conflicts.

• Birdarpa-narayan was succeeded by Garurdhaj, Makardhaj and Udayaditya (1681-1702 A.D).

• In **1702 A.D**, Tamardhaj-narayan became the **Kachari king**. He was **contemporary** to Ahom king Rudra Singha.

• He **declared his independence as a result Ahom army by Barbarua attacked** and occupied **Kachari capital Maibong**.

Tamradhaj-narayan escaped to Khaspur.

• Taking advantage of it, **Jaintia king Ram singha** kept him captive. However, he was **later rescued by Rudra Singha**.

• Following this **Kacharis lost a huge territory** to Ahom kings.

• After the death in **1708 A.D,** Kachari kingdom was ruled by Surdarpa-narayan, harichandra-narayan and Kirtichandra-narayan.

• During the reign of **Rajeswar Singha,** a powerful king named Sandhikari ruled the kachari kingdom. He was succeeded by Harichandra and Krishnachandra. By that time Kacharis had embraced the Hinduism.

Fall of Kachari Kingdom:

• In **1813 A.D, Kachari throne** was **occupied** by Gobindra Chandra.

• During his long reign (1813-1830 A.D), Gobindra Chandra had to face many invasions and internal disturbances.

• In **1818 A.D,** Tularam Senapati revolted and annexed the northern part of Kachari kingdom.

• **Gobindra Chandra took help from the British** to regain his territory from Manipuri king Manjit Singha and Gambhir Singha.

• After his death, **Kachari kingdom and territory of Tularam Senapati was annexed by the British in 1832 and 1854 respectively**.

4.11: AH-2.7: Koch Kingdom

• In 1498 A.D, **Allauddin Hussain Shah** invaded Kamrup-Kamata kingdom and placed his son Danial as the ruler.

• But the **Bhuyan chief got united** against the common enemy and **attacked Danial Garrison** at **Hajo** and destroyed it. After that incident there was not a common king for Kamatapur for a deacde and the internal conflict between the small Bhuyan principalities had started.

• In **1515 A.D, Bisu,** the son of a **Mech chief Haria Mandal** took the advantage of conflicts among Bhuyans and became king under the name Viswa Singha.

• **Viswa Singha** initially defeated the Bhuyans of **Ouguri and Luki** but was repulsed by the **Bhuyans of Phulguri.**

• Later on, he took advantage of the Bhuyan's soldiers being engaged in a festival and killed many Bhuyan chiefs.

• Thereafter he defeated the **Bhuyan chiefs of Bijni** and other places.

• Then **he occupied Guwahati** by defeating the **Bhuyan of Pandu.**

• Later on he defeated the Head-Bhuyan of Baushi and their confederacies in Bajali and Kshetri

• Thus the entire country from Karatoya in the west to Baranadi in the east has became the boundary of Koch kingdom under **Viswa Singha**.

• He **established his capital** at Koch Bihar.

• **Viswa Singha embraced and patronized Hinduism**. He bought numerous Brahmins to Koch kingdom from **Kanauj**, **Benaras** and other places.

• He said to have **many wives and 18 sons** including Malla dev, Shukladhaj, Nar Singha and Gohain Kamal.

• Viswa Singha died in **1540** after a reign of 25 years. At that time **Malla Dev and Shukladhaj were at Benaras for learning** and the **throne** was occupied by **Nar Singha.**

• But he was soon defeated and expelled, **Malla Dev** ascended the throne and **assumed the name** of Nara Narayan.

Koch Expeditions:

• His **brother** Shukladhaj became the **chief commander of Koch army** and met with almost unvarying success. He displayed such promptness of action that he was **nick named** "Chilarai"(Kite King).

• **Chilarai(Shukladhaj)** became very powerful and ascended to the **north bank of Brahmaputra** as far as **Dikhorai river(Sonitpur)**.

• It was followed by **two other engagements of Ahoms at Kaliabar & Sala** during the reign of Suklengmung where the Ahoms were defeated.

• In the *last engagement of the bank* of the **river Pichala**, **Suklengmung defeated the Koch army**.

• In course of these invasions the Koch king constructed an **embankment road** from Koch capital at Koch Bihar to Narayanpur under the supervision of **Gohain Kamal**, the kings brother and was known as "Gohain kamal Ali" (350 miles long). It was completed in **1547 A.D** and following that a **fort was erected in Narayanpur (present day Lakhimpur)**.

• **Chilarai** led Koch expeditions to Kachari kingdom, the **Kachari king Durlabhnarayan** made submission and **paid tribute** consisting of huge quantity of Gold and Silver to Koch king.

• In 1653 A.D, the kingdom of **Jaintia** was also attacked and **Chilarai killed Jaintia king**.

• The kings of **Manipur** and **Syllhet** & the chiefs of **Dimorua and Khairam** also made **submission & paid tribute** to Nara Narayan.

Gauda Attacked:

• In **1565 A.D**, **Chilarai made an attack on Gauda**. But Gauda army commander Kala Pahar defeated him and ascended upto Tezpur and demolished several Hindu temples. Chilarai was held captive.

• Nara Narayan however did not accept this defeat as final.

• Few years later in 1583 A.D, he **joined with the emperor Akbar** in second attack upon the **Badshah of Gaud** and Gauda was divided between the emperor of Delhi and the Koch king. During this attack **Chilarai died of Pox**.

A Brief Account of Koch Kingdom:

• Numerous manuscripts contain accounts of Koch kingdom. **Most detailed account** was **found** in the Darrang Raj Bansabali.

• During the **reign of Nara Narayan**, British traveler **Ralph Fitch (in 1536 A.D) visited Koch Bihar**.

• The reign of Nara Narayan reached, the **Zenith of the Koch power.** He was helped by his brother Bir Chilarai.

- He was a **Shakta** and also sent his men **to arrest Srimanta Sankardeva** after getting complaints but later honoured his instead.
- He patronized Eksarana Dharma of Srimanta Sankardeva and also wanted to be a disciple.
- Sankardeva visited many places of Koch kingdom- Patbausi, Sonpora, Bheladanga etc. to propagate his views.
- Nara Narayan was a **great patron** of learning and patronized several scholars and authors.
- During his rule, Ramsaraswati translated Mahabharat into Assamese, Purushuttam Bidyabagish authored a grammar Ratmala in Sanskrit. Ananta Kandali translated Bhagvat and some other noble ancient texts into Assamese.

He executed many **useful public works**. He built several **roads**, erected several **temples** and caused several **tanks** to be dug.
- Nara Narayan had **restored** the famous temple at Kamakhya which had been **damaged by the Muhammadan invader Kalapahar in 1565 A.D**.
- He introduced a Silver Coin called Narayani Mudra.
- Nara Narayan made Koch Bihar a **centre of excellence of art and culture.**

Decline of Koch kingdom:

- As for a long time **Nara Narayan had no male child** and hence **Chilarai's son Raghu Dev** was regarded as **his heir**.
- But in his *late age,Nara Narayan begot* a son called Lakshmi Narayan.
- After losing the hope of succeeding to the throne, raghu Dev withdraw from the capital Baranagar and rebelled.
- Nara Narayan tried to compel Raghurai to return but failed.

Division of Koch Kingdom:

- He resolved to **divide his kingdom.** The possession of Koch territory from Sonkosh to Barnadi was given to Raghu Dev as a tributary king which came to known as Koch Hajo.
- Nara Narayan kept the western part of the Koch kingdom for himself.
- Raghu Dev **rebuilt** the **Manikut of Haigrib Temple at Hajo**, which was destroyed by Kalapahar.
- At **Nara Narayan's death 1584 A.D**, Lakshmi Narayan ascended the throne of Koch Bihar.

Fall of Koch Kingdom:

- **Raghu Dev** declared independence and was succeeded by his son Parikshit in 1603 A.D.
- He continued a **struggle for independence** and involved in **frequent hostilities** with Lakshmi Narayan.
- Parikshit mounted **cannon at Pandunath** to the west of the Kamakhya hill and built a town at North Guwahati.
- Feeling **helpless Lakshmi Narayan** made his **submission to Mughal in 1596 A.D** and following that **Parikshit asked for Ahom assistance**.
- Homs agreed under a condition that all Koch army be sent to Ahom army which Parikshit refused.
- Ultimately in **1614 A.D, Parikshit surrendered** to the **Mughal Emperor** after a long and desperate war and his dominion upto the Barnadi was annexed to the Mughal empire with head-quarter at Hajo.
- Mughal placed Parikshit's son Chandra Narayan(Bijit Narayan) as the Zamindar of the territory between the Sonkosh and the Manas with establishment at Bijni. He was founder of Royal family at Bijni.

King of Darrang (Darrangi Raj):

- In 1615 A.D, **Parikshit's brother** Bali Narayan fled away and sought **shelter** under the **Ahom King Pratap Singha** he was cordially received by the latter.
- **Pratap Singha** appointed Bali Narayan as the tributary Raja of Darrang and renamed him Dharma Narayan. Dharma Narayan assisted the Ahoms to fight with the Mughals.
- In 1628 A.D, a **Peace-Treaty** was concluded between the **Mughal** commander **Allah Tar Khan** and the **Ahom** General **Momai Tamuli Barbarua.**

Later Kings of Darrang:

- The boundaries between the two powers was fixed on both banks of Brahmaputra-Barnadi on Darrang-Kamrup on the north bank and **Asurar Ali** near Gauhati on the south bank. The treaty was known as Asurar Ali Treaty.
- The territory to the west of Barnadi was given to Mughals and Ahoms were left with the undistributed portion of Koch Hajo which was ruled by Parikshit.

* From that time, **eastern Koch rulers lost their identity** and **western Koch** rulers continued as **vassal king of Mughals.**

Fall of Darrangi Raj:

* **Dharma-narayan** was succeeded by **Mahendra-narayan, Chandra-narayan & Surya-narayan** in 1682 A.D.
* Surya-narayan was **defeated and held captive** by Monsoor Khan and chose **minor Indra-narayan** to the throne.
* On the death of Indra-narayan in 1725 A.D, Aditya-narayan became the king of Darrang.
* During the reign of Aditya-narayan, his brother Madan-narayan occupied a large territory of Darrang and it got divided under two rulers- Buraraja & Dekaraja thereby bringing an end to Darrangi Raj.

4.12: AH-2.8: Jaintia Kingdom

* Jaintia were **ancient and original** inhabitants of **North East India.**
* There is **no considerable materials** found regarding the history of Jaintia Kingdom mostly based *chronicles of Ahoms & Koch* kingdoms.
* As per chronicles, Parbatarai(1500-1516) was said to be the **first king of Jaintia.**
* Koch commander **Chilarai** invaded **Jaintia kingdom** in **1653 A.D**
* In the beginning of the **17th century**, Dhan-manik and his son Jasmanik ruked Jaintia kingdom.
* Dhanmanik & Jasmanik were succeeded by Sundar Rai, Chota Parbat Rai(1635-1647 A.D) and Jashmanta Rai(1647-1669 A.D).
* In 1662 A.D, Jashmanta Rai made a **failed attempt to declare independence**. He was succeeded by Ram Singha, Pralap Singha and Lakshmi Singha.
* Ram Singha was a **famous Jaintia king**. He held Kachari king Tamradharmarayan captive.
* Ramsingha succeeded by Jainarayan, Borgoshai(1729-1770 A.D), Chatra Singha, Jatra-narayan and Bijay-narayan.

Fall of Jaintia Kingdom:

* In 1790 A.D, Ram Singha II became Jaintia king.
* Jaintias did not have major conflicts with Ahoms.
* Rajendra Singha was the **last Jaintia King** and in **1835 A.D, British annexed the territory of Jaintias.**

4.13: AH-2.9: Ahom Dynasty

Advent of Ahoms:

• The Ahoms belong to the **Tai Mao section** of the Tai Race. Tai Race is native to South East Asia.

• As per **Ahom chronicles or Buranji**, the Ahoms were led by Prince (Chao-lung) Sukapha.

• He left Mao-lung (in Thailand) in **1215 A.D** with his followers including several nobles, officers of various ranks, nine thousand men, women and children.

• Ahoms led by **Sukhpha crossed the Patkai in 1228 A.D** and **set up their first territorial** at Khamjang Valley (Nagaland). Some **Nagas attempted to resist Sukapha**. But he defeated the Nagas and launched atrocities on them.

• Following this, all other Nagas in the neighbor-hood made submission to Sukapha.

• After **reaching the Brahmaputra valley**, Sukapha and his followers moved from one place in search of a better one particularly **suitable for rice cultivation.**
They stayed in several places like **Namrup, Dihing, Tipam, Habung, Ligirigaon & Simaluguri.**

• On the other hand, **Sukapha** has organized several other **territorial units** along the bank of rivers Dihing and Dikhow.

• Sukapha finally established the **capital at Charaideo** in **1253 A.D.**

• This is how Sukapha founded a small Ahom kingdom in 1228 A.D bounded by **Patkai Hills and Naga Hills** (South), Buri Dihing (East), Brahmaputra(North) and Dikhow(West).

• This kingdom was inhabited mainly by the **Morans and Borahis**.

• A **few villages** of **Chutiyas and Kacharis** eveidently of **Bodo origin** were also there. **Nagas** were also included in the **hilly region of Patkai**.

• **Sukapha** was an enterprising and brave Prince. With judicious treatment he won over the **chiefs of Morans and Borahis** and **encouraged inter-marriage with them** and appointed some of them in various capacities.

• However Sukapha was got criticized for his atrocities on the Nagas.

- The memory of the wandering of Sukapha is still preserved in various local names and traditions.
- **Sukapha** appointed **two great officers** of the state- Bar Gohain and Burha Gohain.
- Bar Gohain and Burha Gohain exercised power next the king only.
- After the **rule of 40 years Sukapha died** in **1268 A.D.**

The Early Kingdom:

- Sukapha was **succeeded** by his **son** Suteupha.
- He occupied some parts of Kachari territory to the west of Dikhow.
- He also engaged in a war with **Nara Raja**. Initially, Ahom army was defeated but later came in terms with the enemy.
- **Suteupha died in 1281 A.D.**
- He succeeded by Subinpha. He introduced **some reforms** in the Ahom administration. He **died in 1293 A.D.**
- Subinpha was succeeded by the **4th Ahom King Sukhangpha (1293-1332 A.D).**
- During his reign the Ahoms engaged in a war with the ruler of Kamata kingdom. Eventually the Kamata ruler made a peace treaty by offering a **princess named Rajani.**
- Sukhangpha was succeeded by Sukhrangpha in 1332 A.D. During his reign **prince Taosulai rebelled.**
- Sukhrangpha died in 1364 A.D. As he did not have a child or heir to his throne, after his death the nobles ruled for few years upto 1369 A.D.
- Then in **1369 A.D**, the nobles choose Sutupha to the throne. Sutupha got killed in a friendly encounter with Chutiya king.
- Succeeded by Tao-Kham-thi (1380-1389 A.D). He led a successful expedition against the Chutiya king to take revenge of the murder of his brother Sutupha.
- He was succeeded by Sudangpha. He was also known as **Bamuni Konwar** for his birth in the house of a Brahmin at Habung.
- Sudangpha's reign is important in several aspects. The Ahom capital was shifted to Charagua, near the bank of the river Dighing.
- In his **reign Brahmanical influence** had its entry in to Ahom royal palace. Some nobles were dis-satisfied at his sub-ordination to hindu

influence and they reported it to the Tai ruler of Mong Kwang (Mogaung).

• Following this, the Tai ruler sent an expedition to annex the Ahom kingdom.

• But Sudangpha successfully resisted the attack and made a treaty. By this treaty the Patkai was fixed as the boundary between Assam & Mong.

• Sudangpha suppressed a revolt of the Tipamiyas. He asserted his sovereignty over the three eastern dependencies viz, Tipam, Aiton and Khamjang.

• The reigns of successive kings Sudangpha (1407-1497 A.D) covering a period of 90 years were comparatively peaceful.

• However, a brief war with the Dimasa Kacharis was fought in 1490 A.D. The bordering Nagas who made some raids were also kept in check.

• So it has been observed that from 13th to 15th century Ahoms were busy in consolidating their newly acquired territory and protecting it from neighboring powers.

Expansion of Ahom Kingdom:

• The **real expansion** of Ahom kingdom began with the reign of **Suhungmong.**

• He ascended the throne in **1497 A.D.** He was better known as Dihingia Raja as he belongs to the Dihingia Raja (Clan) of the royal family.

• During Suhungmong' reign the Brahmanical influence grew considerably in the Ahom Court.

He was adopted the **Hindu title Swarganarayan**.

• He transferred his capital to Bokota on the bank of Dihing River.

• During his reign the **Saka era** was adopted and census of population was conducted.

• In 1504 A.D, the Aitonia Nagas revolted but defeated by Ahom army led by Bar Gohain and Burha Gohain. He also annexed the Habung territory.

• In **1513 A.D**, Chutiya king **Dhirnarayan attacked Ahom kingdom** but got defeated.

• However, later on the battle of Dihing, Ahoms got defeated.

- In **1524 A.D** taking that advantage of weakening Chutiya kingdom, Suhungmung conquered Sadiya. The Chutiya king Nitipal was killed. Suhungmung annexed the Chutiya territory to the Ahom kingdom & placed frontier officer titled Sadiya Khowa Gohain to administer it.
- In 1525 A.D, Suhungmung appointed frontier officers to administer the frontier provinces Habung, Dihing and Banglung.
- In **1527 A.D, <u>Muslim army led by Bar Ujir and Bit Manik</u>** attacked Ahom kingdom. But they were defeated and Bit Manik was killed. It was the first Muslim invasion to Ahom kingdom.
- Later commander **Turbak ascended up to Singri** with a huge force. In that battle, the Ahom side got defeated including Frachengmung Burhagohain and huge member of soldiers.
  Prince Suklengmung was also got severely wounded.
- However, in 1533 A.D in a renewed war, the Ahoms defeated the army of Turbak in Duimunisila and Turbak was killed.
- To take the revenge of the death of Frachengmung, his wife Mulagabhoru bravely fought against Turbak with exemplary bravery and perseverance and caused major damage to the enemy side and finally laid her life. Her death inspired the Ahom soldiers.
- A large number of arms, cannons, horses and soldiers were captured by the Ahoms. The captured soldiers later settled in Ahom Kingdom and came to known as Moriyas. They were engaged in Brass-metal works.
- Suhungmung also defeated the Kacharis of the Doyang-Dhansiri valley and Kachari royal family moved to Maibong leaving Dimapur.
  He brought the Kachari territory under the Ahom as a province called Marangi and placed an officer titled Marangi Khowa Gohain to administer it.
- After sometime the Kachari king at Maibong was given recognition as Thapia-Sanchita(established and preserved) by Suhungmung.
- He also brought under control the Bhuyans on the north bank.
- The Ahom army marched westward as far as the Karatoya and thus by 1534 A.D, the Ahom liberated Kamrupa and Kamata king.
- Thus Suhungmung extended the Ahom dominion from Sadiya to Karatoya river in the west.

• Suhungmung established the relation with Gauda & the Gauda king offered two of his daughters to Ahom king. Koch king Viswa Singha had also offered presents to Suhungmung.

• Envoys were also sent to Orissa and Manipur and presents were exchanged.

• After the eventful reign of 42 years, Suhungmung died in 1539 A.D.

• **Suhungmung** was succeeded by his son Suklengmung.

• He was better known as **Garhgayan Roja** as he shifted his capital to Garhgaon.

• During his reign there was a series of conflicts between the Ahoms and Koch. Initially, the Koch army led by Chilarai defeated the Ahoms. But later Suklengmung defeated the Koch army.

• During his reign Gargaon Tank was excavated and Naga Ali was built. He was the first Ahom king to strike coins.

• **Suklengmung died in 1552 A.D.**

• Suklengmung was succeeded by **Sukhangpha.** He was also known as **Khora or Lame.** He got injured his foot while out for hunting elephant.

• A plot was was formed against him by **seven (7) princess** soon after his accession to the throne. They were caught by pardoned. But they rebelled again in **1559** and that time they were put to death.

• In **1662 A.D, Chilarai** attacked the Ahom kingdom and occupied Garhgaon and king fled. That is why **Sukhangpha was also known as Bhogoniya Raja.** However the Koch army soon returned after a peace-treaty.

• Sukhangpha also had engaged in war with **Nara Raja**. He also defeated the **revolt** by a Bhuyan ruler and Aitonia Nagas.

• Several earthquakes and epidemics occurred in his reign.

• Sukhangpha died in **1603 A.D** after a long reign of about 50 years.

The Period of Ahom-Mughal Conflicts:

• The history of the Ahoms during the 17th century was mainly the Ahom-Mughal conflicts.

• The conflicts occurred between the **Governor of Bengal** under **Mughal Empire** and **Ahom king**.

• The Mughal Emperor at that period were Jahangir (1605-1627 A.D), Shah Jahan (1627-1658 A.D) and Aurangzeb (1658-1707 A.D).

• The imperial ambition of the Mughal emperors to extend their dominions to further east beyond Bengal and to seek routes to China and Tibet stimulated the series of Mughal invasions to Ahom kingdom.

• After Sukhangpha, **Susengpha alias Pratap Singha** ascended the throne in **1603 A.D.** He got the name of due his great deeds and exemplary bravery in wars.

• Due to his great wisdom, he was called **Buddhi Swarga Narayan.**

• He was also nick-named as Burha Raja as he became king at an old age.

• In **1606 A.D, Pratap Singha** engaged in a war with the kachari king Jash Narayan. But after seeing the Mughals approaching towards the Ahom kingdom, he made a peace-treaty with the Kachari kingdom.

• In 1608 A.D, Pratap Singha married Mangladahi- daughter of Koch ruler Parikshit (son of Raghudev).

• In 1615 A.D, Balinarayan was defeated by Mughals and he fled to Ahom kingdom and Pratap Singha cordially received him.

• The Mughal claimed on the Koch territory to the east of the Barnadi and the trading adventures of Mughal merchants has initiated the

Ahom-Mughal conflicts.

• In 1616 A.D, during Pratap Singh's reign, a Muslim trader was killed in kaliabar of suspicion of being a spy.

• Following this Shekh Kasim- the Governor of Bengal sent expedition to Ahom kingdom led by Saiad Hakim, Saiad Abu Bakkar and Chatrajit.

• The Ahom army resisted the Mughal army in Bharali but got defeated.

• Later, Ahom army made a surprise night attack on the Mughal army both land and water & defeated them and many commanders and soldiers were put on to death. At this victory, Pratap Singha performed the Rikkhvan ceremony.

• A vivid description of the plight of the Mughal soldiers is given in the Baharistan-i-Ghayli by Mirza Nathan- a Mughal general.

• It was followed by a series of campaigns against the Mughals. In 1616 A.D, there was another serious battle at Hajo in which the Ahoms lost nearby 4000 boats, and an equal number of men were killed. The Ahom soldiers retreated.

• At that time Langi Panisiya has been able to restore order among fugitive Ahom soldiers and Pratap Singha rewarded him by offering the newly created post of Barphukan.

• Barphukan was placed in charge of lower Assam went of Kaliabar and also head of diplomatic relations with the west.

• Pratap Singha also created another important post Barbarua. He was placed as the head of the Secretariat and judiciary immediately under the king.

Mumai Tamuli was the first Barbarua of Ahom kinhdom.

• The conflict of Ahom-Mughal however did not stop and continued with the occasional outburst.

• In 1619 A.D, Pratap Singha has defeated the Mughal army on the south bank of Brahmaputra and following this a number of frontier chiefs of Dimarua, Luki, Beltola etc. made submission to him.

• Following that Pratap Singha made an alliance with frontier chiefs and defeated Mughals at Pandu, Saraighat and Agiathuri.

• As per Buranji, a Firangi or European aiding Mughals were captured by Ahom soldiers.

• Ultimately, peace was restored by a treaty by Momai Tamuli Barbaraua and Allah Yar Khan in 1639 A.D. By that treaty, the Barnadi on the north and the Asurar Ali on the south were fixed as the boundary between the Ahom and Mughal territories. This treaty was known as **Asurar Ali Treaty**.

• Pratap Singha introduced the Paik system in Ahom kingdom.

• Notable works of Pratap Singha included construction of several important roads, bridges, excavation of tanks and ramparts.

 He erected several forts and several towns and markets were built. A census was also taken.

• He appointed Hindu Katakis Peons.

• Pratap Singha died in 1641 A.D and he was succeeded by Surampha (1641-1644 A.D) and Sutyinpha (1644-1648 A.D).

• Sutyinpha was known as Nariya (sick) Raja due to his indifferent health.

Reign of Jayadhwaj Singha:

• Nariya Raja was succeeded by the reign of Sutamla.

• Sutamla ascended the throne in 1648 A.D and took the Hindu name Jayadhwaj Singha.

• Soon after his accession, several conspiracies were made against Jayadhwaj Singha. But all were repressed and conspirators were put to death.

• In 1650 A.D, he sent an expedition to control Lakma Nagas. This followed a series of conflicts and eventually after few years, the Naga chief made submission to Jayadhwaj Singha.

• In 1655 A.D Miris killed two Ahom subjects. After that an expedition was sent against the Miris and they were defeated. The Miris agreed to pay tribute to Jayadhwaj Singha.

• In 1658 A.D Jaintia king Pramatta Rai attacked the tributary chief of Gobha and he fled, Jayadhwaj Singha re-established him.

• In the same year Mughal emperor Shah Jahan fell sick and following this, Koch ruler Pran Narayan threw off the Mughal Allegience.

• Jayadhwaj Singha also occupied Gauhati.

• Then Pran Narayan proposed to make an alliance with Ahoms but Jayadhwaj Singha rejected the proposal and also defeated Pran Narayan and drove them across Sankosh.

• After few years as a retaliatory action, Mir Jumla-the newly appointed Nawab of Bengal led huge force to invade Ahom kingdom in 1662 A.D.

• Mir Jumla was accompanied by Rashid Khan.

• It was a huge army with 12000 horses, 30000 foot soldiers supported by a strong Navy mostly manned by Europeans chiefly the Portuguese and the Dutch.

Invasion of Mir Jumla:

• At first, Mir Jumla and his army ruined the defenses put up at Hatichala-Baritala and Jogigopha Fort and occupied Gauhati.

• Then they occupied the Fort at Simlagarh and Samdhara, the Mughal army had a naval victory near Kaliabar on the Brahmaputra.

• The Mughal army advanced towards the Ahom capital Garhgaon.

• So Jayadhwaj Singha with his family and close associates evacuated the capital and fled to Namrup close to the Patkai Hills. Hence, Jayadhwaj Singha was nick named as Bhaganiya Raja.

☐ Then Pran Narayan proposed to make an alliance with Ahoms but Jaydhwaj Singha rejected the proposal and also defeated Pran Narayan and drove them across Sankosh.

☐ After a few years as a retaliatory action, Mir Jumla- the newly appointed Nawab of Bengal led a huge force to invade Ahom kingdom in 1662 A.D.

☐ Mir Jumla was accompanied by Rashid Khan.

☐ It was a huge army with twelve thousand horses and thirty thousand foot soldiers supported by a strong navy mostly manned by Europeans chiefly the Portuguese and the Dutch.

☐ Mir Jumla divided his army into two and advanced east, one division along the north bank and the other along south bank of the Brahmaputra river.

☐ By February 4, 1662, Mir Jumla took possession of Guwahati. The Ahoms took stand at Samdhara (under the Borgohain) and Simalugrah (under Bhitarual Gohain) in the north and south banks respectively.

☐ Mir Jumla now transferred his entire army south and reached Simalugarh at the end of the month and overran it with some effort. The attack so disheartened the Samdhara fort that it was abandoned in haste and the Borgohain adopted a scorched earth retreat.

☐ After a night-long naval battle at Kaliabor, the Ahoms again fell back. Mir Jumla then reached Salagrah, which too was abandoned.

Treaty of Ahom-Mughal

☐ On **Jan 9, 1663**, the **treaty of Ghiladharighat** was drawn up by which – Jayadhwaj became a tributary of the Mughal Emperor and he agreed to pay a huge ncompensation- several thousands tolas of Gold and silver and large numbers of Elephants.

☐ **Jayadhwaj's daughter and daughter of Tipam Raja** was sent to Delhi.

☐ All prisoners to be given up.

Reign of Jayadhwaj Singha

☐ **Mir Jumla** was the first Mughal Commander to occupy Ahom capital.

☐ Mir Jumla was accompanied by a chronicler known as Shihabuddin Talish. He wrote Fatiyah-i-Ibriyah which was a valuable account of

Assam about its climate, population, customs and products found in the capital of Ahom i.e., Garhgaon.

☐ He was the first Ahom king to embrace Hinduism by receiving initiation from a Vaishnava priest. He donated large lands to Satras.

☐ One of his notable achievements was the planned settlement of villages in certain tracts of the country.

☐ Jayadhwaj Singha died in 1663

Reign of Chakradhwaj Singha

☐ His Ahom name was Supungmung.

☐ During his reign two Mughal officials visited his court with reminder that the balance of war compensation was overdue and presented him a gown (Siropa) sent by Mughal court to him as a tributary. But Ahom king refused to wear it.

☐ In 1667 A.D., Mughal administrator of Guwahati, Saiad Firus Khan sent a strongly worded letter , demanding the outstanding indemnity.

☐ After receiving the letter, Chakradhaj Singha decided to fight against Mughasl despite the suggestion from his nobles.

☐ The command was entrusted to the great warrior Lachit Barphukan who was the son of Mumai Tamuli Barua.

☐ The Ahom army led by Lachit Borphukan along with general Aton Burha Gohain first occupied the Mughal outpost at kajali and Bansbari and captured prisoners, horses, cannons and were sent back to Garhgaon.

☐ Soon Guwahati and Pandu were captured by the Ahom army. Guwahati was made the headquarters of Bar phukan and Pandu and Saraighat were strongly fortified.

☐ An inscription in Assamese on the Kanai Barasi Bowa Rock was recorded about the victory. A cannon in Silghat also bears the inscription about the victory of Ahoms.

Invasion of Ram Singha

☐ The Mughal emperor Aurangzeb dispatched a Rajput general Ram Singha with a large force in order to invade Ahom kingdom.

☐ In the engagement in Tezpur, Ahoms got defeated.

☐ However later in a naval war Ahoms defeated Mughals and Mughal army retreated to Hajo.

- The war dragged on for many years and heavy losses were incurred on both the sides.
- Ram Singha offered peace treaty and hostilities were suspended for a short time.
- In 1670 A.D., Chakradhwaj Singha passed away and he was succeeded by Udayaditya Singha.

Battle of Saraighat

- The negotiations between Ahom and Mughal sides continued. But Ram Singha got reinforcement of several thousand troops and war got renewed. The Ahoms also advanced with 2000 troops from Samdhara to Saraighat.
- In 1671 A.D., Ahoms and Mughals got engaged in a two - front war at Saraighat.
- On land, Ahom army successfully defeated the Mughals. But in the naval war Ahom army got defeated by the Mughals and they retreated to Barshila. Seeing this Lachit Barphukan despite his severe sickness arrived with more slips (small vessels).
- The Ahom army acquired a new zeal and defeated the Mughals.
- Facing a disastrous defeat at Saraighat, Ram Singha retreated to Rangamati in March 1671 A.D. Hadira opposite Goalpara became the new frontier outpost of Ahoms.
- In this war, the Garos and the King of Rani assisted the Ahoms. Many other neighbouring hill states also sent their contingents.
- The Battle of Saraighat has a great significance in the history of Medieval India as the great Mughal Power had to face a disastrous defeat in the hands of a comparatively smaller Ahom power.
- Lachit Barphukan died about a year after the victory at Saraighat.

Lachit Barphukan

- He was a great patriot and warrior and his devotion to his land is best reflected in the battle of Saraighat.
- During the preparations for the battle he ordered a fortification to be constructed within one night and employed his maternal uncle as the supervisor. Late in the night when Lachit came for inspection, he found that the work was not progressing satisfactorily. Seeing such negligence

of duty, Lachit became furious that he beheaded his uncle on the spot saying that , " My uncle is not greater than my

nation." The remains of this fortification are still known as "Momai-kota-Garh."

☐ This great warrior Lachit Bar phukan however was defeated by illness and he passed away soon after the victory at the battle of Saraighat.

☐ His remains lie in rest at Lachit Maidaam constructed in 1672 by Udayaditya Singha at Holongapar near Jorhat.

☐ On 24th November each year Lachit Divas is celebrated in Assam as a State holiday to commemorate the heroism of Lachit Bar Phukan.

Period of unstable Ahom Kingdom

☐ After Udayaditya Singha, the nobles chose Ramdhwaj Singha, to the throne and he died in 1675.

☐ He was followed by Suhung, Gobar, Sujinpha(1675-77)and Sudaipha(1677-79). It was a period of weak and unstable Ahom kingdom during which several weak and young kings were placed on the Ahom throne and then quickly removed by ministers and high officials for their own selfish gains.

☐ During this period, Laluksola Bar Phukan handed Guwahati to the Mughals. Many Ahoms were dissatisfied with Sudaipha and allied with Laluksola Bar phukan.

☐ In 1679 A.D., Sudaipha was killed and Sulikpha was chosen to the throne.

☐ Sulikpha was nicknamed as Lora Raja as he became king at a tender age.

☐ At that time, Gadapani Konwar from Tungkhungiya Phoid was the most capable prince to take over as a king.

☐ He fled from Ahom kingdom and sought shelter at Sattras(Vaishnav monasteries) and the adjoining hills outside the Ahom kingdom.

☐ Failing to trace Gadapani, Sulikpha's soldiers brought his wife Joymoti to Jerenga Pathar. Despite horrific torture she refused to reveal the whereabouts of her husband. After continuous physical torture over 14 days, Joymoti died on 27 March, 1680.

☐ She was accorded the honorific Sati due to her supreme sacrifice for the sake of her husband and Ahom kingdom.

 Soon after the death of Joymoti, Laluksola Barphukan was assassinated by his bodyguards Bhutai Deka, Madhav Tamuli and aghuna Kachari and Sulikpha was also killed.

Reign of Gadadhar Singha

 Gadapani was formally chosen by nobles and officers to the throne in August 1681, Kaliabor.

 He assumed the Tai name Supaatapha and Hindu name Gadadhaar Singha.

 He sent huge Ahom forces to reoccupy Guwahati. The Ahom army first occupied the forts and Banshbari and Kajali and Ahoms and engaged in full front war with Mughals led by Monsoon Khan at Itakhuli near Guwahati.

 Defeated Mughal Faujdar Mansoor Khan fled and Ahoms occupied Guwahati.

 This battle of Itakhuli in 1682 A.D., was the last battle between Ahoms and Mughals.

 Gadadhar Singha repressed several conspiracies against him. He also sent expeditions against Miris and Nagas.

 During this period, Vaishnava Sattras have attained remarkable influence in Ahom kingdom and the country became full of Vaishnava followers. Many people who became followers of Sattras only get exemption from the Paik system.

 Moreover Gadadhar Singha had developed a personal grudge against some Gossains or Satradhikaris as they refused to give him shelter during exile.

 So Gadadhar Singha decided to break the power of Sattras and Gossains. At his order, many Gossains were captured and killed. Their properties were also confiscated.

 The disciples of Satras were captured and robbed of their property and forcefully engaged them in various works.

 By engaging the idle(Dhud) followers, a long road on the south bank of Brahmaputra and hence it came to be known as Dhudor Ali.

 The Dhudor Ali is a 212 km long road starting from Kamargaon in Golaghat to Joypur in Dibrugarh touching Mariani, Jorhat and now it is a State highway.

He also initiated a detailed land survey of Ahom kingdom for the first time.

Gadadhar Singha built the Shiva temple on Umananda island.

Other notable public works of Gadadhar Singha are Aka Ali, two stone bridges and several tanks.

He was a Shakta follower.

He died in 1696 A.D.

Joymoti

In the memory of Joymoti, her son king Rudra Singha built the Joysagar Tank and Joy Daul in Sibasagar.

Sati Joymoti Divas is her commemoration day on 27th March celebrated every year. The Annual Award in her name is awarded to women of excellence in fields of works.

The first Assamese movie Joymoti directed by Jyoti Prasad Agarwalla in 1935 is also based on her life.

Reign of Rudra Singha

Rudra Singha was the elder son of Gadadhar Singha and Sukhrangpa was his Tai name.

He reigned for 17 years.

He reversed the policy of Gadadhar Singha towards the Vaishnava Sattras and Gossains. They regained their old positions with one condition to make Majuli their headquarters.

A capital city was constructed in Rangpur(near Sivasagar) and several brick palaces were built.

During his reign, masonry bridges over Namdang and Dimow rivers and roads like Meteka Ali, Kharikatia Ali were constructed.

He created the post of Bezboruah for practicing traditional medicine.

He created the post of Gayan Baruah and Kukura Suwa Baruah to look after music and dance and sports, respectively.

Rudra Singha patronized several scholars and authors. Kabiraj Chakrabarty was the royal poet of the court.

He decided to formally embrace Hinduism and invited Krishnaram Bhattacharya but later he changed his mind. But prior to his death he directed his sons to become disciples of Krishnaram Bhattacharya.

☐ During his reign, Kachari king Tamradhwaj asserted independence. Then Rudra Singha dispatched Bar Barua and Pani Phukan with a strong force and the Ahom forces occupied the Kachari capital Maibong and several other places under Kachari kingdom.

☐ The Ahom forces were recalled in 1707 A.D.

☐ During the attack, Tamradhwaj fled but he was held captive by Jaintia king Ram Singha.

☐ Following that Rudra Singha sent an expedition against Jaintia king. Both Tamradhwaj and Ram Singha were captured by Ahom soldiers and they both were received in a grand durbar at Biswanath on the bank of Brahmaputra.

☐ Rudra Singha announced annexation of both Kachari kingdom and Jaintia Kingdom into Ahom territory.

☐ Rudra Singha had planned to invade Bengal with support of the rulers and chiefs of Tripura, Koch Bihar, Burdwan and Nadia.

☐ Rudra Singha advanced in person to Guwahati and organized a huge army, fleet and cannons.

☐ But unfortunately, he suddenly fell ill and passed away in Guwahati in 1714.

☐ Rudra Singha is considered as the greatest of all Ahom kings.

Reign of Siba Singha

☐ Rudra Singha had five sons- Sib Singha, Pramatta Singha, Rajeswar Singha, Lakshmi Singha and Barjana Gohain. Prior to his death, he directed his sons to ascend the Ahom throne one after another.

☐ Siba Singha became the disciple of Krishnaram Bhattacharya and gave him the management of Kamakhya temple in Nilachal Hills.

☐ The successors of Krishnaram Bhattacharya came to be known as Parbatiya Gossains.

☐ During Siba Singha's reign, Hindu influence grew enormously.

☐ Dhai Ali was built and a number of temples were built and reconstructed.

☐ Survey was initiated in Kamrup and Bakata and recorded in Pera Kagaj (Register).

☐ Bar Raja Phuleswari built Gauri Sagar Daul and Tank. Bar Raja Ambika caused the construction of Siba Daul and Sibasagar Tank.

☐ During the reign, in 1734 A.D., Sukumar Barkaith authored the famous book on medical treatment and training elephants- Hasti Bidyarnav.

☐ Kabiraj Chakravarty authored Sakuntala Kabya. Ananta Acharya authored Ananda Lahiri, Kabichandra Dwij authored Kam Kumar Harana and Dharma puran.

☐ In 1739, four Europeans paid a visit to Siba Singha.

☐ Siba Singha passed away in 1744 A.D.

Reign of Pramatta Singha

☐ Pramatta Singha constructed the masonry Rang ghar- the Royal pavilion to watch animal fights and other sports.

☐ New masonry buildings and gateways were constructed at Garhgaon. The Rudreswar and Sukreswar temples were erected at Guwahati.

☐ His reign was almost peaceful without any major conflict and expedition and after an uneventful reign of seven years, he died in 1751.

Reign of Rajeswar Singha

☐ In 1751, Rajeswar Singha ascended the throne. He assumed the Ahom name Surampha.

☐ In 1758, Dafalas committed several raids in Ghiladharighat.

☐ As a punishment Rajeswar Singha erected forts and prohibited the Dafalas to enter the plains.

☐ Finally, they made submission to Ahom kings and an agreement was made to allow Dafalas to levy taxes from frontier areas.

☐ In 1765, two huge expeditions were sent against the Mikirs as they had stopped paying tribute to Ahom king.

☐ Following that Mikirs came in with tribute and begged forgiveness.

☐ Rajeswar Singha summoned Kachari king Sandhikari but he refused to come.

☐ Following that Kachari king came in and paid tribute to Rajeswar Singha.

 Rajeswar Singha was an able king but he preferred pleasure to state affairs and hence he left the Government in the hands of Kirtichandra Baruah.

 Kirtichandra Baruah became ambitious and caused resentment among nobles.

 Numali Bar Gohain wrote a Buranji named Chakaripheti where it was mentioned that Kirtichandra was from a lower descent.

 Rajeswar Singha fell ill and died in 1769 at Dergaon. Public Works of Rajeswar Singha.

 Rajeswar Singha erected dauls in Baishistasram, Manikarneswar and Nabagrah Dewalaya.

 Construction of Kareng ghar and Talatal Ghar were his best notable works.

 Kareng Ghar- It is a seven storied palace constructed in Garhgaon in 1752.

 Talatal Ghar- Also known as Rangpur palace, is located in Rangpur.

Reign of Lakshmi Singha

 He ascended the throne in 1769 and he assumed the name Sunyeotpha.

 He was nicknamed Kalsoliya Gohain because of his dark complexion.

 His reign was disrupted by the Revolt of Moamariyas. The Moamariyas were the disciples of Mayamara Satra.

 The relation between the Ahoms and Moamoriyas started to degrade since the reign of Pratap Singha.

Moamariya Revolt

 During Siba Singha's reign, Bar Raja Phuleswari tried to impose Shakta rituals on the Mahantas.

 Kirtichandra Baruah provided physical punishment to Moran Chief Nahar who came to the annual offer of elephants. Nahar was offended at this and was looking for an opportunity to take revenge on Barbarua.

 In 1769, Moamariyas defeated the Ahom soldiers in several engagements and the moamariya rebels occupied the capital Rangpur.

 Lakshmi Singha was captured and held captive in Jayasagar Daul and Kirtchandra Baruah was put to death.

 Raghab (Moamariya) assumed the post of Bar Barua and Ramakanta son of Moran Chief Nahar was chosen to the Throne.

 Coins were minted in Ramakanta's name in 1769.

 They retained the structure of the Ahom government and didn't bring any change.

 Initially they didn't face any opposition but later Ahom nobles along with Queen Kuranganayani planned to overthrow the Moamariya regime.

 Finally, in 1770, taking advantage of the Bihu festival Raghab Barbarua was killed.

 Lakshmi Singha was released from captivity and was reinstated to the throne. A large number of Moamariyas were captured and killed at Lakshmi Singha's order.

 In 1780, Lakshmi Singha died at the age of 68 years.

Reign of Gaurinath Singha

 The Ahom kingdom began to decline from the time of Gaurimnath Singha.

 Gaurinath Singha was very cruel and vindictive but he did some good work like abolition of human sacrifice at the Kechaikhati temple at Sadiya.

 In 1782, moamariyas revolted and increased hostilities.

 In the same year, Purnanda Burha Gohain was appointed, he was a brave and efficient Ahom officer. He advised Gaurinath Singha to adopt liberal policy towards Moamariyas.

 In 1785, Gaurinath Singha allowed Moamariyas to have a Guru and Pitambardev was appointed as Moamariya Mahanta.

 After some time of peace, Moamariyas under the leadership of Harihar Tanti advanced towards Rangpur and defeated many Ahom soldiers.

 Gaurinath Singha sought assistance from Manipur, Kachari, Jaintia , but before the help arrived, the rebels occupied Rangpur.

 At Rangpur, the Moamarias set up Bharath Singha as king and Hatisungi Morans set up Sarbananda as their king of the territory to the east of Dihing and both minted coins in their names.

 Then the Ahom administration was shifted to Doichoi (Jorhat) and from there Purnanda Burhagohain continued to fight against Moamarias.

 Krishnarayan of Darrang rebelled and occupied North Guwahati.

 At that time several petty chiefs declared independence and finally Gaurinath Singha had to seek British Assistance.

He appealed for help of men and materials to the British East India Company.

In response to this, Governor General Lord Cornwallis dispatched Captain Thomas Welsh with the sepoys and he arrived at Goalpara in 1792.

The meeting between Gaurinath Singha and Captain Welsh took place at Nagarberra on the Brahmaputra.

Operation of Captain Thomas Welsh

Captain Welsh suppressed the rebellious elements at Guwahati and on the north bank.

He also pacified Darrangi Raja Krishnanarayan and expelled many of the Burkandazes who assisted him.

Then Captain Welsh advanced to Jorhat, then he defeated the moamarias in Rangpur and restored the authority of Gaurinath Singha at Rangpur in 1794.

Soon after this success, Capt. Welsh left Assam as he was recalled by the new Governor General Sir John Shore.

During his stay, Capt. Welsh concluded a commercial treaty in 1793 by which commerce between Assam and Bengal was sought to be put on reciprocal basis.

Reign of Kamaleswar Singha

During his reign, there were many localized revolts by the Khamtis, Pani noras, Miris, Moamariya in league with dafalas nut those were suppressed.

The most notable revolt occurred in Kamrup and it was led by Haradatta and his brother Birdatta. They organized some Barkundez(north Indian) soldiers. The local people called them Dumdumiya and the revolt was known as Dumdumiya or Donduwa Droh.

The Donduwa Droh was soon repressed and Haradatta and Birdatta were killed by Kalia Bhomora Barphukan. So he was offered the title Pratap Ballav by Kamaleswar Singha.

☐ Kalia Bhomora Barphukan also decided to build a bridge over Brahmaputra near Silghat. The second bridge over Brahmaputra 'Kolia Bhomora Setu' (1987) connecting Kaliabor and Tezpur has been named after him.

☐ In 1805, there was a fresh rising of Moamariyas under Sarbanada Singha. Moariyas also brought Burmese army twice for assistance. But Purnanda bribed the Burmese and sent them back.

☐ Finally Purnananda burhagohain concluded a treaty with Moamariyas and they settled in between Brahmaputra and Buridihing which came to be known as 'Matak' state. Their chief was given the title,'Bor Senapati'.

☐ Kamaleswar Singha connected the new capital Jorhat by constructing several new roads like, Na-ali, Rajabahar Ali, Mohabandha Ali, Kamarbandha Ali, etyc.

☐ He also built a copper house at kamakhya.

☐ Kamaleswar singha died in 1810.

Reign of Chandrakanta Singha

☐ He assumed the Ahom name Sudenpha.

☐ His reign saw the Burmese invasion.

☐ Chandra Kanta Singha developed a great friendship with Satram who soon became greedy and insolent and plotted assassination of Burhagohain. He was captured and banished to Namrup.

☐ By that time Kalia Bhomora Barphukan died and Badanchnadra was appointed as the Barphukan.

First Burmese Invasion- 1816 A.D.

☐ Badanchandra Barphukan was very corrupt and soon conflict developed between Purnanda Buragohain and Badan Chandra Barphukan.

☐ Finally Burhagohain sent men to arrest Badan Chandra but he fled and went to Calcutta and sought British assistance. British refused to intervene.

☐ The Badan Chandra went to the Kingdom of Ava(Myanmar) ruled by the Burmese and requested help to fight against the Burhagohain.

☐ The Burmese Monarch Bodoupaya already had his eyes on Assam.

 Bodoupaya took the opportunity and in 1816 he dispatched a huge Burmese army of about sixteen thousand men with Badan Chandra to Assam. It was the first Burmese invasion to Assam.

 Purnananda Burhagohain sent the Ahom army to resist the Burmese army.

 At that juncture, unfortunately he died of heart attack. Purnananda's death was a big blow to Ahom kingdom. He was succeeded by his son Ruchinath Burhagohain.

 The first battle of Ahom and Burmese took place at Ghiladharighat and Burmese defeated the Ahom army.

 Burmese army arrived at Jorhat. On their line of March, Burmese army burnt thousands of villages.

 In April 1817, the Burmese returned to their country and took with them an Ahom girl named Hemo Aideo and a huge amount of presents.

 After the departure of Burmese, Barbarua and Badan Barphukan involved in conflicts.

 The king's mother Numali Rajmao, Nirbhay Narayan Bargohain took side with Barbarua.

 Finally, Badanchnadra was assassinated in 1818.

 Ruchinath Burhagohain decided to place Brajnath Singha in Ahom throne. But he was ineligible for further accession to the throne.

Second Burmese Invasion -1819 A.D.

 News of assassination Barphukan Burmese monarch. He sent a huge force under Alu Mingi and they reached Assam in 1819.

 It was the second Burmese invasion to Assam.

 In the battle near Nazira, initially Ahom army successfully resisted the Burmese. But later the Ahom army retreated and Burmese army advanced to Jorhat.

 Purandar Singha and Ruchinath fled to Guwahati. Purandar Singha reached Calcutta and appealed to the British East India company to assist him but they refused to intervene.

 Chandra Kanta Singha was once again restored to the throne by the Burmese. He was the only nominal ruler and the real authority was vested on Burmese army commander.

In 1819, Alu Mingi returned to Burma. Some Burmese soldiers remained in Ahom kingdom under Mingimaha Tilowa.

After the departure of the Burmese, Chandra Kanta Singha secretly started erecting a fort at Jaipur against further Burmese invasion. It was supervised by Patal Barbarua.

Third Burmese Invasion

In 1821Burmese Monarch Bagidaw sent a Burmese force with presents of ornaments and dress to Chandra Kanta Singha.

When the bUrmese force reached near Jaipur, they saw the preparation for the fort and they killed Patal Barbarua.

Chandrakanta got afraid of this hostile move of Burmese and in 1821, he fled to Guwahati. The Burmese tried to convince him to return but failed.

In 1821, the Burmese placed Jogeswar Singha as a nominal king; the real authority was vested on Burmese commander Mingimaha Tilowa.

Last Battle of Ahom – Burmese and fall of Ahom Kingdom

In 1822, Mingimaha Bandula arrived in Assam with a large reinforcement.

In April, 1822, the battle of Mahgarh took place between Chandra kanta Singha and Burmese but Chandrakanta Singha was defeated.

In June 1822, Chandrakanta fought the last battle of Hadirachaki and there he also got defeated. Chandrakanta fought with exemplary bravery but he was badly defeated due to shortage of ammunition.

After the battle of hadirachaki, the Burmese formally took over the Ahom kingdom.

Chandrakanta Singha fled to Bengal.

Period of Burmese rule (Manor Din) (1821-1824)

The period from 1821-1824 is called a period of Burmese rule.

During that period, the Burmese devastated the country and committed atrocities by plunder and killing of innocent people. People were burnt alive, some portions of their bodies were cut off alive. Their oppression was so horrific which can not be described in words.

In addition to that the Singphos allied with Burmese and made constant raids and carried off helpless Assamese people as their Slaves.

☐ Even after many years Burmese left, people remember Manor din with horror.

Friction between Burmese and British

☐ The Burmese started demanding the surrender of refugees including Chandrakanta Singha and their supporters.

☐ In that time, the border conflict in the East India Company's Chittagong frontier with the Burmese empire also took a serious turn.

☐ Bengal was the most prized possession of British and anticipating a Burmese invasion on Bengal, British Governor Lord Amherst decided to fight.

☐ Governor General Lord Amherst declared war in March 1824 against Burma(Myanmar) under the command of General Archibald Campbell.

Anglo Burmese War

☐ This is the first Anglo Burmese War which lasted for nearly two years.

☐ The British army entered the Goalpara frontier of Assam, defeated the small Burmese garrisons in Lower Assam and advanced to Upper Assam.

☐ The British army in Brahmaputra Valley was led by a civilian (agent of Governor General) David Scott, Colonel Rechards and Captain Neufville.

☐ At first British troops occupied Moramukh- main establishment of Burmese.

☐ In Jan 1825, British army occupied Rangpur and martial law was declared. David Scott was appointed as civil officer in charge of civil matters and Col. Richards in charge of the army.

☐ In 1824Colonel Innes with the help of Gambhir Singh drove out the Burmese from Manipur.

☐ In June 1825, Captain Neufville defeated the allies of Burmese and Singphos. The Burmese were expelled and Singphos submitted. In that mission, Captain Neufville rescued around Six thousands Assamese captives.

☐ Narrative of Burmese War by Wilson provides a detailed account of Anglo Burmese War.

Treaty of Yandaboo, 1826

By 1826, all the Burmese army in Assam and nearby areas were driven out.

Finally on 24 February 1826, a treaty of peace and friendship was concluded between the British and the Burmese at Yandboo.

By this treaty of Yandaboo, The Burmese monarch renounced all claims upon and promised to refrain from all interference with Assam, Manipur and Arakan and also recognized Gambhir Singh as the Raja Manipur.

British keptr Assam under its occupation. It was constituted as the province of Assam and British administration was introduced.

CHRONOLOGY OF IMPORTANT EVENTS

- Beginning of Ahom rule – 1228 A.D.- Syu Ka Pha
- First Ahom Mughal Conflict – 1527 – Pratap Singha
- Invasion of Turbuk- 1532- Suhungmung
- Koch Hajo annexation by Mughals- 1613
- Mir Jumla's Assam invasion- 1662- Jaydhwaj Singha
- Treaty of Ghildaharighat- 1663- Jaydhwaj Singha
- Death of Joymoti- 1680- Sulikpha
- Battle of Itakhuli- 1682- Gadadhar Singha
- Lota Kota Ran- Rajeswar Singha
- First Moamariya Rebellion- 1679- Lakshmi Singha
- Captain Welsh's Mission- 1792- Gaurinath Singha
- Dondowa Droh- 1795- Kamaleswar Singha
- First Burmese Invasion- 1817- Chandraknata Singha
- Second Burmese Invasion- 1819
- Treaty of Yandboo- 1826

BRIEF ACCOUNT ON THE AHOM KINGDOM
Ahom Administration

The system of Government was partly monarchical and partly aristocratic.

The king or Swargadeo was the supreme head of the state. All honours, titles offices originated from him.

- There were several establishments or clans of princes introduced by Suhungmung namely- Charingiya, Tipamiya, Tungkhungiya, Dihingya, Samaguriya, Parbatiya and Namrupiya.
- Each of these princes had their own estates and dependents. All of them belonged to the Ahom royal family and given the title Raja.
- There were two qualifications to become a king - no one could ascent the throne if

a) he is not a prince of the blood

b) He has a noticeable scar mark, blemish or defect in his body.

- The ceremony of installation was of great importance.
- The king wore the Somdeo(image of their deity) carry Hengdan(ancestral sword) and entered Singari Ghar.
- The Ahom king acted according to the advice of three great councilors or GohainBurhagohain, Bargohain and Barpatra Gohain.
- These posts were hereditary in nature but only kings could appoint.
- Syu Ka Pha created the posts of Burhagohain and Barhgohain.
- Suhunmung created the post of Barpatra Gohain equivalent to Burhagohain and Bargohain. Konseng was the first Barpatra Gohain.
- Provinces assigned to the three Gohains where they can exercise powers independently.
- Pratap Singha created the posts of Barphukan and Barbarua.
- Barphukan was placed in charge of lower Assam from Kaliabor upto western boundary with headquarters at Guwahati. He was also head of diplomatic relations with the west(Bengal,Bhutan, etc). He possessed more independent power as he stayed in Guwahati.
- Barbarua was placed as the head of the secretariat and judiciary immediately under the king. He was also the Chief Executive Officer of the entire western region of the Ahom kingdom.
- These posts were not hereditary like the Gohains.
- Ahom king appointed local governors or frontier officers such as Sadiya Khowa Gohain, Marangi Khowa Gohain, Solal Gohain, Kajali Gohain were appointed for the administration of the outlying areas of the country such as Sadiya, Marangi, Sala, Kajali.
- Respectable Ahom families also held higher ranks. Among them was the Phukan. – Nauboicha Phukan, Bhitarual Phukan, Dihingiya Phukan,

Deka Phukan, Na Phukan, Neog Phukan formed the council of the Barbarua.

☐ Next rank was the Barua. There were twenty Baruas- Duliya Baruas, Bez barua, Hati barua, etc.

☐ There were twelve Rajkhowas who commanded three thousand men.

☐ There were several other small posts. Katakis acted as agents or messengers.

☐ Kakati were the writers, Dolois practiced astrology, Bairagi acted as spy, Khaund supervised the cremation of kings and nobles. Bairagi and Khaund travelled from place to places and provided valuable information to the king.

Paik System

☐ It was the backbone of the Ahom administration.

☐ The Paik system was introduced by **Pratap Singha** and was structured by **Mumai Tamuli Barbarua.**

☐ It was not the usual practice in Ahom kingdom to pay the revenue in cash.

☐ The whole male population of Ahom kingdom from 15-50 years had to provide service for the nation instead of paying the revenue in cash.

☐ They were called Paiks.

☐ Females were exempted from the Paik system.

☐ Some paiks were exempted from rendering service under Paik by paying taxes and they were called Chomuwas. Vaishnava Mahantas and disciples pof Sattras were also exempted from the Paik.

☐ Paiks were organized into Gut(group) having 3-4 paiks and they were further higher groups called Khel.

☐ Twenty paiks were commanded by a Bora. Hundred paiks were commanded by Saikia. Thousand paiks were commanded by Hazarika.

☐ As reward to their services, each paik was allotted two puras of best land for rice growing. One could hold additional land by paying taxes.

☐ The people who did not cultivate had to pay taxes. Eg., Artisans, fisherman, Brass workers.

☐ There were no separate standing army in the Ahom kingdom and every active and efficient paik participated in battles as soldiers.

☐ Mughal commander Ram Singha admitted that every Assamese soldier was an expert in rowing boats, shooting arrow digging trenches and cannons and he did not find such specimens of versatility in any part of India.

Law and Justice

☐ The criminal law was characterized by harshness such as mutilation, branding with hot iron. In civil matters traditional laws were followed and later Hindu laws were followed.

Customs and Literature

☐ Sudangpha- Brahmanical influence had its entry to the Ahom palace.

☐ Suhungmung- Adoption of Hindu name. saka era was adopted. Buranjis were written in Assamese.

☐ Suklengmung- First Ahom king to strike coins.

☐ Jayadhwaj Singha- Embraced Hinduism by receiving initiation from a Vaishnava priest.

☐ Rudra Singha- Put an end to burying servants with dead kings in maidams. Celebrated bihu festival in his palace.

☐ Kabiraj Chakrabarty- Royal poet of Rudra Singha's court.

☐ Siba Singha- Unprecedented growth of Hindu religious proclivities.

☐ Gaurinath Singha- Abolition of Human sacrifice in Tamreswari Temple, Sadiya.

Sanskrit Tools for learning

• Sukumar Barkaith- 'Hasti Bidhyarnav'.

• Kabiraj Chakrabarty- Sakuntala kavya

• Ananta Acharya- Ananda Lahiri

• Kabichandra Dwij – Kam Kumar Harana and Dharma puran.

Ahom capitals

▪ Syu ka Pha- Charaideo

▪ Suhungmung – Bokota (bank of Dihing)

▪ Suklengmung – Garhgaon

▪ Rudra Singha- Rangpur

▪ Gaurinath Singha- Dichoi (Jorhat)

Ahom Architecture

☐ **<u>Rang Ghar</u>** – It is located in Rangpur. Rang Ghar is the royal sports Pavilion with two storeys. The Royal family and nobles enjoyed sports such as Elephant Fight, Buffalo fight and other performances from Rang Ghar.

- A Rang Ghar was initially built with wood and bamboo by Rudra Singha which got destroyed.

- The present day masonry built Rang Ghar was constructed by Pramatta Singha in 1746.

- The playground in front of Rang Ghar is known as Rupahi pathar. King Rudra Singha invited young dancers to perform Bihu dance in Ranghar.

□ **Talatal Ghar** – It is located in Rangpur. It was the royal palace of Ahom kingdom.

- It was constructed from 1751-1769 by Rajeswar Singha.

- The palace is said to have seven floors- Four above and Three below the ground with two underground tunnels to Dikhow river and Garhgaon palace or Kareng Ghar.

- However, at present only three overground floors can be seen consisting of thirty six chambers. The palace is enclosed by three ramparts- Bajgarh, Bhitargarh and Tolagarh.

□ **Kareng Ghar (Garhgaon Palace)** – It is located in Garhgaon at Nazira.

- It was the Royal palace constructed in 1752 by Rajeswar Singha.

- At present four floors can be seen over the ground.

□ **Namdang Stone Bridge-** The bridge is carved out from a single solid rock over river namdang. It was constructed in 1703 by Rudra Singha.

□ **Maidams-** The maidams are pyramid-like burial tombs of members of the Ahom royalty. The best known are some 40 tombs at Charaideo. Moidam of Lachit Barphukan is in Hologapar(Mariani) and king Purandar Singha and Purnanda Burhagohain are in Jorhat.

□ **Sivasagar tank and Temple-** Sivasagar Tank dug in 1734 by Queen Ambika to commemorate the victory of Siva Singha. On its banks three temples are located – Shiva doul, Vishnu doul and Devi doul.

□ **Gaurisagar Tank and Temple-** Gaurisankar Tank was dug during the reign of Queen Phuleswari and was dedicated to Goddess Durga.

- **Rudra Sagar Tank and Temple**- Built in 1773 by Lakshmi Singha in memory of his father king Rudra Singha.
- **Joy Sagar Tank and Joy Doul**- Excavated by Rudra Singha in memory of his mother Joymoti. Ranganath Doul, Haragauri Doul, Gaurivallabh Doul and Fakua Doul – the burial place of Jaymoti built by Rudrasimha and the subsequent rulers are located in Rangpur area.

Ahom Monuments and Public Works in Jorhat

- **Roads- Seuni Ali** – Jayadhwaj Singha; Kharikatia Ali, Mahabandha Ali Kamarbandha Ali- Kamaleswar Singha.
- **Tanks**- Rajmao Phukhuri, Mitha Pukhuri, Bongal Pukhuri,- Chandrakanta Singha.
- **Ramparts**- Landoigarh, Mohgarh – Pratap Singha, Borgheta garh.
- **Maidams**- Roja maidam- Maidam of Kamleswar Singha and Purnanada Burhagohain.

Characteristics of Ahom monument

- At that time, the Artisans of Ahom kingdom were not too skilled. So for building the brick monuments. Artisans were mostly brought from Bengal.
- In the brick buildings, instead of cement a mixture was used as a binding agent. The mixture of Egg, Borali Fish, Mati Mah, Bora Saul(Waxy Rice) Lime was applied to walls of monuments.
- Another important feature of Ahom age Tanks is that water levels of the tanks remain higher than the surrounding places. For construction of tanks an expert known as Mati Cheleka used to test the soils.

4.14: AH-2.10: Archaeological Ruins And Places Of Importance

PLACES OF IMPORTANCE

Suryapahar Region

- The Suryapahar region is located in Goalpara.
- In Suryapahar many sculptures and ruins from the 8th-9th century were discovered.
- Vishnu, Hari Hara, Lord Shiva with twelve hands, Goddess Durga etc.

- A number of solid Buddhist stupas, images of Jain Tirthankaras of the 8th - 9th century are also there.
- It is an important archaeological site as remains belonging to different faiths were found at a common place.

Rangpur (Sivasagar)

- Originally founded as the Ahom capital by Rudra Singha in 1699.
- Rangpur area include Jaysagar and Gaurisagar and has a lot of temples, tanks, stone bridges.
- In Rangpur, there exists the royal palace Talatal Ghar and two storied pavilion Rang Ghar.
- Near Talatal Ghar, there is the Jayasagar tank, Fakua Daul, Ranganath temple.

Charaideo

- It is the place where Sukapha set up the first Ahom capital in 1253.
- Charaideo was divided into different areas. The burial area contains innumerable tumuli(Moidams) where kings and members of the royal household were buried.
- The place of worship contains the Deosal with eight columns and the Langkuri Dol. Garhgaon
- Located in Nazira, Sivasagar.
- Established by Suklenmung Garhgaon Raja in 1540.
- Famous Kareng Ghar is located there.
- In Garhgaon there were three large gateways – Barduar, Paniduar and Chunparaduar.

Chargua

- Chargua, the second capital of the Ahoms was set up by Sudanpha.
- At present it contains two large Moidams as well as traces of household compounds.
- Maduri is another region near Jaisagar- Nazira Road and it has altogether 10 moidams.

Sarupathar and Barpathar

- In Nagajari- Khanikar Gaon near Sarupathar, a stone inscription of the 5th century and rocks bearing Brahmi scripts has been recovered.

- Duboroni village near Barpathar has yielded a number of sculptures belonging to the 8th century.

Tezpur

- The present Tezpur town and peripheral region was the capital of Harrupeswar of Salasthamba dynasty (655-900 A.D.)
- A hillock named Bamuni Pahar contains ancient brick and stone ruins. The ruins are famous for their exemplary artistic finesse and date back to the 9th – 10th century.
- Mahabhairab Temple (9th Century) – It is located in the heart of town. The ruins of the old temple are found around the present modern temple.
- In Da – Parbatiya, ruins of the door frame of a temple were found. Its carving resembles the characteristics of early Gupta school of sculpture.
- Others- Hazara Pukhuri, Bhairavi temple, bricks remains of Dhenukhuwa parvat, Mukhalingam known as Tingeswara.

Guwahati

- Guwahati has a number of ancient and medieval period temples.
- Kamakhya Temple, Sukra-Janardana temples, Chatrakara temple, Basistha Temple, Umananda Temple, Navagraha Temple, Ugratara Temple.
- The north Guwahati region has a number of 18th century brick temples namely Asvakranta temple, etc.

Biswanath

- It is situated on the north bank of Brahmaputra in Biswanath district.
- In the medieval period, Ahoms had a regular camp in this region.
- It is popularly known as 'Gupta Kashi'.
- There were several temples of the late medieval period in Biswanath but only two have survived now.
- There is also a Shiva daul in Biswanath.
- The area contains a river islet known as Umatumoni where once existed a brick temple of Goddess Uma. The islet also has a lot of inscriptions engraved on the rock face.

Baihata

- This area is 40km from Guwahati. The famous architectural ruins of Madan Kamdev are located here.
- It is believed that there were 20 temples in this area.

- The ruins of Madan Kamdev belonged to the 10th- 12th century when Pala dynasty ruled Kamarupa.
- The ruins are basically ramparts, walls, pillars, lintels and door frames decorated with flowers, animals, images of Lord Shiva and most importantly sculptures of men, women and animals in erotic postures.

Hajo

- It is located on the north bank of Brahmaputra. It has altogether six temples built during different times.
- The Hayagriva temple is the principal and the oldest temple of the locality dated back to the 8th century situated in Monikut Hill.
- The Lamaists Buddhists also consider Hajo as the place of Mahapanirvana of Sakyamuni or the Budha.
- The 16th century dargah of Ghiyassudin Auliya is also located in Hajo popularly known as Poa Mecca.

Maibang

- It is located on the east bank of the Mahur river in the northern part of Cachar district.
- Maibang was the second capital of the Kachari kingdom.
- It was set up by Kachari around 1676 after they were driven out of their first capital at Dimapur by the Ahoms.
- There is a monolithic Chandi Mandir carved in 1761.

Khaspur

- It is located near Silchar in Cachar.
- It is the last capital of the Kachari kingdom.
- It was established in the 18th century when their former capital at Maibang was sacked by the Ahoms.
- It houses the Archaeological ruins of a king's palace, a Lion Gate and Sun Gate which belong to Kachari Kingdom.

Numaligarh- Deopahar

- Numaligarh region constituted a part of the Kachari kingdom.
- There exists on a hillock the ruins of a 12th century temple, known as Deopahar ruins and also evidence of brick and stone ruins in the vicinity.

Jangal Balahu garh

- It is located in Raha, Nagaon.

- It is a fortified area assigned to Jongal Balahu- the alleged son of Arimatta.

Amtala

- A village near Dabaka in Nagaon.
- A large tank with bricks, ruins of stone temples are discovered dated back to 10th - 12th century.

Important Inscriptions

☐ Umachal Rock Inscription- The rock cut inscription of Surendravarman- the sixth ruler of the Varman dynasty. It is the earliest inscription discovered in Assam dated back to the 5th Century.

☐ Kanaibarashi -bowa Rock Inscription (North Guwahati)- It records the invasion of the Turuska(Muslim) army in 1128. It refers to Muhammad-bin-Bakhtiyar who was confronted and worsted by the army of Bartu or Prithu.

☐ Hayunthal Copper Plate Inscription- It is dated back to the 9th century and it gives the genealogical list of Salasthambha dynasty down to Vanamala, son of Harjavarman.

☐ Nagajari- Khanikar Gaon Stone Inscription- It is a fragmentary inscription belonging to the 5th century. It records the donation of land.

☐ Tezpur Copper Plate Inscriptions of Vallabhadeva- These plates are dated back to 1185 and give the names of four rulers, Bhaskara, Rayarideva, Udayakarna and Vallabhdeva himself.

Coinage of Ahom Age

☐ Shu-Klen-Mung was the first Ahom king to strike coins in 1543. It was in Ahom or Tai script.

☐ Jayadhwaj Singha introduced Sanskrit script in his coins.

☐ Gadadhar Singha is the first Ahom king to annually issue coins and this practice was followed up to the fall of Ahom kingdom. He also re introduced Tai scripts in coins.

☐ Rani Phuleswari is the first queen to strike coins in her name.

☐ Rajeswar Singha issued coins in Assamese, Devnagri and Persian script.

☐ Usually Ahom coins are Octagonal or Square in shape.

☐ Rajeswar Singha introduced coins of different shapes.

☐ Cowrie coins were mostly in use.

☐ During the Moamariya rebellion, coins in the name of Bharat Singha and Sarbananda -two Moamariya leaders were issued from 1791-1795.

Other Coins issued by other Kingdoms

☐ Nara Narayan was the first Koch king to strike coins in his name. His coins were of silver. The half-rupee Koch coins minted were known as Narayani Mudra. Koch coins were round in shape.

☐ Yasodarnarayan Dev and Pratap Narayan Dev of Kachari kingdom issued coins.

☐ Last Kachari king Gobinda Chandra issued a coin of modern type.

4.15: AH-3.1: British Rule & Freedom Struggle

Overview of British Rule in Assam

☐ After the Treaty of Yandaboo in 1826, the British East India Company restored the kings of Cachar, Jaintia and Manipur but continued their occupation in Assam.

☐ Assam was divided into two regions- Lower Assam and Upper Assam.

☐ Lower Assam comprised of Kamrup, Nowgong and parts of Darrang with its headquarters in Guwahati.

☐ Upper Assam comprised of Darrang, from Biswanath to the river Buridihing with its headquarter at Rangpur.

☐ Lower Assam was brought directly under the british control as revenue income from Lower Assam was high.

☐ Upper Assam was under direct military control. David Scott was appointed as the agent of Governor General of the North Eastern frontier and Commissioner (Senior of Assam). He was entrusted with the interest of civil and revenue administration and the extension of British dominion into Assam.

☐ Col. Richards was appointed as the Commissioner (Junior) of Upper Assam. Later the post of Junior Commissioner was scrapped and the post of political agent was introduced.

☐ In 1833, the Ahom prince Purandar Singha was set up as a vassal king and the entire Upper Assam except Sadiya and Matak territories placed under him.

☐ However, based on the reports of Commissioner Jenkins, Purandar Singha;s territory by the British in September 1838. It was divided into two districts- Sibasagar and Lakhimpur.

☐ Then, British annexed Cachar.

☐ Thus, one by one all the principalities of Brahmaputra Valley were annexed to the company's dominion in two decades.

☐ Similarly, Jaintia was annexed in 1835 and Manipiur was restored to its ruling dynasty.

☐ Khasi Hills was annexed in 1834.

☐ Due to the outrages committed by the Bhutias on the british subjects, the British Government also attached all Assam duars in 1841.

Meanwhile on the recommendation of T.C. Robertson in March, 1833, the province of Assam was divided into four districts- Goalpara, Kamrup, Darrang and Nagaon.

In 1842, British Annexed both Sadiya and Matak territory and combined them with Lakhimpur district and Dibrugarh was made the headquarters.

In 1898, British took possession of the Lushai Hills and placed them under the Assam administration.

Between 1835-1851, ten military expeditions were sent to the Naga hills and by 1866 the British annexed the area of Naga Hills.

In 1854, the territory of Tularam(successor of Kachari King) was annexed and added to the North Cachar sub – division.

In 1874, the province of Assam was created after combining with the Cachar and Sylhet district and a Chief Commissioner was appointed as the head.

The headquarters of the newly created Assam province was established in Shillong in 1874.

In 1905, Lord Curzon combined the eastern Bengal with Assam (Partition of Bengal) and formed a new territory. Later in April, 1912, Assam was restored to its former territorial position.

In 1921, Assam was given the status of a Governor's province (Government of India Act, 1919).

In 1935, Assam was granted provincial autonomy (Govt of India Act 1935). A bicameral legislature was formed in Assam.

On 15th August 1947 along with other parts of India, Assam also got independence from the British occupation and became a part of Indian Union.

British Civil Administration in Assam
Administration of David Scott

In 1828, Martial law was lifted from Upper Assam and David Scott was appointed as the Commissioner of Assam and all matters- civil, criminal, justice, revenue administration, police, etc. was placed under him.

David Scott organized the administration in general outline and retained many old indigenous systems prevalent at that time.

☐ In Upper Assam, the old Paik system and Khel system was retained. Barbarua was appointed to collect the tax.

☐ In Lower Assam, the Pargana land division- system was retained.

☐ Each Pargana was placed under the charge of the Choudhury to collect taxes. Professional tax, rent tax, stamp duties were among the various taxes imposed on people of Lower Assam.

☐ Scott recommended the restoration of Ahom monarchy in Upper Assam rather than its annexation. Accordingly, the Ahom prince Purandar Singha was enthroned as the Raja of the Upper Assam under an agreement

i) The Raja would pay a sum of Rs 50,000 annually as tribute.

ii) The Raja would act accordingly to the advice of the British Political agent.

iii) The Raja would be protected against any foreign aggression.

Administration of T.C. Roberston

☐ David Scott died in 1831 and he was succeeded by T.C. Roberston in 1832 as the Agent to the Governor -General and Commissioner of Assam.

☐ T.C. Roberston divided Lower Assam into four districts. Each was placed as a Principal Assistant vested with the powers of a Collector, Judge and Magistrate.

☐ Roberston brought about radical changes. In 1832, he abolished additional compulsory taxes. But tax on land at various rates was imposed on the peasants. Choudhuries, Patgiris and Baishyas were appointed the revenue officers.

☐ In 1834, the post of agent of Governor General for the north eastern frontier was scrapped.

☐ Captain Francis Jenkins was appointed as the commissioner of Assam. During his administration, Upper Assam was annexed to the British territory in 1838.

☐ The post of Deputy Commissioner was created in 1839 to relieve the commissioner as Civil Judge with judicial powers. He acted as district and session judge.

British Civil Administration in Assam

⬜ Each district was placed in charge of a Principal (Senior) Assistant assisted by a Junior Assistant and a Sub-Assistant.

⬜ The old Khel system was abolished and new taxes like tax on 'barimati' were introduced.

⬜ In 1861, Deputy Commissioner was re-designated as Judicial Commissioner; Principal Assistant as Deputy Commissioner, Junior assistant as Assistant Commissioner and Sub-Assistant as Extra Assistant Commissioner.

⬜ In 1874, Assam was created as a separate province and a Chief Commissioner was appointed.

⬜ Colonel R.H. Kitting became the first Chief Commissioner of Assam.

⬜ In 1880, a commissioner was appointed for Brahmaputra valley and in 1905 commissioners were appointed for Cachar, Surma and Hill districts.

⬜ On 16th October 1905, Assam became the part of the new born composite province of Eastern Bengal and Assam. Later in 1912 Assam was again restored as a Chief Commissioner's province. In 1912 the first Assam Legislative Council was created.

⬜ In 1921, Assam was given the status of Governor's province and Sir Nicholas Dodd Beatson Bell became the first Governor of Assam.

British Judicial Administration in Assam

⬜ Initially Barphukan looked after judicial administration.

⬜ There was a civil judicial establishment consisting of one Principal Sadar Amin, Sadar Amnis and Munsiffs.

⬜ In each district, there were two courts- the munsif and the panchayat.

⬜ The munsif's court tried original cases from one hundred to five hundred rupees and heard appeals from the panchayat court. The panchayat court tried minor cases of up to one hundred rupees.

⬜ The separate establishment of Sadar Amin and Munsiffs was abolished in 1872.

⬜ After the creation as a separate province in 1874 separate Faujdari (criminal matters) and Diwani (civil matter) courts were established in each district of Assam.

☐ To maintain law and order and protect lives and properties in the interiors thanas were established with a thanadar or daroga in charge. It consisted of one Daroga, one Jamadar and a number of constables.

☐ The darogas could arrest suspected persons, detain them and even hold preliminary trials before sending them to sadar station.

☐ British abolished cruel punishment and practices such as chopping off ears, noses, abduction of young women, forced labour. But at the same time, the judicial system became a costly affair. Court cases lawyers these things became out.

☐ On failure to pay taxes, property of the defaulting peasants was confiscated with the result that peasants at times could not save their farming land and home.

Trade, Commerce and Communication

☐ Gaurinath Singha signed a commercial treaty with Captain Welsh in 1793. It had allowed the merchants of Bengal to engage in trading in Assam.

☐ Indigenous tea of Assam was discovered by Mr. Robert Bruce in 1823.

☐ In 1839, Assam company was established by the British and set up the first tea garden at Nazira. By 1858, Lakhimpur, Sibsagar and Cachar were covered by this company for tea plantation.

☐ C.A. Bruce and Maniram Dewan played a great role in tea plantation of Assam during the initial period.

☐ Import of labour from outside(Chotanagpur, Jharkhand, Odisha) took place for expansion of the tea industry.

☐ Avenues of employment both in office and trade caused an inflow of population from the districts of Sylhet, Dacca, Mymensingh and Rangpur to Assam.

☐ First coal mining was done in 1882 at Ledo in Assam Railway & Trading Company.

☐ First oil well at Digboi drilled in 1889 and the first refinery at Digboi started functioning in 1901 under Assam Oil Company Limited.

☐ The first railway line in Assam was the Dibru Sadiya line (constructed in 1882-1884). To evacuate tea, oil timber produced in Assam.

☐ In 1892, Assam Bengal Railway was incorporated.

In 1841, Steam boat was launched by Assam Tea Company for navigation in Brahmaputra.

In 1842-43 the Assam trunk Road was constructed and after around ten years North trunk road was constructed.

Official Language

Between 1826 and 1837 the Assamese language had been in use in Assam in literature and official purposes.

British encouraged the establishment of English schools in Assam as they needed English knowing people to help run the administration.

The services of the English educated and Bengali people from Bengal became very important in the revenue and judicial departments and newly started Government schools.

Eventually, in 1837 Bengali language was made the official language in Courts, got. Department and medium of instruction in the school of Assam.

Anandaram Dhekial Phukan was the first voice of protest against the imposition of Bengali as the medium of instruction and pleaded for its replacement by Assamese.

Finally, many educated Assamese and Christian Missionaries protested and Assamese was re -introduced as the official language in 1871.

The long period of 1837 to 1871 is called the Dark age of Assamese language.

Development of Education

Primary Education- David Scott promoted of indigenous system of education in Assam and he started eleven schools mostly in lower Assam. He also opened a school in Garo Hills and expanded primary education among the hill tribe. In 1926, the first compulsory Primary Education Act was passed.

Secondary education- In Assam secondary education started in the year 1835.

- Captain Jenkins established the first English High School in 1835 in Guwahati known as 'Guwahati Seminari' and later 'Guwahati School' which is the present Cotton Collegiate School in Panbazaar.

- From 1912-1947 the number of Middle English school and Middle Vernacular schools increased to 742 and High schools increased to 191.

- The Matriculation examination was conducted by Calcutta University.

  Higher Education- In May 1866 the Collegiate section was open at Guwahati School with affiliation to the first examination in Arts stream.

- In 1882, Sir Charles Elliot introduced a scholarship to all Assamese students who passed the entrance examination and went for F.A. and B.A. examination at any college in Bengal.

- In 1899 Manik Chandra Barua, made a strong demand for establishment of a college at Guwahati.

- Chief commissioner Sir Henry Cotton decided to establish a Government college at Guwahati in May 1901, the 'Cotton College' was formally opened. Fredric Willium Sudmersen was the first principal of Cotton College.

- From 1914-1935 the following colleges were established in Assam- Earle Law College at Guwahati(1914), Jagannath Barua College at Jorhat(1931) and Lady keane College at Shillong(1935).

- In 1945, Dibrugarh College was established. (now known as DHSK college).

FREEDOM STRUGGLE
Initial Anti British – Plots and Rebellions

● In 1826, Assam was formally handed over to the British East India Company.

● British gradually started introducing a new system of civil revenue administration and the Ahom royal families and other nobles had lost their rights and privileges and it caused great resentment.

● In 1828, some of them organized a revolt under the leadership of Dhananjoy Piyoli Borgohain. That was the first revolt against British in Assam. The rebels decided to place Gomadhar Konwar on the throne. The Khasis and the Singphoes were also prepared to revolt against the British. They organized some soldiers and advanced towards Rangpur.

● At Bassa, Gomadhar was formally enthroned. But soon they lost the battle against the British who were led by Lt. Rutherford. Gomadhar was arrested and imprisoned. Dhananjoy was captured and provided death penalty but escaped to Motok state.

- In 1829, Dhanonjoy again organized another revolt against British. He was assisted by his sons Harakanta and Haranath and Jiuram Duliya Barua.
- Later many others from Ahom noble families joined them. Piyali Barphukan the son of Badan Borphukan also took lead in organizing the revolt.
- Rupchand Konwar, Brajnath Konwar, Deoram Dihingiya Phukan also took part in the plot.
- Piyoli Barphukan and Piyoli Bargohain addressed letters to the chiefs of the Khamptis, Singphos, Moamarias, Manipuris, Nagas, Khasis and Garo for help and combined action against the british. Khasi leader Teerut Singh himself had joined the rebels.
- In 1830, the rebels advanced towards Rangpur.
- But Sadiyakhowa Gohain betrayed the rebels and handed over some secret letters to British officials.
- The British got alerted and launched precautionary measures and in January 1830. Haranath was apprehended by the British officials.
- Piyoli Bargohain and other leaders launched an attack upon Rangpur on the night of March 1830.
- Capt. Neufville immediately sent troops and Piyoli Barphukan , Jiuram Duliya Barua, Rupchand Konwar were arrested.
- They were brought to trial at the first instance in the Sadar panchayat Court at Sibsagar.
- They were all found guilty of treason and convicted.
- Death penalty was provided to Piyali Barphukan and Jiuram Barua. In August 1830 Piyali Barphukan and JIuram Duliya Barua were publicly hanged to death in the bank of Sivasagar tank.
- The properties of other rebels were confiscated and banished for 14 years.
- This was the last organized rebellion against British rule by the upper classes in Assam. Those initial revolts were unable to gain support of common people because they had lost faith in Ahom rule and preferred to remain under British rule.

Anti- British Movement – 1857 Revolt

• The rule of the East India Company ended in 1858 and the whole India came under the direct control of British Crown.

• The assessment of land revenue was increased and income tax stamp duties were also imposed by the new administration. The government carried on trade in opium and salt in the State and started earning considerable profits.

• It was followed by the association of Assam in Sepoy Mutiny and Maniram Dewan was taking lead in Assam.

• In 1839, Maniram became the Bar Bhandar Barua(finance minister) of Purandar Singha. Later he became the Dewan of the Assam Tea Company but he resigned.

• In 1853 Moffat Mills came to Assam to review the economic condition.

• Again in 1857 Maniram proceeded to Calcutta to plead the Government to restore the kingdom to Kandarpeswar Singha. But he didn't not get any response and eventually turned into a rebel in 1857.

• Maniram Dewan from Calcutta sent secret letters through conveyors (known as Bhat) to several individuals in Assam to organize revolts. Contact was established with Subadars Nur Muhammad and Bhikun Sheikh and a few Jemadars of the Sepoys at Dibrugarh and Golaghat. Bahadur Gaonbura and Sheikh Formud Ali actively joined in the plot.

• But British officers Charles Holroyd came to know about the conspiracy. Soon security measures were tightened up by British and enforced operation and large numbers of arrests took place.

• Piyoli Baruah, Dutiram Baruah, Mayaram Nazir, Marangikhowa Gohain, Bahadur Gaoburah, Shaikh Formund and several others were arrested.

• Kandarpeswar Singha was arrested and dispatched to Calcutta and kept confined as state prisoner in Alipur.

• Maniram Dewan was arrested in Calcutta and brought to Assam.

• On 26th Feb 1858, Maniram Dewan and Piyoli Baruah were hanged in Jorhat Jail.

● The Sepoy Mutiny had also spread also amongst troops of the Kamrup Regiment stationed at Guwahati following which many of them were dismissed from service.

Peasant Uprising

☐ The Government doubled the existing rates of revenue on land after coming under the Queen's crown in 1858.

☐ In 1861, a peasant uprising in Phulaguri Dhawa took place in Phulaguri region of Nagaon. The main cause was the ban of private cultivation of opium and increased rate on Opium.

☐ The people of Phulaguri in Nagaon district are mostly Lalung and Kachari tribes and they were Opium users.

☐ They strongly opposed the ban on the cultivation of poppy through Rajmel (Public meeting) in October 1861.

☐ On 18th October 1861 a young British officer Mr. Singer was lynched to death by an angry mob as he tried to disperse an ongoing Raizmel. Following that incident, the revolt was suppressed. Many leaders were executed and imprisoned.

☐ In 1886, Assam Land and Revenue Regulations were introduced and revenue was increased.

Assam Riots

☐ Following the several peasant uprising took place in 1892-1894 in the Kamrup and Darrang districts. The popular uprising was termed by British as 'Assam Riots'.

☐ The uprisings took place in regions like Bajali, Rangia, Lachima and Patharughat.

☐ The people of Rangia organized Raizmels and ransacked the Rangia market. In 1894, they raised a slogan that they would not pay the increased revenue. On the same day a ban on the 'mel' was imposed by the Deputy Commissioner of Kamrup.

☐ All the leaders were arrested and the Rangia revolt came to an end.

☐ However, taxes were doubled.

☐ The most notable uprising took place in Patharughat (Darrang district), in 1894. In January 1894, 140 protesting peasants were killed in police firing . Berington was the Superintendent of Police.

The Patharughat incident was known as Doli Ron as the peasants pelted Doli (clods of clay) on the armed police.

The uprisings of 1892-1894 had an impact in the imperial Legislative Council where Dr. Rash Behari Ghosh questioned the enhanced assessment of revenue in Assam.

Rise of Socio-political organization

In 1885 the Indian National Congress was formed.

In the second session of the Congress held in Calcutta in 1886 many representatives from Assam joined- Debi Charan Baruah of Upper Assam Association, Kali Kanta Barkakoti of Shillong Association, Satyanath Borah of Nagaon Ryot Association, Kamini Kumar Chanda of Habibganj People's Association.

The Assam Association- It was formed in 1903 by Manik Chandra Barua, Ghanashyam Barua, Jagannath Barua, Phanidhar Chaliha, Faijnur Ali and many others.

In 1905, its first session was held in Dibrugarh and it formally elected Raja Prabhat Chandra Baruah of Gauripur as its President, Jagannath Baruah as Vice-President and Manik Chandra Baruah as General Secretary.

They opposed the partition of Bengal, the grazing tax and realization of money by the government from the immortal trade of opium.

Nabin Chandra Bordoloi presided over the 1917 Association at Dibrugarh. Following a deputation from Assam Association consisting Nabin Chandra Bordoloi and Prasanna Kumar Barua was sent to London to represent Assam before the Selborne Committee of House of Lords and demanded full provincial status of Assam.

In 1917, a delegation of Ghanashyama Barua, Nabin chnadra Bordoloi, Padmanath Gohain Barua, Chandradhar Barua and Prasanna Kumar Barua gave evidence before Montague, Secretary of State of India.

Finally in 1921, Assam Association merged itself with the newly formed Assam Provincial Congress Committee (APCC).

The Assam Chatra Sanmilan- In 1916, the first session of Assam Chatra Sanmilan was held in Guwahati. The president was Lakshminath Bezbarua.

- It was originally a literary organization and not interested in politics, but afterwards they got involved in the freedom movement. They urged people for use Swadeshi goods and to boycott foreign goods. They also demanded separate universities for Assam.

- The Assam Chatra Sanmilan created a cadre of student leaders- Chandranath Sarma, Omeo Kumar Das, Hem Chandra Barua, Padmadhar Chaliha and many others.

☐ Later Tarun Ram Phukan became president of APCC and constituted APCC and Gopinath Bordoloi, Bimala Prasad Chaliha, Chandranath Sarmah, Krishna Nath Sarmah and Kanak Chandra Sarmah as members of All India Congress Committee.

☐ Under the initiative of the new committee Mahatma Gandhi was invited to Assam in 1921 to propagate the message of non-cooperation amongst the masses of Assam.

Non-Cooperation Movement

☐ Mahatma Gandhi launched the Non-Cooperation Movement in 1920.

☐ In Assam both Hindu and Muslim equally responded to the cause of Khilafat.

☐ Nabin Chandra Bordoloi appealed to the people of Assam to accept NonCooperation.

☐ In 1920, Tezpur session of Assam Association chaired by Prasanna Kumar Barua accepted the resolution of non-cooperation.

☐ In 1921, Provincial Congress Committee of Assam was formed. Kuladhar Chaliha was the first President of Provincial Congress.

☐ Mahatma Gandhi visited Assam with Ali Brothers- Shaukat Ali and Mohammad Ali in August 1921. The lawyers, government officers, and teachers left their jobs to devote themselves to the cause of the nation.

☐ There was also a strike against the opium habit. The Congress volunteers made a door to door campaign.

☐ In March 1921, there was a labour strike in Halem Tea Estate in Darrang.

☐ Another labour strike in the tea gardens in Sylhet and Cachar in Surma Valley about the middle of 1921 when the non cooperation movement was in full swing. There was a general exodus or mass departure of thousands of labourers from the garden in protest against incredibly low wages.

☐ This was termed as Chargola exodus.

☐ The Guwahati Bar Association at the initiative of young lawyers even decided to boycott the Viceroy's visit. Almost all the district level Association took a decision to boycott Council elections and also raised objections to take titles, honour and honorary posts from British Government.

☐ The boycott agitation of the students had almost automatically led to the demand for setting up national schools and national colleges in the province.

☐ However, the Non Cooperation movement met its abrupt end as Gandhiji suspended it after the Chauri-Chaura incident in 1922.

☐ In March 1922, Omeo Kumar Das attended All India Congress Committee meeting and was informed about severe repression which was then going on in Assam. Following that Rajendra Prasad and Pandit Madan Mohan Malviya visited Assam in May 1922 and submitted a report.

Period of Political Unrest

☐ By the end of 1922, Provincial Congress suffered from organizational weakness.

☐ This led to the formation of a wing of the Swarajya Party in Assam in 1923. Tarunram Phukan was elected its president and Gopinath Bordoloi the secretary.

☐ They contested council elections in 1923 and finally eight Swarajya Party members were elected to the Assam Legislative Council in 1924. Traunram Phukan was elected to the central Legislature.

☐ In 1926, Nabin Chandra Bordoloi was also elected to the central legislature.

☐ Assam Sangrakshini Sabha was founded by Ambikagiri Roy Choudhury. He also started publishing a monthly journal 'Chetana' and demanding protection of rights of the Assamese people against aggression of outsiders.

☐ Padmanath Gohain Barua and Nilmoni Phukan subscribed to Assam Sangrakshini Sabha and it later became Asom Jatiyo Mahasabha.

Pandu Session of Indian National Congress

In 1926, 41st session of Indian National Congress was held in Pandu Guwahati. The president of the session Sri Nivas Iyengar.

In 1929, in the Lahore Congress Session the National Congress Committee declared the demand for complete independence. In response to that Assam spontaneously celebrated 'Independence Day' on 26th January 1930.

Civil Disobedience Movement in Assam

Assam congress joined the Civil Disobedience Movement. The struggle in Assam took the form of a boycott of foreign clothes, drugs, and shops selling such goods. Picketing was resorted to.

Sri Bishnuram Medhi, Tyagbir Hemchandra Barua, Dr. Bhubaneswar Barua, Omeo Kr. Das, Pitambar Goswami and others played a great role.

Women also played a great role. Chandra Prabha Saikiani, Durgaprava Barua, Girijabala Gupta. Rani Gaidinlu from Nagaland also organized a revolt against British. Later in 1933 she was imprisoned for life.

To mobilise women across Assam, Assam Mohila Samiti was formed in 1930.

In 1937, as per the provision of the Government of India Act 1935, general elections were held in Assam.

A United People's Party was formed by Tarun Ram Phukan and Rohini Kumar Choudhury to contest the elections.

By that time, a local agitation named Assam University League for the establishment of a separate Assam University for Assam was also set up with K.N. Dutt as President.

Saadullah Ministry

In 1937 elections, Congress won 33 seats out of 108 seats in Assam. But Congress did not form the Ministry in Assam. In the same year Jawaharlal Nehru visited Assam.

Sir Muhammad Saadullah formed a coalition ministry with support of the European group and other groups became the Chief minister of Assam.

But soon the Govt. headed by Sir Muhammad Saadullah started allowing influxes of landless peasants from East Bengal and opened up fallow waste lands in Assam for cultivation for them a section of Assamese nationalists got alarmed.

Congress Ministry in 1938

The Assam Sangrakshini Sobha began to demand for vindication of the rights of the Assamese people, the children of the soil, as against aggression of outsiders.

On 13th sept, 1938, the ministry headed by Sir Md. Saadullah had to resign because of its communal policies.

Congress formed the Ministry in Assam and Gopinath Bordoloi became the Chief Minister of Assam.

The Bordoloi ministry immediately stopped opium cultivation, reduced the land revenue, and restricted illegal immigrants.

In 1939, The digboi Labour Strike took place involving nearly 10,000 labourers. There was dispute between the Assam Oil Company(A.O.C) and A.O.C. Labour Union.

In Nov, 1939, the Bordoloi ministry in Assam resigned and Sir Syed Saadullah again formed a Coalition ministry.

In December 1941, a students demonstration was held by the students of Cotton College at Guwahati Judge field against Government initiative for collection of money for the war fund. Police Lathi charge was launched on them and several students were injured.

This incident led to the resignation of the Saadullah ministry on 24th December 1941.

Quit Movement (August Revolution)

After the civil disobedience movement a campaign of individual Satyagraha was launched under the leadership of Mahatma Gandhi.

In Sibasagar, the individual Satyagraha movement was started by Moulana Tayebulla, the President of the Asom Pradesh Congress Committee. Gopinath Baordoloi, Bishnuram Medhi , Omeo Kumar das and many others also took part in the individual Satyagraha and got arrested.

After that in 1942, the World War II took a serious turn and to meet the situation the British Government sent the Cripp's Mission to India but his proposals were not accepted by the Congress and the Muslim League.

☐ In 1942, the Congress Committee adopted the famous 'Quit India Revolution'.

☐ Assam jumped into the movement within a week of declaration of the Quit India resolution in August 1942.

☐ Gopinath Bordoloi, Md. Tayabullah, Fakaruddin Ali Ahmed, Bishnuram Medhi, Debeswar Sarma, Dr. Harekrishna Das, Lila Barua with many others were arrested by the British as preventive measure.

☐ All organisations including Ryot-Sabhas which subscribed to the Congress fund were declared unlawful.

☐ The Mrityu Bahini carried out serious acts of sabotage and violence destruction of railways and bridges, and set fire to Govt. properties. Other leaders were Gahanchandra Goswami, Jyotiprasad Agarwalla.

☐ Another organization Shanti Bahini was formed for non violent protests.

☐ On 20th September 1942, a procession of unarmed villagers marched towards Gohpur Police Station to hoist the National Flag and Kanaklata Baruah and Mukunda Kakoti were shot dead by police.

☐ Madan Barman and Rawta Kachari lost their lives in the police firing in Bajali.

☐ In Dhekiajuli Thana, police opened fire on a crowd. Kahuli Devi, Kumali Devi, Tileswari Barua and three others were shot dead.

☐ At Brahmpur(Nagaon) due to police firing Bhogeswari Phukanani, Phuleswari Konwari, Thagi Sut, Hemram Patar and others embraced death.

☐ On 10th October 1942, a military train derailed at Sarupathar Golaghat by Mrityu Bahini and British soldiers lost their lives.

☐ Following that Kushal Konwar was arrested, convicted of sabotage and hanged to death in Jorhat Jail in 1943.

☐ Kushal Konwar was the only martyr to be hanged in the Quit India Movement.

☐ In December 1945, Jawaharlal Nehru made a tour to Assam making an impact in the public mind in favour of the Congress.

☐ In January 1946, Mahatma Gandhi visited Guwahati along with four other leaders of Assam and performed mass-prayers. This was his last visit to Assam.

Elections were held in 1946 and the congress won over 50 seats out of 108 seats. Two independents joined later and the congress ministry with Gopinath Bordoloi as the Premier was formed on 10th February 1946.

Cabinet Mission and Grouping Plan

In 1946, three members of British reached India under the Cabinet Mission. It arbitrarily divided British India into three groups A,B,C.

As per grouping plan Assam and Bengal were to be clubbed together in group C creating a predominantly Muslim zone in Eastern India.

But it was strongly resented by the people of Assam. The Assam Provincial Congress resisted Assam's inclusion in the grouping system.

Assam Jatiya Mahasabha revealed an underground conspiracy of Maulana Bhasani group from Eastern Bengal to invade Assam through population migration.

Assam Jatiya Mahasabha under the leadership of Ambikagiri Roy Choudhury organized mass protests across Assam.

In July 1946, The Assam Legislative Assembly adopted a resolution moved by the Chief Minister Gopinath Bordoloi himself expressing disapproval of the grouping plan.

By the same time, Syed Saadullah and Gopinath Bordoloi participated in the constituent assembly on behalf of Assam. They have put efforts in incorporating the Sixth Schedule in the constitution.

Independence of Assam

On 3rd June 1947, the Mountbatten Plan was accepted. This plan was formulated after Indian National Congress, The Muslim League and the Sikh community came to an agreement with Governor General Lord Mountbatten.

On the basis of Mountbatten's plan the Indian Independence Bill, 1947 was passed on 18th July 1947.

India was divided into India and Pakistan. Pakistan won freedom on 14th August 1947 and India on 15th August 1947.

Akbar Hydari became the First Indian Governor of Assam.

Gopinath Bordoloi became the first Chief Minister of Assam in Independent India.

4.16: AH-3.2: Bodo Accord

Context- With an aim to bring permanent peace in Bodo-dominated areas in Assam, the Centre on 27th January 2020 signed a tripartite agreement with the dreaded insurgent group National Democratic Front of Bodoland (NDFB) and two other outfits, providing political and economic benefits without acceding to the demand for a separate state or Union Territory.

• The All Bodo Students' Union (ABSU), which has been spearheading a movement for a Bodoland state since 1972, and the United Bodo People's Organisation were also signatories to the Comprehensive Bodo Settlement Agreement – Bodoland Territorial Region (BTR).

• Important Points- In the presence of Union Home Minister Amit Shah, the tripartite agreement was signed by top leaders of the four NDFB factions, the ABSU and the United Bodo People's Organization (UBPO); Joint Secretary in the Home Ministry Satyendra Garg; and Assam Chief Secretary Kumar Sanjay Krishna.

• Assam Chief Minister Sarbananda Sonowal also signed the pact as one of the witnesses. Soon after the agreement was signed, Prime Minister Narendra Modi said it would usher in a new dawn of peace, harmony and togetherness.

• Bodos, who believe to be the earliest settlers of Assam, are an ethnic and linguistic group which is a sub-group of the Bodo-Kachari family.

• The Bodo conflict, which dates back to the pre-Independence era, gained momentum from 1987 when the ABSU launched an agitation for a separate state. Some prominent armed separatist groups were founded during the 1980s.

• Bodos have advanced a number of reasons for wanting a separate state. They have called the territory they inhabit home for centuries, and want to protect their ethnic identity, way of life, and language. They also sought better governance and development.

Timeline of major events in the long standing problem of Bodo conflict

• 1929: Bodo leader Gurudev Kalicharan Brahma submitted a memorandum to the Simon Commission asking for reservations in the

Legislative Assembly and for a separate political entity for his people. He efforts failed him.

• 1960s and 1970s: There were calls from Bodos and other tribes for a separate state of Udayachal as unauthorized occupants were accused of encroaching on Bodoinhabited lands.

• Late 1980s: A demand for a separate state for Bodos – Bodoland – and for Assam to be divided "50-50" were raised. Despite Bodo leader and then ABSU president. Upendranath Brahma adopting a "peaceful" approach, separatist groups like the Bodoland Liberation Tigers (BLT) and the The National Democratic Front of Bodoland (of which NDFB(S) is a faction) were founded during the same time.

• 1993, February: The Centre, Assam government and the ABSU sign a tripartite agreement, following which the Bodoland Autonomous Council (BAC) was constituted.

• 2003, February: The separatist BLT was disbanded and another agreement was signed between the Centre, the Assam government and the BLT. This led to the formation of the Bodoland Territorial Council (BTC).

• The BTC administered the Bodoland Territorial Area – an entity based on the idea of a 'state-within-a-state' and created by the reorganization of seven Assamese districts into four contiguous districts – Kokrajhar, Chirang, Udalguri and Baksa.

• Hagrama Mohilary, who currently heads the Bodo Territorial Council, was a leader in the now defunct armed separatist group Bodo Liberation tigers.

• 2005: The National Democratic Front of Bodoland (NSFB) agreed to a ceasefire with the Assam government and the Centre. After the treaty was signed, the group had split into three factions. One of those factions, the NDFB (S), continued to carry out violent attacks within the state.

• 2012: The Bengali-speaking Muslims and Bodos in Bodoland Territorial Area got involved in ethnic riots, thereby killing 100 and rendering four lakh homeless. This isn't an isolated incident. Bloody clashes between Bodos and non-Bodos, especially Bengali-speaking Muslims, have been routinely reported in the region.

● May, 2014: Acting on assumption that people did not vote for their candidates in Lok Sabha polls held in April, 2014, the Bodo terrorists killed 30 people in Kokrajhar and Baksa districts.

● December, 2014: Further attacks by Bodo terrorists killed at least 81 people, including 76 adivasis. As many as 2 lakh people were rendered homeless after the attacks.

● Both the May and December 2014 attacks were allegedly carried out by NDFB (S).

● Post the December incident, the Centre launched an Operation All Out – a largecale military operation involving the Army, the Air Force, Assam state police and paramilitary forces – with an aim to eliminate NDFB(S) completely.

● August, 2016: Fourteen civilians were killed in Kokrajhar district by terrorists. The NDFB(S) were suspected to be behind the attack.

● August, 2017: The movement group comprising ABSU, NDFB (P) and People's Joint Action Committee for Bodoland Movement (PJACBM) supported by Ranjan Daimaryled NDFB faction, which is currently under peace parley with the Government of India, had announced the series of movement seeking early solution to the Bodoland issue.

● A crucial meeting of the movement group was held at Bodofa House, Baganshali in Kokrajhar on 20 August, 2017, and discussed the future course of action and movement strategy.

● In the press meet held after, the president of the ABSU, Promod Boro said the movement group was compelled to undertake the series of agitation as the NDA government at the Centre had been giving lukewarm response towards the solution of Bodoland issue even after promising a resolution prior to the 2014 parliamentary election. He had said that there would be a 10-hour highway blockade by women on 28 August, 12-hour Assam bandh on 12 September, mass hunger strike from 1 October, 24-hour railway blockade in October and indefinite economic blockade from November.

● 27, January 2020: As the ABSU continued with its movement for creation of a Bodoland state and NDFB carried out hit-and-run operations, several rounds of negotiations with New Delhi, four factions of NDFB and the ABSU on Monday led to the signing of the third Bodo accord. Now, there are going to be 60 members in the Bodoland Territorial Region.

☐ Though Amit Shah and the Bodo leaders are euphoric with the Bodo accord 2020, it is definite that it can never be the end of movements in Bodoland.

4.17: AH-3.3: Language Movement in Assam

Official Language Movement

☐ The demand for making Assamese the official language in Assam, after the independence of India had been raised since 1950, following the States Reorganization Act, 1956 the movement gained a new momentum.

☐ The inclusion of Assamese in the Eighth Schedule to the Constitution of India also helped increase a sense of confidence.

☐ The Assam Sahitya Sabha passed two resolutions, one in 1950 and another in 1959, stressing the need to make Assamese the official language in Assam.

☐ The April 1959 resolution, demanding that Assamese be made the sole official language in Assam- sparked political reaction.

☐ During a visit by the then Prime Minister of India, Jawaharlal Nehru to Gauhati University, the students made the same demand.

☐ The Assam Pradesh Congress Committee (APCC) passed a resolution supporting it. Students organized processions, strikes and meetings for the cause.

☐ This move to make Assamese the official language was however, protested against by a group of non-Assamese speakers in Assam. Following the APCC resolution, a procession was led out by non-Assamese students in Shillong to oppose the decision to make Assamese the sole official language in Assam.

☐ The Shillong students' procession was in turn opposed in Upper Assam- in areas such as Sivasagar, Dibrugarh, Golaghat and Jorhat, where they supported the acceptance of Assamese as the official language.

☐ After a tenuous situation, as colleges and the university reopened, the agitation became pronounced in Lower Assam and Guwahati.

The Silchar and Karimganj Bar Associations on the other hand passed resolutions demanding President's Rule in the state.

On 4 July 1960, an Assamese student was killed and 6 others injured in police firing.

The government of Assam, under the then Chief Minister Bimala Prasad Chaliha proposed the Assamese Official Language Bill in the Assembly on 10 October 1960. The Bill provided for two official languages- Assamese and for an interim period, English. It was passed on 24 October 1960.

Protests in the Barak Valley region- including Cachar, Karimganj etc. against the bill on 19 May 1961 led to the death of a number of protesters.

In Cachar itself, on the other hand, the Muslims, the Manipuris and the indigenous Cacharis formed the 'Shanti Parishad' which in a memorandum to the Home Minister urged that Assamese should be the sole official language in Assam.

Clashes between the two groups led to deaths and insecurity. A circular was released in 1961 stating that "without prejudice to the provisions contained in Section 3, the Bengali language shall be used for administrative and other official purposes up to and including district level" as the bill was amended on 7 October 1961.

This move is associated with the 'Shastri Formula'- named after the then Union Home Minister Lal Bahadur Shastri. Provisions regarding the autonomous districts in the state were also made, where English is the official language.

Medium of Instruction Movement

In 1970, the Gauhati University decided to introduce Assamese as the medium of instruction in all colleges under its jurisdiction, except a few, including colleges in Cachar, Manipur, Nagaland, the NEFA and the then newly proposed Meghalaya. English was allowed as an alternative and no deadline was set to shift to Assamese too.

With the possibility of other universities taking a similar decision in the near future, political resentment got pronounced in Cachar through press statements, public meetings etc.

⬜ In March 1972, the university released a circular that also allowed students to write answers in Bengali in examinations. A section of the Assamese students protested. While they had no objection to students from Cachar writing exams in Bengali, they opposed the application of this in the Brahmaputra Valley.

⬜ The Assam Sahitya Sabha backed this position. The university in response, quickly changed its stand and declared that only Assamese and English shall be accepted in examination answer-scripts.

⬜ This resulted in protests in Cachar again and the matter reached the Supreme Court of India, where it was alleged that Article 30 of the Indian Constitution, providing certain rights to linguistic minorities, was violated. The court released a stay order while the Government of Assam supported the idea that a new university shall be set up for the Barak Valley.

⬜ People in the Brahmaputra Valley opposed the government's stand, as they believed it would make the state clearly bi-lingual. The people of Cachar also did not support the stand because it diluted their demand for making Bengali an option for colleges even in the Brahmaputra Valley.

⬜ The All Assam Students Union in the Brahmaputra Valley opposed the stand believing that it was against the suggestion of the States Reorganization Commission, 1956, which suggested Assam as an Assamese speaking state.

4.18: AH-3.4: Assam Agitation

• **Context of the news:** "Our state has witnessed several movements in the past. But this is perhaps the biggest one after the Assam Movement. People are coming out on the streets on their own, opposing the Bill. There are protests in some parts of the state every day," said Lachit Bordoloi, a human rights activist and a member of the Asom Gana Parishad (AGP), who had closely witnessed the Assam Movement.

• A brief introduction: Students' movements are synonymous with Assam. India's northeastern state witnessed the world's longest such movement between 1979 and 1985 when lakh of students took to the streets seeking detection and deportation of illegal foreigners in the state.

• The All Assam Students Union, called for putting off the election till 'names of foreigners' were struck off the electoral rolls. This was the start of a six-year agitation that culminated in the Assam Accord.

Prafulla Kumar Mahanta was named president of AASU in 1979. In August the same year, the All Assam Gana Sangram Parishad (AAGSP) was formed. It was constituted by the AASU, and joined by the Assam Sahitya Sabha, among other organizations.

• AASU had, through a memorandum dated February 2, 1980, conveyed to then Prime Minister Indira Gandhi its "profound sense of apprehensions regarding the continuing influx of foreign nationals into Assam and the fear about adverse effects upon the political, social, culture and economic life of the State".

• Talks with the centre break down repeatedly on the issue of the cut-off date for citizenship, with Indira Gandhi's government adamant on keeping it March 25, 1971 – after the formation of Bangladesh – and the AAGSP and AASU insistent on 1951.

The Nellie Massacre:

• At Nellie, 71 km from Guwahati, in fourteen villages, over two thousand Muslims, mostly children, women and old people, are massacred and their homes set on fire in a matter of hours.

• The attackers are local Axomiya Hindus and Tiwa tribesmen who use spears, sickles, and firearms on the victims.

• Hearing rumours of imminent violence, a delegation of Muslims had asked for police protection two days previously. The police allegedly did not act.

• The Illegal Migrants (Determination by Tribunal) Act is passed by parliament in 1983. Rather than requiring an accused individual to prove s/he is not a foreigner, it shifts the burden of proof to an accuser and the police.

• Formal discussions resumed in March 1985, when Rajiv Gandhi was PM. Earlier, several rounds of informal talks had been held in 1984.

• The Accord was finally signed later in 1985.

The signing of Assam Accord

The Assam Accord: Important clauses

• Clause 5:

– It was agreed that "for purposes of detection and deletion of foreigners, 1.1.1966 shall be the base data and year", and that "all persons who came to Assam prior to 1.1.1966, including those amongst them whose names appeared on the electoral rolls used in 1967 elections shall be regularized".

• Foreigners who "came to Assam after 1.1.1966 (inclusive) and upto 24th March, 1971 shall be detected in accordance with the provisions of The Foreigners Act, 1946, and The Foreigners (Tribunals) Order, 1964", and their names "will be deleted from the electoral rolls in force".

• While, "On the expiry of a period of ten years following the date of detection, the names of all such persons which have been deleted from the electoral rolls shall be restored".

• Foreigners who came to Assam on or after March 25, 1971 shall continue to be detected, deleted and practical steps shall be taken to expel such foreigners."

Clause 6: It deals with safeguards for the Assamese people.

Constitutional, legislative and administrative safeguards, as may be appropriate shall be provided to protect, preserve and promote the culture, social, linguistic identity and heritage of the Assamese people.

Clause 7: Economic Development

• The Government takes this opportunity to renew their commitment for the speedy all round economic development of Assam, so as to improve the standard of living of the people. Special emphasis will be placed on education and science & technology through establishment of national institutions.

4.19: AH-3.5: MCQs – Assam's History (251-350)

H 251. Who founded the Koch Dynasty?

a) Naranarayan

b) Shva Singha

c) Biswa Singha

d) Chilarai

Ans- c) Biswa Singha

H 252. Who was the greatest king in the Varman Dynasty?

a) Bhaskar Varman

b) Pusya Varman

c) Harshabardhan

d) Sandhya

Ans- a) Bhaskar Varman

H 253. Who was the first Ahom King who embraced Hindu Religion?

a) Suhungmung

b) Suhanpha

c) Supipha

d) Suklengmung

Ans- a) Suhungmung

H 254. Who was the last Ahom King?

a) Rudra Singha

b) Purandhar Singha

c) Jayadhaj Singha

d) Lakshmi Singha

Ans- b) Purandhar Singha

H 255. The battle of Pichalapariya was fought between __________

a) Ahom & Kachari

b) Ahom & Chutiya

c) Ahom & Koch

d) Ahom & Bhuyans

Ans- c) Ahom & Koch

H 256. Who was the First Ahom King accepted the title "Swargodeo"?

a) Sudangpha

b) Susengpha

c) Sukapha

d) Suhungmung

Ans- d) Suhungmung

H 257. Name the first king of Pal Dynasty?

a) Brahmapal

b) Ratnapal

c) Indrapal

d) Dharmapal

Ans- a) Brahmapal

H 258. Who wrote the book "Buranji Vivek Ratna"?

a) Surya Kumar Bhuyan

b) Maniram Dewan

c) Sarbananda Rajkonwar

d) Jagannath Barua

Ans- b) Maniram Dewan

H 259. What is the old name of Assam?

a) Pragjyotishpur   b) Kamatapur
c) Ahom   d) Guwahati
Ans- a) Pragjyotishpur

H 260. Durlav Narayan was the king of ___________.
a) Darrangi Raj   b) Kamrup-Kamata
c) Koch Bihar   d) Mattak Rajya
Ans- b) Kamrup-Kamata

H 261. Which king of Ancient Assam performed the Ashwamedha Yagna?
a) Mahendra Varman   b) Bhaskara Varmana
c) Narakasura   d) Bhagadutta
Ans- a) Mahendra Varman of Varmana Dynasty was the first king of Assam to perform Aswamedha Yagna

H 262. Who among the following was the last ruler of Varmana Dynasty?
a) Pushya Varmana   b) Bhaskara Varmana
c) Bhuti Varman   d) Hajara Varman
Ans- b) Bhaskara Varman

H 263. Chinese traveller Huen Tsang visited Kamarupa in which of the following period?
a) 4th Century   b) 5th Century
c) 6th Century   d) 7th Century
Ans- d) 7th Century

H 264. Who among the following was the first king of ancient Assam?
a) Naraksura   b) BHaskara Varmana
c) PushyaVarman   d) Mahiranga
Ans- d) Mahiranga

H 265. Who founded the Pala Dynasty in Kamarupa?
a) Brahmapala   b) Nityapala
c) Ratnapala   d) Jaypala
Ans- a) Brahmapala

H 266. During the first Muslim invasion to Kamarupa, the king of Kamarupa was –
a) Bhaskara Varmana   b) Prithu
c) Sandhya   d) Mahiranga

Ans- b) Prithu

H 267. Pushya Varmana was contemporary to which of the following famous rulers in North India?

a) Babar

b) Samudragupta

c) Ashoka

d) Chandragupta

Ans- b) Samudragupta

Explanation- Samudragupta was the fourth ruler of the Gupta Empire.

H 268. Harshavardhan was contemporary to which of the following rulers in Kamarupa?

a) Arimatta

b) Bhaskara Varmana

c) Hajara Varmana

d) Vaidyadeva

Ans- b) Bhaskara Varmana

H 269. Umachal Rock Epigraph belongs to which of the following dynasty?

a) Salstambha

b) Pala

c) Varman

d) Kamata

Ans- c) Varmana dynasty

H 270. The capital of Salstambha dynasty was

a) Haruppeswar

b) Kundli Nagar

c) Pragjyotishpur

d) Kamatpur

Ans- a) Haruppeswar

Explanation- During the rule of the Salstambha dynasty the capital city was located at Haruppeswara (Tezpur). Salastambha (655-675 A.D.) established the Salstambha dynasty.

H 271. Who among the following is said to have built the Kamakhya temple in Guwahati?

a) Bhaskara Varmana

b) Sandhya

c) Narakasura

d) Arimatta

Ans- c) Narakasura

Explanation- Narakasura was one of the most powerful rulers of ancient Kamrupa. He made Pragjyotishpur the capital city.

H 272. The book Tabaqat- i – Nasiri provides a brief account of which of the following events?

a) Invasion of Ghiyasuddin -Iwas – Khilji

b) Invasion of Muhammad – bin- Bakhtiyar

c) Invasion of Mir Jumla

d) Invasion of Ram Singha

Ans- b) Invasion of Muhammad – bin- Bakhtiyar

Explanation- It was written by Minhajuddin.

H 273. Who among the following was the first ruler of Chutia Kingdom?

a) Dharmadhapal　　　　　　　b) Birpal

c) Ratnapal　　　　　　　　　d) Nityapal

Ans- b) Birpal

H 274. During the reign of which dynasty, the Hazara Pukhuri in Tezpur was excavated ?

a) Varmana　　　　　　　　　b) Salstambha

c) Ahom　　　　　　　　　　d) Koch

Ans- b) Salstambha

H 275. Which of the following Muslim ruler invaded Kamrup for the third time?

a) Ghiyasuddin-Iwas Khilji　　　b) Mir Jumla

c) Tughril Khan　　　　　　　d) Nasiruddin

Ans- d) Nasiruddin

H 276. Which of the following Ahom kings got killed at the hands of Chutiya?

a) Sutupha　　　　　　　　　b) Subinpha

c) Sudangpha　　　　　　　　d) Supatapha

Ans- a) Sutupha

Explanation- Sutupha was killed by the Chutiya king during a friendly encounter in Dikhow river in 1376. Sutupha was the sixth Ahom king.

H 277. Which amongst the following Ahom king conquered Sadiya and annexed Chutiya Kingdom into Ahom Territory?

a) Sudangpha　　　　　　　　b) Suhunmung

c) Jayadhwaj Singha　　　　　d) Rudra Singha

Ans- b) Suhunmung

H 278. Sati Sadhani Divash is commemorate in Assam every year on

a) 24th February　　　　　　　b) 27th March

c) 21st April　　　　　　　　d) 24th November

Ans- c) 21st April

H 279. Who among the following was the last ruler of Khen dynasty in medieval Assam?

a) Nilambar

b) Niladhwaj

c) Chakradhwaj

d) Mriganka

Ans- a) Nilambar

H 280. Which of the following rulers established the Kamata Kingdom?

a) Prithu

b) Sandhya

c) Nidhwaj

d) Arimatta

Ans- b) Sandhya

H 281. Who among the following was the queen of Rajeswar Singha?

a) Ambika

b) Sarbeswari

c) Kuranganayani

d) Hemo Aedeo

Ans- c) Kuranganayani

Explanation- Kuranganayani was the daughter of Manipuri King Jai Singha. She was married to Rajeswar Singha.

- Rajeswar Singha helped Manipuri king Jai Singha to fight against the Burmese. So he offered lots of presents and his daughter Kuranaganayani to Rajeswar Singha.

H 282. Which Ahom king created the post Barpatra Gohain?

a) Suhungmung

b) Syu Ka Pha

c) Pratap Singha

d) Rudra Singha

Ans- a) Suhungmung

Explanation- Suhungmung created the post of Barpatra Gohain. Barpatra Gohain was equivalent to Bar Gobhain and Burha Gohain.

H 283. Mulagabharu fought against which Mughal commander?

a) Mir Jumla

b) Turbuk

c) Ram Singha

d) Saiad Abu Bakkar

Ans- b) Turbuk

Explanation- During the reign of Suhungmung Muslim commander Turbuk defeated Ahom army and several Ahom generals including Frachengmung Burhagohain got killed. To take revenge for the death of Frachengmung, his wife Mulagabhoru bravely fought against Turbuk with exemplary bravery.

H 284. In which of the following places, the last battle between Ahoms and Burmese took place?

a) Hadirachaki

b) Itakhuli

c) Hajo

d) Duimunisila

Ans- a) Hadirachaki

H 285. The Poki Rang Ghar was built during the reign of Ahom king?

a) Rudra Singha

b) Pramatta Singha

c) Rajeswar Singha

d) Gadadhar Singha

Ans- b) Pramatta Singha

Explanation- During the reign of Pramatta Singha, the masonry or Poki Rang Ghar was built. Before Pramatta Singha, his father Rudra Singha constructed the Rang Ghar using Bamboo and Wood.

- Rang Ghar was the royal sports pavilion for watching buffalo fight and other sports.

H 286. Who amongst the following Ahom kings was known as Lora Raja?

a) Suhenpha

b) Susenpha

c) Sutupha

d) Sulikpha

Ans- d) Sulikpha

Explanation- Sulikpha became king at a tender age and hence he was nicknamed as Lora Raja. (Boy King)

H 287. The treaty between Mir Jumla and Jayadhwaj Singha was concluded in which of the following places?

a) Kaliabor

b) Rangpur

c) Biswanathghat

d) Ghiladharighat

Ans- d) Ghiladharighat

Explanation- Mir Jumla occupied Garhgaon on March 1662. Soon, the Mughals started facing great hardships. So in January 1663, a treaty was concluded in Ghiladharighat between Mughals and Jayadhwaj Singha.

H 288. Which Kachari King was received by Ahom King Rudra Singha by organising a durbar at Biswanath?

a) Maha Manikya

b) Nirbhaynarayan

c) Tamradhwaj

d) Indranarayan

Ans- c) Tamradhwaj

H 289. Who among the following was the royal poet during the reign of Rudra Singha?

a) Ram Saraswati

b) Kabiraj Chakrabarty

c) Kabichandra Dwij

d) Ananta Kandali

Ans- b) Kabiraj Chakrabarty

H 290. The Talatal ghar was built during the reign of Ahom king?

a) Rudra Singha

b) Pramatta Singha

c) Rajeswar Singha

d) Gadadhar Singha

Ans- c) Rajeswar Singha

H 291. Which among the following authors wrote the book Hashti Bidyarnava?

a) Sukumar Barkaith

b) Kabiraj Chakrabarty

c) Kabichandra Dwij

d) Ramasaraswati

Ans- a) Sukumar Barkaith

H 292. Which of the following books was written by Sihabuddin Talish?

a) Tabaqat-i- Nasiri

b) Fatiyah-i-Ibriyah

c) Baharistan-i-Ghayli

d) Nadir-ul-Asra.

Ans- b) Fatiyah-i-Ibriyah

H 293. Which of the following Ahom kings was known as Bhaganiya Raja?

a) Lakshmi Singha

b) Purandar Singha

c) Jayadhwaj Singha

d) Gaurinath Singha

Ans- c) Jayadhwaj Singha

H 294. In which of the following year, the first Burmese invasion to Assam took place?

a) 1815 A.D.

b) 1817 A.D.

c) 1819 A.D.

d) 1821 A.D.

Ans- b) 1817 A.D.

H 295. The masonry bridge over Namdand river was built during the reign of which Ahom king?

a) Rudra Singha

b) Pramatta Singha

c) Rajeswar Singha

d) Gadadhar Singha

Ans- d) Gadadhar Singha

H 296. Which among the following authored Chakarapheti Buranji?

a) Sukumar Barkaith

b) Numali Bargohain

c) Kabichandra Dwij

d) Purushuttam Bidyabagish

Ans- b) Numali Bargohain

H 297. Which of the following was the Burmese Commander in the Second Burmese invasion?

a) Mingimaha Tilowa   b) Alu Mingi

c) Mingimaha Bandula   d) Bagidyaw

Ans- b) Alu Mingi

H 298. The first Moamariya Revolt took place during the reign of which Ahom King?

a) Lakshmi Singha   b) Purandar Singha

c) Jayadhwaj Singha   d) Gaurinath Singha

Ans- a) Lakshmi Singha

H 299. The Donduwa Droh took place during the reign of which Ahom King?

a) Lakshmi Singha   b) Kamaleshwar Singha

c) Nariya Raja   d) Sudangpha

Ans- b) Kamaleshwar Singha

H 300. Which Mughal Emperor sent a Siropa(Gown) to Ahom king Chakradhwaj Singha?

a) Aurangzeb   b) Jahangir

c) Shah Jahan   d) Akbar

Ans- a) Aurangzeb

H 301. Who among the following was the first Barphukan of Ahom Kingdom?

a) Lachit   b) Badan Chandra

c) Kalia Bhumura   d) Langi Panisiya

Ans- d) Langi Panisiya

H 302. Which Ahom king created the post of Bezbaruah?

a) Rudra Singha   b) Syu Ka Pha

c) Suhungmung   d) Pratap Singha

Ans- a) Rudra Singha

Explanation- Bez Baruah was the physician of Royal Ahom family and practiced traditional medicine.

H 303. Which Ahom king belonged to the Tungkhungiya phoid?

a) Suhungmung   b) Gadadhar Singha

c) Syu Ka Pha   d) Suteupha

Ans- b) Gadadhar Singha

H 304. Who among the following authored the book Baharistan-i-Ghayli?

a) Sihabuddin Talish
b) Mirza Nathan
c) Said Hakim
d) Said Abu Bakkar

Ans- b) Mirza Nathan

H 305. The Kareng Ghar was built during the reign of which Ahom king?

a) Rudra Singha
b) Pramatta Singha
c) Rajeswar Singha
d) Gadadhar Singha

Ans- c) Rajeswar Singha

H 306. The Lata Kata Ran took place during the reign of which Ahom king?

a) Suhungmung
b) Rudra Singha
c) Pratap Singha
d) Rajeswar Singha

Ans- d) Rajeswar Singha

H 307. Who was the independent Ahom king?

a) Jogeshwar Singha
b) Purandar Singha
c) Chnadrakanta Singha
d) Kamaleshwar Singha.

Ans- b) Purandar Singha

Explanation- Purandar Singha ruled from 1818- 1819.

H 308. Which of the following Ahom kings shifted Ahom capital to Dichoi or Jorhat?

a) Rudra Singha
b) Gaurinath Singha
c) Suklengmung
d) Suhungmung

Ans- b) Gaurinath Singha

H 309. On which of the following days, Sati Joymoti Divas are commemorated?

a) 24th November
b) 24th February
c) 27th March
d) 21st April

Ans- c) 27th March

Explanation- During the reign of Sulikpha, Joymoti was put to continuous physical torture over 14 days as she did not reveal the whereabouts of her husband Gadapani Konwar and she died on 27th March, 1680. - To honour her supreme sacrifice, every year 27th March is commemorated as Sati Joymoti Divas.

H 310. The mission of Captain Thomas Welsh to Assam took place during the reign of which Ahom king?

a) Prandar Singha
b) Gaurinath Singha
c) Jogeswar Singha
d) Chandrakanta Singha

Ans- b) Gaurinath Singha

H 311. After the treaty of Yandaboo, British introduced who among the following as a vassal king?

a) Purandar Singha
b) Chandrakanta Singha
c) Kandarpeswar Singha
d) Gomadhar Konwar

Ans- a) Purandar Singha

H 312. In which year, Assam was declared as a Chief Commissioner's Province?

a) 1858
b) 1861
c) 1874
d) 1912

Ans- c) 1874

Explanation- In 1874, the province of Assam was created after combining with the Cachar and Sylhet district and a Chief Commissioner was appointed as the head.

H 313. Who among the following was the first Chief Commissioner of Assam?

a) David Scott
b) Col. Richards
c) T.C. Robertson
d) Col. Kitting

Ans- d) Col. Kitting

H 314. In which year, Assam was given the status of a Governor's province?

a) 1912
b) 1920
c) 1921
d) 1937

Ans- c) 1921

H 315. Which of the following forces was created by British to protect British settlements in the hills areas in Assam?

a) Assam rifles
b) Assam Regiment
c) Border Security Force
d) Sashastra Seema Bal

Ans- a) Assam Rifles

H 316. The first revolt in Assam against British which took place in 1828 was led by

a) Piyali Barphukan   b) Piyali Borgohain

c) Maniram Dewan   d) Jiuram Duliya Barua.

Ans- b) Piyali Borgohain

H 317. In which year, Piyali Barphukan and Jiuram Duliya Baruah were hanged?

a) 1828   b) 1830

c) 1857   d) 1858

Ans- b) 1830.

H 318. In which year, Mofat Mills visited Assam?

a) 1826   b) 1831

c) 1853   d) 1857

Ans- c) 1853

Explanation- In 1853, Moffat Mills came to Assam to review the economic condition. He was a judge of Calcutta High Court. Maniram Dewan explained the evil effects of the British rule and pleaded to restore Upper Assam to Kandarpeswar Singha.

H 319. Who among the following was a martyr of Sepoy Mutiny in Assam?

a) Piyoli Baruah   b) Piyoli Phukan

c) Farmud Ali   d) Kushal Konwar

Ans- a) Piyoli Baruah

H 320. In which year, Phulaguri peasant uprising took place?

a) 1861   b) 1874

c) 1892   d) 1894

Ans- a) 1861

Explanation- In 1861, an peasant uprising 'Phulaguri Dhawa' took place in Phulaguri region of Nagaon. The main cause was the ban on private cultivation of opium and increased rate on opium by Govt. The tribal peasants of Phulaguri organised several Raizmel(public meetings) against British in October, 1861.

H 321. The peasant uprising of Patharughat took place in which year?

a) 1861   b) 1874

c) 1894   d) None of the above

Ans- c) 1894

Explanation- Several peasant uprisings took place in the Kamrup and Darrang districts in 1892-1894 against British revenue policies. On January 28, 1894, around 140 protesting peasants were killed in police firing in Patharughat (Darrang district).

H 322. Who among the following was the first President of Assam Provincial Congress Committee?

a) Tarunram Phukan
b) Nabin Chandra Bordoloi
c) Kuladhar Chaliha
d) Bimal Prasad Chaliha

Ans- c) Kuladhar Chaliha

H 323. Who among the following joined the second session of Indian National Congress held in 1886?

a) Devicharan Baruah
b) Gopinath Bordoloi
c) Tarunram Phukan
d) Kuladhar Chaliha

Ans- a) Devicharan Baruah

Explanation- Many representatives from Assam joined- Debi Charan Baruah of Upper Assam association, Kali Kanta Barkakati of Shillong Association, Satyanath Borah of Nowgong Ryot Association, Kamini Chanda of Habiganj People's Association.

H 324. Who among the following established the Gyan Paradayani Sabha?

a) Jagannath Baruah
b) Anandaram Dhekial Phukan
c) Manikchandra Barua
d) Hemchandra Goswami

Ans- b) Anandaram Dhekial Phukan

Explanation- In 1857-59, Anandaram Dhekial Phukan established the Gyan Pradayini Sabha at Nagaon with the objective of spreading advanced knowledge among people.

H 325. In which of the following year Sarbajani Sabha was formed?

a) 1884
b) 1886
c) 1903
d) 1912

Ans- a) 1884

H 326. Who among the following was the first President of the Assam association?

a) Manikchandra Baruah
b) Prabhar Chandra Baruah
c) Hagannath Baruah
d) Ghanashyam Baruah

Ans- b) Prabhat Chandra Baruah

H 327. Who among the following went to London to represent Assam before the Selbourne committee of the House of Lords?

a) Nabin Chandra Bordoloi   b) Gopinath Bordoloi

c) Tarun Ram Phukan   d) Jagannath Barua

Ans- a) Nabin Chandra Bordoloi.

Explanation- A deputation from Assam Association headed by Nabin Chandra Bordoloi was sent to London to represent Assam before the Selbourne committee of House of Lords and demanded full provincial status for Assam. As the result of the meeting, Assam acquired the status of a full - fledged Governor's province.

H 328. Who among the following was the first president of Assam Chatra Sanmilan?

a) Chandrakumar Agarwala   b) Lakshminath Bezbaruah

c) Gunaviram Baruah   d) Hem Chandra Baruah

Ans- b) Lakshminath Bezbaruah

Explanation- In 1916, the first session of Assam Chatra Sanmilan was held in Guwahati. It was originally a literary organisation and not interested in politics, but later they got involved in the freedom movement. Other members- Chandranath Sarma, Omeo Kumar Das, Hem Chandra Braua, Padmadhar Chaliha.

H 329. In which year Mahatma Gandhi visited Assam for the first time?

a) 1912   b) 1921

c) 1922   d) 1926

Ans- b) 1921

H 330. Who was the president of Swarajya Party in Assam?

a) Tarunram Phukan   b) Nabin Chandra Bordoloi

c) Gopinath Bordoloi   d) Chandra Nath Sharma

Ans- a) Traunram Phukan

H 331. Who was the President of Pandu session of Indian National Congress?

a) Jawaharlal Nehru   b) Dadabhai Naoroji

c) Sri Nivas Ayengar   d) Vinoba Bhave

Ans- c) Sri Nivas Ayengar

H 332. In which year, the infamous Cunningham Circular was notified in Assam?

a) 1905   b) 1930

c) 1932   d) 1942

Ans-b) 1930

Explanation- In 1930, 'Cunningham Circular' was implemented by J.R. Cunningham (Director of Education Department). The circular demanded an undertaking to abstain from joining politics from students and guardians.

H 333. Who among the following founded the Asom Sangrashini Sabha?

a) Anandaram Baruah   b) Ambikagiri Roy Chaudhary

c) Traunram Phukan   d) Omeo Kumar Das

Ans- b) Ambikagiri Roy Chaudhary.

Explanation- Ambika Giri Roy Choudhary founded Asom Sangrashini Sabha to demand for vindication of right of the Assamese people the children of soil as against aggression of outsiders.

H 334. In which year Assam ryot Association was formed?

a) 1885   b) 1921

c) 1933   d) 1938

Ans- c) 1933

H 335. In which year Assam Desh Hitaishini Sabha was formed?

a) 1884   b) 1885

c) 1886   d) 1887

Ans- b) 1885.

Explanation- In 1885, Assam Desh Hitaishini Sabha was formed at Sibsagar under supervision of Anandaram Barua and Gunabhiram Barua.

H 336. In which year, the first Assam Legislative Council was formed?

a) 1905   b) 1912

c) 1919   d) 1921

Ans- b) 1912

H 337. Who among the following was the first Governor of Assam after independence?

a) Md. Akbar Hydari   b) Jairamdas Daulatram

c) Sri Prakasa   d) Saiyid Fazal Ali

Ans- a) Sir Muhammad Saleh Akbar Hydari

H 338. In which year did the Digboi Labour Strike take place?

a) 1921   b) 1927

c) 1939　　　　　　　　　d) 1942

Ans- c) 1939

H 339. In which year Mahatma Gandhi visited Assam for the last time?

a) 1946　　　　　　　　　b) 1945

c) 1939　　　　　　　　　d) 1926

Ans- a) 1946.

H 340. Who among the following is a martyr of the Quit India Movement?

a) Kushal Konwar　　　　　b) Maniram Dewan

c) Piyali Baruah　　　　　d) Jiuram Duliya Baruah

Ans- a) Kushal Konwar

H 341. When was the teaty of Yandaboo signed?

a) 1826　　　　　　　　　b) 1626

c) 1771　　　　　　　　　d) 1871

Ans- a) 1826

H 342. What is the earlier name of Dimapur?

a) Maibang　　　　　　　b) Hidimbapur

c) Rangpur　　　　　　　d) Ratanpur

Ans- b) Hidimbapur

H 343. Who constructed the Gohain Kamal Ali?

a) Naranarayan　　　　　b) Rudra Singha

c) Gadadhar Singha　　　　d) Rajeshwar Singha

Ans- a) Naranarayan

H 344. Where did Sukapha first establish his capital?

a) Rangpur　　　　　　　b) Bokota

c) Sivasagar　　　　　　d) Charaideo

Ans- d) Charaideo

H 345. Who excavated the Rudrasagar Tank?

a) Lakshmi Singha　　　　b) Rudra Singha

c) Gadadhar Singha　　　　d) Rajeshwar Singha

Ans- a) Lakshmi Singha

H 346. Who was the Ahom General during the battle of Saraighat?

a) Momai Tamuli Barbarua　　b) Lachit Barphukan

c) Gamdhar Konwar　　　　d) Langi Gadapani

Ans- b) Lachit Barphukan

H 347. Where was the battle of Sessa-mukh taken place?

a) 1520

b) 1521

c) 1523

d) 1522

Ans- c) 1523

H 348. Who was the first to implement land Survey in Assam?

a) Sukapha

b) Swarganarayan

c) Gadadhar Singha

d) Shiva Singha

Ans- c) Gadadhar Singha

H 349. Who built the Joysagar and Joy Doul?

a) Shiva Singha

b) Rajeshwar Singha

c) Paramatta Singha

d) Rudra Singha

Ans- d) Rudra Singha

H 350. Who built the Kareng Ghar at Sivasagar?

a) Shiva Singha

b) Rajeshwar Singha

c) Paramatta Singha

d) Rudra Singha

Ans- b) Rajeshwar Singha

5. ASSAM'S ART AND CULTURE

Index

5.1: AC-1: FESTIVALS OF ASSAM

Bihu

Bihu is the **most important festival** of Assam and is celebrated by all people irrespective of caste, creed and religion, faith. Bihu festival is basically a seasonal festival and celebrated in three different seasons. They are –

    a) Bohag Bihu or Rongali Bihu (Month of April)
    b) Kati Bihu or Kongali Bihu (Month of September)
    c) Magh Bihu or Bhogali Bihu (Month of January)

a) Bohag Bihu or Rongali Bihu

- It is a festival of joy celebrated with the **advent of spring**.
- Usually it is celebrated in the **Bohag month** in the **Assamese** calendar.
- Bohag Bihu signifies the **beginning of the Assamese New Year** and the **sowing season** in Assam.
- Bohag Bihu has its **roots in fertility cult**.
- Bohag Bihu is celebrated for **Seven (7)** Days. The **first day** is dedicated to **Cattle** and known as Goru Bihu. **Next day** is called **Manuh Bihu** and the **third day** is **Gosain Bihu** – dedicated to God, Fourth Day is Kutum - dedicated to Families, 5th is Senehi/Jiyari – daughters come to their parent's house, 6th is Mela Bihu & 7th is Chera/Bohagi Bidai Bihu.
- Bihu dance and **'Husari'** are important components of Bohag Bihu.

b) Kati Bihu or Kongali Bihu

- It is celebrated on the **last day** of the month of **'Ahin'**.
- During that time, the food grains stored in the granary deplete and the new crops are not ready for harvesting. There is a **scarcity of food grains** and other resources and that is why it is called Kongali Bihu.

- **Prayers are the most significant** part of Kati Bihu. People offer prayers for a good harvest in the coming season. There is a ritual of offering prayers before Tulsi plants.
- Earthen lamps are lit in granaries and paddy fields to welcome Goddess Laxmi. In paddy fields, lamps are placed at tips of bamboo posts known as 'Akash Banti'.

Magh Bihu

- Magh Bihu is a harvest festival which is celebrated in the Sankranti of 'Pooh' month (mid January) after the harvest is collected.
- Also called Bhogali Bihu – a Bihu known for feasting and enjoyment. The eve of the **Magh Bihu is called Uruka**, people build makeshift cottages called Bhelaghar and Meiji where community feasting is celebrated during night. The rituals performed in Magh Bihu are related to **Agni- God of Fire.**
- Buffalo fight, Egg Fight(Koni Kuj) are some fun activities performed in this Bihu.

Daul Utsav or Falgutsav

- **Daul Utsav or Falgutsav** commonly known as Phakua is celebrated in Assam like other parts of India in the month of **Phagun.**
- Basically, it is a festival of colours where people smear each other with Faklua or Abir of different colours.
- It has been celebrated since ancient time and the original purpose is to promote fertility of men, animals and crops. It is also believed that colour used is an antidote to pox.
- As per **Hindu mythology**, Daul Utsav has its **origin at Gokul** where Sri Krishna played Holi with the Gopis.
- In the **Satras of Assam** particularly in Barpeta, Bordowa and Majuli, Daul Utsav is celebrated as per **Satriya Parampara.**
- It is believed that **Falgutsav was first introduced** by Shankardeva himself in the Bardowa Than. Some Borgeets also narrate how Lord Krishna played with color with his fellow friends.
- Usually it is celebrated from three to five days. The image of Lord Krishna is taken in a procession (Daul Jatra) to the adjoining areas and the devotees take part in that. It is also termed as Gosain Fakua. After the Daul Yatra, devotees play Holi with each other.

Ambubachi Mela

- It is the most important festival of **Kamakhya temple** of Guwahati and is held every year during the month of **'Saavan'(Mid June)**.
- During Ambubachi Mela the doors of the <u>temple remain closed for three days</u>. It is believed that **Goddess Kamakhya undergo menstruation** in that period and Earth becomes impure. During this time no farming work is undertaken.
- The Ambubachi Mela is held with great festivity on the **fourth day when the doors** are **opened** and the <u>devotees are allowed to enter inside the temple for worship</u>. Thousands of devotees from all over the country and abroad visit this mela.

Me-Dum-Me-Phi

- The Me-Dum-Me-Phi is the **ancestor worship** observed by the Ahom community. This festival is performed annually on 31st **January** and helps to develop social contacts and community feelings among the Ahoms.
- Colourful processions with devotees in traditional finery are also taken out on occasion.
- It is believed that if Me-Dum-Me-Phi is not celebrated in the customary way, the deities will be displeased and there will be crisis in the State like political rivalry, increased activities of militancy, natural hazards like floods and earthquakes resulting in loss of human lives and property.

Other festivals

- **Bhatheli-** It is a popular festival mainly in Kamrup, Nalbari,Goalpara and so on. It is **also known** as Sori, Suari, Pawra festival. It is <u>celebrated during Bohag month</u>. In Batheli, Bamboo is worshipped with some traditional rituals.
- **Moho Ho festival-** It is celebrated in the **month of Aghon** and is popular mainly in <u>all districts of Lower Assam</u>. It is traditionally associated with the driving of mosquitoes. It is also believed that this festival was <u>originally associated with tiger-hunting.</u> The term <u>Moho-Ho</u> may have come from Bodo language.

Festivals of Tribes in Assam

Festival of Bodo Tribe- The seasonal festivals of Bodo tribe are- Baisagu, Domashi and Katrigacha. These three festivals are similar to the three Bihus.

• Among the **religious festivals** of the **Bodos**, the **'Kherai'** is the most famous and usually understood to be the national festival of the Bodos.

• Among other religious festivals of the Bodos the 'Sibrai Langamara Puja', the 'Apeswari Puja', the 'Haul Kheta' are well known.

Festival of Mishing Tribe- Ali – ai- Ligang is the most important festival of Mishings. It is related to agriculture.

• It is a springtime seed sowing festival. The festival is usually celebrated in the month of Phagun. The goddess of Paddy is worshipped in this festival.

Nara Siga Bihu and Po Rag – These are harvest festivals of Mishing people. Po Rag conveys the meaning of grand re-union and is celebrated every three to five years at the end of a good harvest. The 'Amrok' festival is observed when food from the harvested crop is offered.

Festival of Rabha tribe- The 'Baikho' or 'Khosi Puja' is the most important festival of Rabhas and it is observed in the month of Baisakh. Rabha people also observe a number of Puja festivals- 'Kechaikhaiti' Puja, 'Langa' puja or Dinga Puja, Maeri puja etc, 'Hana Ghora' is a festival of merriment.

Festival of Deori Tribe- Two major festivals are observed by the Deori people 'Bhoagiyo Bisu' and Maghaya Utsava. The Bohagiyo Bisu celebrated in Bohag and lasts for seven days. Maghaya Utsava is observed in the first Wednesday of the month of magh. Bisu puja is a special feature of the Deori Bihu festival.

Festival of Karbi Tribe- 'Rongker' and 'Hacha Kekan' are two main festivals related to agricultural seasons. Rongker is celebrated before the Jhum cultivation starts in winter and again in summer just prior to the planting of rice.

- The 'Great Rongker' is celebrated after an interval of five years. In Rongker only the males are allowed to participate.

- The Hacha Kekan is celebrated at the end of the planting season. Public feasting and elaborate dances are organised to mark this festival.

- **Festival of Tiwa Tribe-** The main festivals of Tiwas are three 'Bisus' (Bihu) , Barat Utsav, Sagra Misua, Wansua and Jon Beel.
- The **Barat Utsav** is the community festival which bears a religio-cultural character and is observed in the month of 'Puha'. 'Sagra Misawa' is a spring festival celebrated with music and dance.
- The **Jon Beel Mela** is organised during Magh Bihu at Jon Beel in Morigaon district. This is basically a traditional 'Haat' or market for where the hill people and plains people exchange commodities. On the preceding day of the Mela, the 'Gova Raja' enjoys a community feast on the banks of the Jon Beel.
- **Festival Dimasa Tribe-** 'Busu' a harvesting festival similar to Bihu is the main festival of Dimasa people. Rajini and Harni Gabra are festivals related to productive work.
- **Festival of Kuki Tribe-** The main festivals of Kukis are Ai- San, Sel Bonchon, Lom KIvah etc. Ai San is related to hunting. Sel Bonchon is about wrestling with Mithun. A few young boys then wrestled with the Mithn and try to excite the animal. Lom Kovah is another festival of Kukis from ancestor's time. C having – Kut is celebrated at the end of the harvesting season.

Calendric Festivals

- Like other parts in India, different Calendric festivals are celebrated in different months, Sankranthi, tithis and days.
- **Some festivals like** Durga Puja, Lakshmi Puja, Kali puja, Diwali, Shivaratri are celebrated in different parts of Assam.
- Festivals belonging to **Muslim community** such as Muharram, Sabe barat, Ramzan and Id- uz- Zuha are also celebrated.
- Similarly **Chirstian people** celebrates Good Friday and Christmas.

5.2: AC-2: DANCES OF ASSAM

Satriya Nritya

- Satriya Nritya is the **classical dance** of Assam. This dance form has been nurtured and preserved by the Vaishnav Satra and therefore it has been named as Satriya.
- Satriya Nritya has been given the recognition of 'Classical Dance' by the **Sangeet Natak Akademi** on 15th **November, 2000.**
- It was introduced in the **15th Century A.D.** by Srimanta Shankardeva as a medium for propagation of Neo-Vaishnavism faith.

- The **main theme** of Satriya Nritya is the legends and **mythologies of Lord Krishna** particularly from texts such as the **Bhagavata Purana**.
- Satriya Nritya has **two** distinctly separate **streams.**
- The **first one** is related to **Natya i.e., Ankiya Bhaona** such as Sutradhar, Gayan Bayan to the Kharmanar Nritya.
- The **second one** is related to **Nritya or dance numbers** which are independent such as Chali, Rajagharia Chali, Jhumura, Nadu Bhangi, Apsara Nritya, Dasavatara Nritya.
- Satriya Nritya is accompanied by **musical instruments** mainly **Khol, Taal and Bahi(flute).**

Bhortal Nritya

- Bhortal Nritya is a dance form which is performed using **Bhortal (a kind of cymbal**) in both hands by the dancer. This dance **originated at Barpeta** and a **part of Satriya culture.**
- It is performed in a group of **six or seven dancers**. The dancers carry the Bhortal which they play to the fast beat of the **Thiya Naam** accompanied by **Nagara (percussion).**
- Different **gestures (mudras)** expressing the underlying meaning of the verse with the melody and rhythm by the dancer are the unique characteristics of Bhortal.

Oja Pali

- Ojapali is one of the unique forms of performance which involves art forms- Song, Dance and Drama.
- It is performed by a group of **4 or 5 men** of whom the chief performer is called Oja(Ojah) who is **supported by 3 to 4 Palis** and hence the name Oja pali.
- The instrument played by Ojapali is **Khutitaal (palm sized Cymbal).** The performers wear long sleeved **white gowns, silver jewellery** etc. and **Nupur**(bundle of tinny metal percussion played by body vibrations).

Dances of Bodos

Bagarumba

- The Bodo tribe of Assam has many folk dances. The most popular and attractive one is Bagarumba dance.
- It is usually practiced during **Bwisagu- festival** of the Bodo people in the Bishuba Sankranti or Mid -April.

• Dancers are usually **young girls** who assemble in a particular area of village. The dancers **move forward and backwards** in a swinging motion by holding the ends of their colourful scarves around their necks. After dancing the **young** people reverentially **bow down to their parents and elders.**

Kherai Dance

• It is a Bodo religious dance and is an essential part of *Bathow* worship.

• **Bathow** is actually <u>Lord Shiva</u>. Usually villagers celebrate the Bathow worship once in a year where Kherai is performed in 5 stages.

• **First**, the place is made sacred for dancing and then the dancers dance covering the place and praise the Gods.

Bordoishikhla Dance

• It is a very **special folk** art form dedicated to the **Goddess of Storm (Bordo)** and **water (Shikla)**. The dancers perform with Khanjani (Bamboo Clappers) in their hands.

Muchalangnai Dance- It is another dance of Bodos.

Dance of Rabhas

Hamzar Dance

• Hamzar refers to the **age-old agricultural tradition of cultivating paddy** on land cleared of forests in the hills and plains which is known as **'Jhum'** or **'Slash'** and **'Burn'** cultivation.

• The tradition of Hamzar has well – defined roles for the Rabha man and Rabha woman.

Santhar Dance

• It is an <u>integral part</u> of the Baikho Puja.

• The dance describes the <u>**joys of youth and love**</u> and it is also a medium for conveying proposals for marriage.

Farakanti Dance

• It is a <u>**very ancient**</u> dance form. It is performed **after the death of a person** in the presence of the relatives of the deceased and community. Through the dance prayers are offered **to show respect** to the **departed soul.**

Dhaowa Dance

• In earlier times the <u>**brave Rabha**</u> people have fought battles with other **hostile groups.**

- The Dhaowa Dance is performed **ceremonially** just before Rabha warriors set out for the battlefield.
- This dance **symbolises** the bravery of the Rabha people.

5.3: AC-3: LANGUAGES, LITERATURE, NEWSPAPER AND JOURNALS

LANGUAGES OF ASSAM

Key statistics on Languages in Assam (2011 census)

☐ The major <u>scheduled</u> languages spoken in Assam are- Assamese, Bodo, Bengali, Nepali, Santali, Odia, Hindi.

☐ 2.89 crores (92%) of population in Assam speak **scheduled** languages.

☐ Some major <u>non-scheduled</u> languages in Assam are- Rabha (1.01 lakhs), Dimasa (1.31 lakhs), Deori(27 thousand), Karbi(5.11 Lakhs), Garo(1.72 lakhs), Munda(71 thousand), Hajong(71 thousand), Lalung(33 thousand).

☐ Some other languages in Assam with a small speaking population are- Tai, Hmar, Khasi, etc.

Some major Languages

☐ **Assamese-** Assamese is the <u>lingua franca of Assam</u> and it is the <u>**official language of Assam.**</u>

- The Assamese speaking population in Assam is 1.59 crore.

- 1.53 crore people (1.26%) of the population of India use Assamese as their Mother Tongue.

☐ **Bengali-** Bengali speaking population in Assam is 90.24 lakhs.

- In **1961**, <u>**Bengali was declared as an official language**</u> in **Barak Valley-** Cachar, Hailakandi and Karimganj.

☐ **Bodo-** It is a scheduled language of India **(included in 2003)**. The Bodo speaking population in Assam is 14.16 lakhs.

- It also includes the Kachari and Mech languages.

☐ **Santali and Odiya-** Mainly spoken by the Tea Tribes community of Assam. Oriya speaking population is 2.18 lakhs and Santali speaking population is 2.13 lakhs.

☐ **Hindi-** Hindi speaking population is around 2.1 lakhs.

LITERATURE

Literature of Assam can be categorised into three categories-

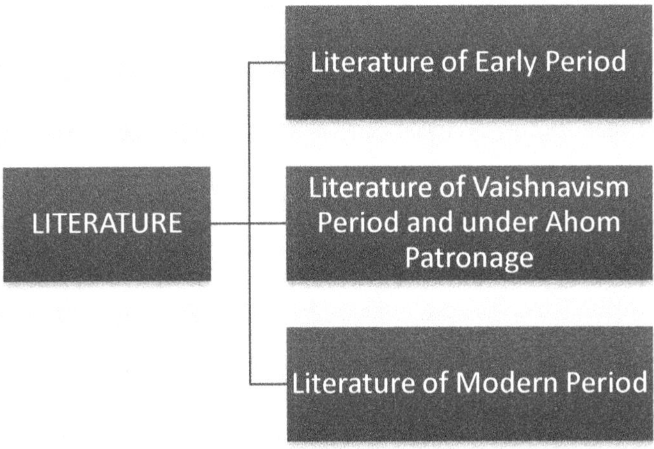

Early Period

□ Charyapads- These are one of the earliest written literature found in Assam. Charyapads are also known as Doha.

□ Charyapads are believed to be composed by Buddhist Siddhacharyas in between 8th and 10th Century mainly to propagate the ideals of Buddhism. The meaning of Charya is acharan or practice.

□ The language used in Charaypads are commonly called Sandhyabhasa which represents the earliest forms of some Indo Aryan languages-Bengali, Assamese and Oriya.

□ In the **medieval period**, the kingdom of Kamarupa and Kamata was a centre of learning. Many poets enjoyed royal patronage.

□ Harihar Vipra, Rudra Kandali, Hema Saraswati, Kaviratna Saraswati, Madhav Kandali are noteworthy among them.

□ Harihar Vipra authored Babrubahanar Judha and Lava Kushar Judha and their stories are based on the Mahabharata.

□ Hema Saraswati authored Prahlad Charit and Hara Gauri Samvada. The stories of these kavyas are based on the Puranas and folklore of land.

□ Kaviratna Saraswati authored Jayadratha Vadha and Rudra Kandali authored Satyaki Pravesh.

□ **All mentioned poets** enjoyed **Royal Patronage** of Kamata kingdom.

□ In the 14th Century with the **encouragement of Kachari King Mahamanikya**, Madhav Kandali **translated Ramayana into Assamese.**

□ Madhava Kandali also composed a kavya named Devajit.

□ Poet Durgabar patronised by Visawa Singha authored Giti Ramayana.

☐ Narayandeva is a great Manasa poet of Assamese literature. He is known as Sukabi. He composed famous Beula Lakhindar songs in the 17th century in the court of King Dharmanarayan of Darangi Rajya.

☐ Beula Lakhidar's songs are also known as Sukananni.

Literature of Vaishnavite Period

☐ The period from **15th – 17th century** is considered to be the Vaishnavite period.

☐ Mahapurush Srimanta Shankardeva initiated a new literary genre. He wrote poetry, songs mainly in Assamese to reach out to the uneducated masses.

☐ **<u>Translation of Bhagavata</u>** was the great literary task of Vaishnavite period.

☐ Shankardeva has translated a number of sections of **Bhagavata into Assamese** as book **I, II, III, and so on.**

☐ He allotted different sections for translation to his disciple.

☐ Ananta Kandali, Gopalchandra Dwij, Anirudha Kayastha translated different sections of Bhagavata.

☐ The **<u>book X or Dasham</u>** is the most important work and attained universal popularity. Dasham describes the incidents of Sri Krishna's early life.

☐ Kirtan Ghosa is a collection of lyrics speaking about God's glory.

☐ Sankardeva authored Harishchandra Upakhyan and Balichalan.

☐ **<u>Ankiya Nat</u>** and **<u>Borgeets</u>** are the great contribution of Sankardeva. Borgeets are devotional songs which are sung with raags.

☐ 37 Borgeet composed by Sankardeva have been found.

☐ Sri Madhabadeva is the **<u>favourite disciple</u>** of Srimanta Sankardeva.

☐ Janmarahasya is the **first literary** work of Madhabdeva. Bhakti Ratnawali, Rajasuya Kavya, Adi Kanda Ramayana are some other notable works of Madhabdeva.

☐ Nama Ghosa is considered as the **<u>greatest work of Madhabdeva</u>**. It is a collection of thousands of Ghosa. It is also called the Hazari Ghosa.

☐ He also composed a few Ankiya Nats which are known as Jhumura namely Chordhara, Pimpara Guchuwa, Bhumi Letuwa, Bhujan Behar.

☐ In the same period under the **patronage of Koch king** Naranarayan, Kavi Ram Saraswati translated **Mahabharata into Assamese**. His another kavya is **Bhim Charit.**

☐ Ananta Kandali is another great author of Vaishnavite period. He completed the unfinished half of Bhagavata Purana. Other notable works are Hari Har Judha, Kumarharan Kavya, Vrittasur Badha.

☐ Sridhar Kandali was another disciple of Sankardeva. His noted work is 'Kankhowa'.

☐ Sarvabhaum Bhattacharya is another noted author.

☐ Baikunthanath Bhattacharya is a very renowned author of popularly known as Bhattadeva and considered as the pioneer of Assamese prose. He authored the famed **Katha Gita** and **Katha Bhagavata**.

☐ Charit Puthi is an important type of literature which contains biographies of Srimanta Sankardeva. **Madhabdeva has introduced** the **practice of composition** of Charit Puthis.

☐ **Kotha Guru Charit** is an important Charit Puthi which includes biographies of both Sankardeva and Madhabdeva. Sankar Charit, Damodar Charit are other examples.

Literature in Ahom Period

☐ During the Ahom age, poets like Raghunath Mishra, Kaviraj Chakravarti, Ruchinath Kandali received royal patronage from Ahom kings.

☐ The Ahom kings introduced the practice of writing of chronicles or Buranjis. Deodhai Assam Buranji, Tungkhuniya Buranji, Purani Assam Buranji all these are compilation of the Brtanjis written during the Ahom age.

☐ A number of Puranas were translated in the Ahom age which provided kings and common man mythology.

☐ Raghunath Mishra translated the **Vishnu Puran**.

☐ Siva Singha and his queen Ambika and Phuleshwari patronised a number of poets.

☐ Kaviraj Chakravarti translated Brahmavartya Purana. He also authored Sakuntala Kavya, Sankhasura Badh, Gita Govinda.

☐ Notable works Kavichnadra Dwij are Dharma Purana and kam Kumar Haran.

- Ananta Acharya authored Ananda Lahiri.
- Following the direction of Queen Phuleshwari, Sukumar Borkaith authored Hashti Vidyarnava. It is an illustrative book on the treatment and training of Elephants.
- Ghoar Nidana another book of the same period.

Literature in Modern Period

- After the **Treaty of Yandaboo** in 1826, British rule started in Assam. By that time **American Baptist** missionaries had already arrived at Assam with the aim of spreading Christainity.
- In collaboration with the Baptist missionaries, **Pandit Atmaram Sarma** translated the **Bible into Assamese** and it was published from Serampore in 1813. It was the first printed Assamese book.
- In **1836**, **Assamese** was **replaced by Bangla** as the official language in the courts and schools of Assam. In the same year **Nathan Brown** and **Oliver T Cotter** arrived in Assam. They have established a Baptist Mission Press in Sibasagar.
- A number of notable books were compiled and published by the missionaries at that time.
- A Grammar of Assamese language (1839) W. Robinson
- Grammatical Notice of Assamese language (1848) by Nathan Brown.
- Dictionary in Assamese and English (1867) by Miles Bronson. It is the first published Assamese dictionary. Although **Jaduram Deka Baruah** has **compiled a dictionary, it was never published.**
- The missionaries also compiled a number of school textbooks in Assamese.
- Anandaram Dhekial Phukan, Hem Chandra Baruah and Gunaviram Baruah literary stalwarts of that period. Anandaram Dhekial Phukan authored Asomiya Lora Mitra (1849), a few remarks of Assamese language (1855).
- Hem Chandra Baruah has compiled a **dictionary Hemkosh (1900).** His other notable works- Grammar of the Assamese language(1856), Kaniyar Kirtan (1869), Bahire Rong Cheng Bhitore Kuwa Bhatore, Adipath, Pathmala, etc.
- Gunaviram Baruah authored Ramnavami, Assam Buranji(1884), Soumar Brahman, etc. He also edited the journal Assam Bondhu.

 Nidhi Levi Farwell, Jaduram Deka Baruah and many others also contributed to Assamese literature at that period.

 In January 1846, the **first Assam Journal** Arunoday was published. It contained articles related to science, current affairs, astrology, history and many more.

 Purani Assam Buranji, Kamraupar Buranji, Chutia Buranji were published in the pages of Orunodoi.

 Yatrikar Yatra, Kamini Kanta, Phulamani and Karuna were other notable publications of Orunodoi.

 In 1888, Asomiya Bhasa Unnati Sadhni sabha was formed in Calcutta.

 In **1889**, an Assamese journal Jonaki was published and it marked the beginning of a new era of Assamese literature.

 The period from **1889-1940** known as age of **Romanticism or Jonaki era** under the leadership of the **romantic trio Chandra Kumar Agarwala, Hem Chandra Goswami, Lakshminath Bezbaruah.**

 Chandra Kumar Agarwala was the first editor of Jonaki.

 Articles like Jatiya Unnati by Kamala Kant Bhattacharya, Asomiyar Unnati, Assamar Unnati, Jatiya Prem by Phanindranath Gogoi, Asomiya Bhasa by HemChandra Goswami, Asomiya Bhasa Lakshminath Bezboruah.

 The satirical writings of Bezboruah under his pen-name Kripabar Baruah such as Kripabar Barbaruar Kakotor Tupula, Kripabar Barbaruar Vabor Burburoni were published in Jonaki.

 The biographies of John Stuart Mill, Nanak, Rajendralal Mitra, David Livingstone were also published. Jonaki reviewed several books in the column Puthir Gunagun.

 Jonaki was last published from Calcutta in 1898. After that it was published from Guwahati from 1901 to 1904 and discontinued.

 Bijuli(1891)- Published from Calcutta by members of the Assamese Literary Club namely the 'trio' Krishnaprasad Duara, Padmanath Gohain Barua and Denudhar Rajkhowa.

 Banhi- Periodical magazine and the brainchild of Lakshminath Bezbarua. Published from 1909-1940.

 Awahon(1929) – Published from Calcutta edited by Dinanath Sarma.

☐ **Jayanti (1938)** – First published from Guwahati. Founding editor Raghunath Choudhary.

☐ The period from 1940-1970 is termed as Post war era of Assamese literature which was centred around the magazine Ramdhenu and hence also termed as Ramdhenu age.

☐ Ramdhenu was first published in **1951**. It was last published in 1996.

GENRES OF ASSAMESE LITERATURE

Poetry

☐ Modern Assamese poetry made its debut in Orunodoi. Jonaki set a new literary trend in poetry writing.

☐ Bholanath Das, Bladev Mahanta, Kamalakanta Bhattacharya, (Agni Kabi) are pioneers of modern Assamese poetry.

☐ **Kamalakanta Bhattacharya-** His poetry speaks about patriotism, philosophy and social reforms. Poem collections are- Chintanal and Chintaratnagiri.

☐ **Chandrakumar Agarwala-** His poems speak of love of beauty and joy of living. He wrote the first Assamese romantic poem Bonkuwari. Pratima and Been Boragi are collections of poems.

Notable poets

☐ **Hemchandra Goswami-** Romantic poet and wrote a few poems-Priyatomar Chithi(First Assamese Sonnet) Kaku Nibilao Hiya.

☐ **Lakshminath Bezbaruah-** Composed poems- Been Boragi, Priyatoma, Dhanbor aru Ratani, etc.

☐ **Padmanath Gohain Baruah-** Phular Chaneki is an anthology of descriptive nature poems.

☐ **Hiteswar Barbarua-** Wrote long narrative poems. Malas, Sakulu are sonnet sequences. Malas is the first Assamese sonnet sequence.

☐ **Raghunath Chaudhuri-** Bihogi Kabi of Assam. Collection of his poems are- Sadari, Keteki, Dahikatara.

☐ **Ambikagiri Roychaudhuri-** Wrote several poems on love and patriotism. Collection of poems – Tumi, Bina, Bandi ki Chandere, Anubhuti, etc.

☐ **Jatindranath Duara-** Essentially a love poet. Apun Sur, Bonphool, Omar Tirtha. Kotha Kobita is his another novel work.

☐ **Nalinibala Devi-** Sandhiyar Sur, Parasmoni- collection of poems.

Novel

☐ **Yatrikar Yatra** (translation of Pilgrim's progress) and Kamini Kanta published in Orunodoi are similar to novels.

☐ **Bhanumati**(1891) written by Padmanath Gohain Baruah is considered as the first Assamese novel. He wrote another novel Lahiri.

☐ **Rajanikanta Bordoloi** – Renowned novelist and known as Upanyas Samrat. His novels are Miri Jiyori, Manomati,. Rangili, Rahdoi ligiri.

☐ **Birinchi Baruah**- Jibonor Batot (1945) is his best creation. Wrote novels under pen names Bina Baruah and Rashna Baruah.

☐ **Birendra Kumar Bhattacharya**- Authored Yaruingam, Mrityunjai (Jnanpith Award winner 1979)

☐ **Mamoni raison Goswami**- Her novels are Mamore Dhora Tarowal (Sahitya Akademi, 1982). She won the Jnanpith Award in 2001.

☐ **Nirupama Borgohain**- She authored Dinor Pisot Din, Abhiyatri, Ejon Burha manuh.

Important Facts on Assamese Literature

First Autobiography: Mor Jiwan Sowaran- Lakshminath Bezbaruah

First Modern Biography: Anandaram Dhekial Phukanar Jiban Charitra

First Sahitya Academy: Award Banphool- Jatindranath Dowerah

First Assamese Modern Play: Ram Navami- Gunaviram Baruah

First Jnanpith Award: Mrityunjay- Birendranath Kumar Bhattacharya

First Assamese Travelogue: Switzerland Bhramana- Birinchi Kumar Baruah

First Assamese Children Magazine: Lora Bondhu (1888)

First Assamese Woman Magazine: Ghor Jeuti(1927)

Authors and Titles

Author	Title
Laksminath Bezbaruah	Sahityarathi, rasaraj(Asom Sahitya Sabha)
Upanyas Samrat	Rajanikanta Bordoloi
Bihogi Kobi	Raghunath Choudhary
Agni Kobi	Kamalakanta Bhattacharya
Nijorar Kobi	Sailadhar Rajkhowa
Bonphoolar Kobi, Bhangoni Kobi	Jatindra Nath Duara
Sewali Kobi	Ratnakanta Borkakati
Natasurya	Phani Sarma

Newspaper

☐ The first Assamese periodical '**Orunodoi**' was published in **1846**. Its first editor was American missionary Dr. Nathan Brown . 'Orunodoi' is considered as the first Assamese Newspaper.

☐ In 1871, '**Assam Bilashini**'- the **second newspaper** of Assam was published. It continued religious themes for twelve years from 1871-1882.

☐ The '**Assam Mihir**' is considered as the **first** known **weekly newspaper in Assamese** language. It was published from Guwahati in 1872.

☐ '**Assam darpan**' was published as a **monthly magazine** from **Tezpur** in 1873-74.

☐ **Prabhati**- A Bengali fortnightly, was the first newspaper from Barak valley.

☐ In the year 1871, the owner of Sri Duttadeb Goswami Prabhu brought '**Dhamiaprakash Tantra**' – the second printing machine of Assam from Calcutta.

☐ In 1876, another newspaper '**Assam Dipak**' was published from Guwahati by 'Dhamiaprakash Tantra'.

☐ In 1882, the editor **Hemchandra Baruah** published '**Assam News**'.

☐ In 1894, a weekly newspaper Asam was published from Guwahati. **In 1895, Times of Assam**- an English weekly was published from Dibrugarh edited by Radanath Changakakoti.

☐ Other publications are Asom Bandhu(1885), Mou(1886).

☐ The **first daily newspaper of Assam** was '**Dainik Batori**'. It was founded as a weekly named Batori in 1929.

☐ In 1935, it became a daily and came to be known as 'Dainik Batori'.

☐ The 'Dainik Asamiya' published in 1946 was the second daily newspaper in Assamese.

☐ In 1939, the Assam Tribune was published by Radha Govinda Baruah.

☐ Currently prominent Assamese dailies are- Asomiya Pratidin, Dainik Janambhumi, Dainik Asom, etc.

☐ English dailies are- The Assam Tribune, The Sentinel, Eastern Chronicle, The Northeast Times.

Literary Organisations in Assam

Asom Sahitya Sabha

☐ It is a non-profit organisation in the field of Assamese Literature and culture of Assam.

☐ Its **head office** is at **Jorhat** District of Assam.

☐ It was founded in **December, 1937** as **Asom Sahitya Sanmilani**. Later the present name was adopted.

☐ Its first conference was held in December, 1937 and the President was Padmanath Gohain Baruah. Sarat Chandra Goswami was the first General Secretary.

☐ From 1999, the tenure of the President has been made two years.

☐ The song 'Siro Senehi Mur Bhasa Janani' composed by Mitradev Mahanta is used as the official song of Asom Sahitya Sabha.

☐ It institutes many awards and honours. It confers two important titles Sahityacharjya and Sadashya Mohain.

☐ The 2018 conference was held in **Bordumsa**, Tinsukia. The President was **Paramanda Rajbongshi**.

☐ The 2019 conference was held in **Raha**. The President was **Paramanda Rajbongshi**.

☐ The 2020 conference was held in **Sualkuchi**. The present President was **Kuladhar Saikia**.

Other Sahitya Sabhas

☐ **Bodo sahitya Sabha-** The literary organisation for development of Bodo Literature and culture. It was formed in 1952. Head office is at Kokrajhar.

☐ **Mishing Sahitya Sabha-** The literary organisation for preserving the Mishing language. It was formed in 1978. Tabu Taid was the first President.

☐ **Karbi Sahitya Sabha-** It was formed in 1966. First conference was held in 1973. Dhaniram Rangpi was the first President.

☐ **Rabha Sahitya Sabha-** It was formed in 1973.

☐ **Assam Lekhika Sangstha-** This literary organisation is formed to support Women writers in the field of Assamese literature. It was founded in 1976. Suchibrata Rai Chowdhary and Preeti Baruah were the first President and General Secretary respectively.

☐ **Sodou Asom Lekhika Samaroh Samitee**- The literary organisation of women writers in Assamese language. It was founded in 1974 in Tezpur, Assam.

5.4: AC-4: SONGS AND PERFORMING ARTS

SONGS

Songs of seasonal festivals

☐ *Bihu Geet*- Bihu songs are mainly associated with Bihu festival. They are also sung on other occasions.

☐ Bihu song describes the beauty of nature and the beloved. It glorifies the youth and also represents frustration and sorrow.

☐ Bihu songs are sung along with a number of musical instruments- Dhol, Taka, Pepa, Gagana, etc.

☐ Most of the tribal communities in Assam have their own festivals similar to the Bihu . They sing their own songs to celebrate.

☐ *Oi Nitam*- These folk songs of the Mishing community. Oi Nitam basically loves poetry with elements of sadness.

☐ *Kaban*- It is another folk song of Mishing.

☐ *Chatkamin Chathar*- These folk songs of Rabha community which are like dialogues between young men and women.

Songs of religious and devotional content

☐ **Bor Geet**- These are collections of devotional songs of Vaishnavism in Assam. These songs are considered to be of high regard thus, their name Bor geet (Great Songs).

- Themes of Borgeet are basically different stories of Sri Krishna.

- Borgeets were composed by Srimanta Sankardeva and Shree Madhabdeva in the 15th and 16th centuries.

- The language of Borgeet is Brajavali.

- The Borgeets are written in pada form of prose.

- The ragas are namely Bhatiyali, Shree, Dhanashree , Ashowari, etc.

- Some compositions are strictly sung in the morning while some are sung during the midday and evening, The singing of Borgeet is accompanied by playing Khola percussion instrument.

☐ **Bhatima**- Bhatima is basically a eulogy written in praise of someone.

- Sankardeva has composed three types of Bhatima- a) Deva Bhatima(in praise of God), b)Nat Bhatima(used in plays), c) Raj Bhatima(praise of king).

- Sankardeva has composed Tutoi and Sopoi.

☐ **Holi geet**- These songs are an essential part of Daul utsav celebrated in Barpeta. They are devotional songs and reveal heavenly qualities of Lord Krishna.

- Some Borgeets composed by Madhabdeva are regarded as Holi songs by the devotees of Barpeta.
- In 20th century some modern writers like Prasannalal Choudhary, Prushuttom Das, Prahlad Chandra Das, Girish Das etc., composed a number of holi songs.

☐ ***Deh Bichar Geet or Tokari Geet-*** These are songs with philosophical contents usually sung by wandering mendicants locally known as Boiragis.
- The literal meaning of Deh Bichar is 'consideration of body'. These songs find the hidden significance of a body and speak about the individual souls in body.
- The Boiragis sing these songs with the tune of a stringed folk instrument called Tokari or Dotara. Hence these songs are also referred to as Tokari Geet.

☐ ***Zikir-*** Zikir are devotional songs of Assamese Muslims. Zikir is believed to have originated from Arabic word Ziqr.
- Zikirs are originally composed by a Sufi poet and Muslim saint named Ajan Fakir in the late 17th century. Hence, the Zikirs are also known as Ajan Fakir geet.
- Zikirs are fully Islamic in ideal. But the influence of Vaishnav naam and Tokari can be seen in terms of literary and musical idioms.
- A typical Zikir speaks of Allah, the Devotees and worthiness of the body.

☐ ***Nam-*** Naam is basically the community singing of hymns both by Men and Women in Assamese society. It basically signifies the reciting or singing in praise of God or any particular deity.
- Naam singing by men Is more vigorous and usually accompanied by the beating of nagara and Taal. Women perform Nam simply with rhythmic clapping of hands.
- Nam singing is held on special religious occasions mostly associated with Vaishnava culture.
- Different Naam is there for different occasions such as Ai Nam, Biya Nam, etc.

Folk Songs

☐ **Goalporiya Geet-** It refers to the lyrical songs of Goalpara that are not associated with any religion or rituals.
- Pratima Pandey Baruah was the most renowned Goalpariya lokageet singer and she has raised the genre to the national level.
- Different themes are- Bhawaiya, Chatka, Moishali(grazers of buffalo) and Mahut(Elephant driver) songs, etc.

☐ **Kamrupi Lokgeet-** It is a popular form of folk music of the Kamrup region.

- Kamrupi Lokageet sung to the humble dolara and dagar(Khanjari).

- Rameshwar Pathak was an acclaimed Kamrupi singer.

☐ **Traditional Ballads or Malita**- Malitas are songs with a story element and once they were an important genre of Assamese oral folklore. Examples of ballads which have been collected so far are Barphukanar Geet, Haradatta geet, Manikonwar Phulkonwar geet, Kamala – Kuwarir geet, etc.

☐ **Nisukani Geet**- The lullabies are known as 'Nisukani Geet' and the nursery rhymes are called 'Dhainam'.

- These songs take children in a different world of moon stars, trees , etc.

- These songs help children to establish relationships with nature and amuse them.

☐ **Songs of Humour**- In lower Assam region specially in Kamrup region, professional entertainers called 'Bhaoriyas' sing humorous songs to entertain the audience. Tamul – Chorar Geet, Chah- Puraner geet, etc

- In Upper Assam, humorous songs are known as Juna. Pachalar Juna, Kapahar Juna, Nanglar Juna, etc.

☐ **Nanglee**- these are unique to Darrang which are couplets of very informal colloquial words sung by Garakhiyas(Herders).

MUSICAL INSTRUMENTS IN ASSAM

Dhol

☐ Dhol is considered to be the most important musical instrument of Assamese Folk culture.

☐ Dhol is a two faced drum of medium size.

☐ Basically it consists of a wooden barrel with an animal hide stretched over its open ends.

☐ Dhol is played by striking with a stick and a hand.

☐ Assamese dol is smaller than other dhols.

Pepa

☐ Pepa is one of the most important and unique instruments of Assam.

☐ It is made out of Buffalo horns. It is played by blowing with your mouth.

☐ In Bihu dance, Pepa is generally played by a young Bihu performer called the Papuwa and the rest accompany him by clapping hands and playing the Toka.

☐ Pepa is known by different names in different tribal communities of Assam, such as the Mishings call it 'Pempa'. The Dimasas call it 'Xuri', the Rabhas call it 'Singra' and tea tribes call it 'Pepati'.

Taal

☐ Taal is a percussion instrument used in a pair and it is made of bell metal.

☐ Taal are of different sizes and shapes are known as different names namely Khuti, Bhoor Taal, etc.

☐ Khuti Taal is used in Bihu, Husari, etc. whereas Bhor Taal, Borkah are used in auspicious occasions.

☐ The tribes of Assam use different varieties of Taal namely 'Jotha' by Bodos 'Sengso' by Karbis. 'Lupi' by Mishing etc.

Bahi

☐ Baahi is primarily another musical instrument of Assam.

☐ It is extensively used in different forms of Assamese folk.

☐ The Baahi is also known as Muruli, Benu, Baxee, etc in different parts of Assam.

☐ It is made up of Bamboo.

Gogona

☐ Gogona is a popular folk instrument and extensively used in Bihu of Assam.

☐ It is a very tiny instrument made of bamboo and has a split in the middle.

☐ It is held in the mouth to play and vibrated to produce sound. Gogona requires a high level of workmanship.

☐ According the size, Gogona are named differently such as Lihiri Gogona, Ramdhoon Gogona.

Toka

☐ Toka is an important Assamese musical instrument. It is made up of Bamboo.

☐ It has different sizes.

☐ Toka is essential in Bihu dance.

Xutuli

☐ Xutuli is an instrument which looks like the half moon and it is made of clay.

☐ Xutuli imitates the sound of animals and birds and produces the sound of a flute.

☐ In ancient times, Xutuli was very popular among cowboys.

☐ Xutuli is an indispensable part of Jeng Bihu and Bihu predominantly played by young girls.

Khol

☐ The khol is a two drum with a hollow earthen body. The body is made out of clay.

☐ In Assam, Khol is first introduced by Srimanta Sankardeva.

☐ Khol is extensively used in all performing arts of Vaishnava culture such as Ankiya Bhona, Borgeet, Satriya Nritya.

PERFORMING ARTS

Bhaona and Ankiya Nat

☐ Bhaona is a traditional form of performing art and associated with Vaishnavism in Assam.

☐ Bhaona is basically the staging of Ankiya Nats. It is a creation of Mahapurusha Srimanta Sankardeva in the early **16th century** mainly to convey messages of Vaishnavism to villagers through entertainment.

☐ Cihnayatra is the first Bhaona produced by Sankardeva.

☐ Usually Bhaona are staged in village Namghar in auspicious occasions – different Tithis, Janmastami, full moon nights. The Bhonas are performed in the Assamese and Brajavali languages.

☐ There are different characters like Sutradhar, Gayan Bayan , Bhoriya, etc.

☐ Masks are essential parts of Bhona. In the first Bhona Chihnayatra a mask was used for Garuda.

☐ Different types of masks are-

i) Masks representing frightful characters- Ravana, Yamraj.

ii) Masks for animal characters- Garuda, Monkeys, Jatayu, Kaliya Serpent.

iii) Masks for comic characters.

Puppetry

◻ The string puppetry of Assam is called Putala Nach. Putola Nach in Assam is in existence **since the 10th century** and finds mention in **Kalika Purana.**

◻ In Lower Assam, Puppetry is known as Putala- Bhoriya. In some areas, it is influenced by Bhaona and known as Putola- Bhaona.

◻ In Majuli, small wooden puppets are used in the style of the Ankia Nat. It is also known as Boti Putola, Tatek Naat.

◻ Sutradhar is the narrator of the whole story and Baazigar is the artist who handles the movements of Puppets.

Bharamyaman or Mobile Theatre

◻ The mobile theatres in Assam is a unique form of performing arts where mobile groups travel from place to place and stage plays or dramas.

◻ Mobile theatres were developed in the last decades of the 20th century and Pathshala Town is the home of mobile theatre.

◻ The **theme** of these plays over the years are mythology, classic Greek tragedies, popular novels, etc.

◻ In **1931, Brajanath Sarmah** formed 'Kohinoor Opera Party' – a mobile theatre group and it gave its first performance in 1933.

◻ The present form of commercial mobile theatres can be traced back to 1963 when Nataraj Theatre Company was started by Achyut Lahkar. **Nataraj Theatre** has introduced the use of mikes, lights, cinematic effects in mobile theatres.

◻ At present, **Bhramyaman Theatre** is one of the key profit making entertainment industries in Assam.

Cinema

◻ Joymoti is the **first Assamese cinema** produced and directed by Jyoti Prasad Agarwalla in **1935.**

◻ The screenplay of Joymoti was based on Joymoti Kunwari play of Lakshminath Bezbaruah.

◻ In **1939**, Jyoti Prasad Agarwalla made his **second and last film** Indramalati.

◻ The next Assamese films are Manomati (1941)- Rohini Kumar Barua, Rupahi (1946), Badan Barphukan (1947)- Kamal Narayan.

◻ Siraj is a notable film directed by Phani Sharma.

◻ Puberun was the first Assamese film to enter the Berlin Film Festival and win a President's silver medal.

◻ Lachit Barphukan (1961), Maak aru Morom (1957), Ranga Police(1958), Era Batar Sur(1956) – Dr Bhupen Hazarika are some notable Assamese films.

▢ Nip Baruah was a renowned film director who directed 14 films.

▢ Pramathesh Chandra Barua, the prince of Gauripur was another renowned filmmaker.

▢ Bhaiti(1972), Kamal Choudhary is the first Assamese coloured film.

▢ Renowned filmmaker Dr. Bhabendranath Saikia has taken Assamese films to a new level.

▢ Sandhyaraag(1977) , Anirban(1981), Agnisnan(1985) – National award for best screenplay.

▢ Ajoli Nobou, Kokadeuta, Nati aru Hati, Ghar Sansar, Son moina, Buwari are some commercial hits.

▢ Halodhia Choraye Baodhan Khai- Swarna Kamal Award, Konikar Ramdhenu are some of the best films of Jhanu Baruah.

▢ Filmmaker Munin Baruah has directed around 16 movies which are commercial hits.

▢ In spite of its long history and its artistic successes , the Assamese film industry is still struggling to compete with the market.

5.5: AC-5: TRADITIONAL CRAFTS IN ASSAM

Traditional Crafts in Assam

Personal Crafts

- Bell Metal & Brass Works
- Bamboo & Cane Works
- Wood Craft
- Weaving
- Pottery
- Mask Making
- Boat Making
- Fire Works

Old Crafts

- Ivory Works
- Manuscript Paintings

Crafts in Assam

▢ Bamboo and Cane works

Cane and Bamboo grows naturally in Assam and people of Assam traditionally inherit the knowledge of utilizing bamboo and cane for different purposes.

- The professional artisans involved in Bamboo and Cane works are called 'Barhoi'.

- The cottage industries of Bamboo and Cane produce household items are Pasi, Dola, Bamboo mat, fishing equipment - Jakoi, Karahi, Kula, Saloni, FurnitureMurha. Musical instruments- Bahi, Gagana, etc.
- Bamboo is extensively used in traditional dwelling houses in Assam both in hills(Chang ghar) and plains for boundary fencing(Jewra).

Japi

- It is the traditional headgear made out of leaf and bamboo . Traditionally Japi was used by open air workers in fields.
- Fulam Japis are embroidered and ornamented Japis and are considered precious possession.
- There are many types of Japis, like – Halua japi, Sorudoiya Japi, Bordoiya Japi.
- Japis are produced in Nalbari, kamrup, Nagaon,Darrang, Sivasagar, Lakhimpur.

Bamboo Mats

- Bamboo Mats are also produced in Assam on a commercial basis. Locally known by different names- 'Dhara, Jharia.
- Well known places for Bamboo Mat production are Bokajan(Karbi Anglong), Phokoli gaon(Nagaon), Borbila(Goalpara), Koyakuchi (Barpeta) .
- Large scale production done in Karimganj district.

Wooden Craft

- The carpenters create decorative items made out of wood.
- In Assam, traditional carpenters are called Barhoi.
- Carved wooden articles were common in olden days- Furniture like Palang, Salpira, Barpira, Para, Dola.
- Most of the Sattras were patrons of good Sutra who used to craft Guru Ashan Thagis, Wooden figures.
- The Guru Asana, in Namghars and sattras is an excellent example of wooden craft in Assam.

Metal Crafts

☐ **Bell Metal and Brass crafts**- As per records, in the 7th century, Kumar Bhaskar Varman presented Bell metal articles to King Harshabardhan.

- The artisans are called 'Kahar' or 'Oja' and assistants are called 'Bhagias'.
- Sarthebari in Barpeta is well known for this Bell Metal where around 1500 artisans are engaged in cottage industry.
- Hajo in Kamrup is known for Brass articles. Cooper and Brass cups of Goalpara district known as Kansas are of great significance.
- The Sorai and Bata have been in use for centuries to offer betel nut and paan and Xorai is often used as a decorative item as a gift.
- Idols of different Gods and Goddess are also made by Bell metal and Brass.

Pottery

☐ Pottery is a traditional form of cottage industry in Assam.

☐ It is practiced by the successive generations of the community members. Kumar, Hira are the main communities associated with it.

☐ Glutinous clay is obtained from the river banks of the Brahmaputra and its tributaries are the main raw material of Pottery.

☐ The well-known places of pottery are Asharikandi in Dhubri, Hajo in Kamrup and Majuli in Jorhat.

Blacksmith

☐ Blacksmith is an important cottage industry in Assam. It is invariably found as the hereditary occupation of the household concerned.

☐ The Blacksmiths are called 'Kamar'.

☐ A large number of blacksmiths are found in Karanga in Jorhat district.

Gold and Silver Smith

☐ The industry of Gold and Silver is mainly concentrated in the urban areas.

☐ The materials used for jewelry were gold, silver, cooper, and embar.

☐ Indigenous jewelers make traditional ornaments such as Dugdugi, Lokapara, Jonbiri, Keru, Thuria, Gamkharu.

Weaving

☐ Assam has early traditions of producing cotton clothes.

☐ Cotton weaving is the most common household handicraft in Assamese society especially of the womenfolk. Hand spinning of cotton yarn is also done. The weaving equipment is indigenous to Assam, Tatsaal, Ugha, Chereki, Mako, Jotor.

☐ Assamese women produce the certain types of cloth mekhela, Chadar, Cheleng, etc.

☐ Mahatma Gandhi once remarked 'Assamese women are born weavers, they can weave fairy tales in their clothes.

☐ Traditionally Muga, Eri, Pat silkworms are reared in the household in Assam. The silk yarns are extracted from cocoons of Silkworms and beautiful silk fabrics are produced.

 Sualkuchi in Kamrup district is the Centre of weaving . It is called the **'Manchester of Assam'.**

Mask Making

 Mask making is one of the famous traditional crafts of Assam and Majuli is the centre of this craft.

 It is mainly practiced by the Vaishnav Sattras. At present the Chamaguri Satra and Uttar Kamalabari Sattra have recognition in making masks.

 Mask making was initiated by Srimanta Sankardeva to depict mythological characters so that devotees can enjoy and associate with Bhaona in a better way.

 Usually masked characters Hansa, Garuda, Jatayu, Kaliya Naag, Bakasura, Jambuban, Narasimha are made.

 As per tradition natural products Hengul(Vermillion), Haital,(Yellow Arsenic), Neel, Dhalmati, Balichanda(Mica) are used as colours.

 Traditionally three types of masks are made-

i) Mukha- Face masks.

ii) Lotokia Mukha- Type of mask is used to move lips, eyes and hands.

iii) Bor Mukha- Nearly life-size or even larger in special cases.

Boat Making

 Crafts related to boat making have been practiced in Assam since ages.

 Majuli, Nagaon are some important centres of boat making.

 Some boats are made of a single piece of log such as Gutiya Nao – a small boat used by a single person. Chellengi Nao- very little weight and high speed, used for fishing, riding etc.

 Some types of boats were Dinga Nao – large boats with covers used by merchants, Khel Nao – racing boats with long and serpent shapes. Bajra Nao- Large beautiful used by rich merchants, landlords.

Manuscript Painting

 The art of manuscript painting was developed in Majuli and is associated with NeoVaishnavism movement.

 This art was also patronized by the Ahom kings.

The most common carriers of manuscripts were Sanchipat made from bark of the Agar tree and Tulapat- sheet made from wood pulp.

The preparation of Sanchipat requires a laborious process of curing, seasoning and polishing of raw slices Agar tree barks in order to retain the ink.

Tulapat was made from wood pulp of some specific trees e.g. Nuni. The Tulapat making process is indigenous to Assam introduced by Ahoms.

Manuscripts on muga and other silk were also common in Assam.

The oldest painted manuscripts on Tulapat are the Phung Chin(1437 A.D) and the Suktanta Keyompong both in Tai language and script.

Earliest Manuscript in Assamese is the Adi Dasama. Lanka Kanda Ramayan, KOtha Guru Charit are other fine examples.

Ivory Works

The ivory crafts in Assam can be traced back to ancient age. The Harsacharita of Banabhatta also records the splendid presents made of Ivory sent by Bhaskaravarman.

Ivory carving was an important handicraft in Ahom rule and practiced by a group of Khanikars.

It was largely practiced in Barpeta.

Used in hilts and handles of weapons and legs of furniture. Ivory was used for making various kinds of boxes, combs, ornaments.

Even mats prepared with ivory strips were produced and one such mat is still being preserved in Auniati Satra.

Fireworks Craft of Barpeta

This traditional craft goes back to 130 years ago.

Late Lakshiram Pathak of Majorhati had started fireworks craft in Barpeta after going through a Bengali book on Chinese Fireworks published in 1885.

Queen Victoria was satisfied with his work and gave him a gold medal and donated two bighas of land for his trade.

After Pathak's death, his son Late Narahari Pathak and other family members Manoranjan Pathak, Nalini Pathak and Achinta Pathak established separate fireworks units.

Currently there are five units at Majorhati, Brindaban Hati, Bilator Hati in Barpeta producing traditional fireworks.

The Assam government has also allotted land to set up a Barpeta Atosbazi Village.

Around **31 varieties** are produced like Fanush, Asman Gola, Phulijari , Patta Lori.

5.6: AC-6: TRIBES OF ASSAM

TRIBES AND COMMUNITIES OF ASSAM

Bodo Tribe

◻ The Bodo Tribe of Assam is the largest ethnic tribe of Assam and they belong to the Indo-Mongoloid group. Mythologically, they are related to the 'Kiratas' found in Mahabharata.

◻ The population of Bodo Tribe in Assam is around 20 lakhs. The Bodo people mostly inhabit the districts of Kokrajhar, Baksa, Udalguri, Chirang (**BTAD**), Darrang and Sonitpur.

◻ Bodo villages are situated in the plains of the valleys and rice growing is their traditional occupation. Bodo people are experts in bamboo and acne crafts.

◻ Bodos have their own language called Bodo which is one of the 22 scheduled languages of India. It has also been introduced as the medium of instruction in educational institutes especially in the BTAD regions. The script is Devanagari.

◻ Bodo literature is mostly indigenous and was composed orally or in folk songs.

◻ The Bodo Sahitya Sabha was formed in 1952.

◻ The seasonal festivals are – Baisagu, Domashi, Katrigacha.

◻ Among the religious festivals of the Bodos, the Kherai is the most famous.

◻ Bagrumba is a famous folk dance of the Bodos.

◻ Usually the Bodo family structure is patriarchal.

◻ Traditionally Bodo religious faith rests on 'Bathou' analogues to Lord Shiva. The Sizu plant which is known for longetivity is planted in front of the Bodo courtyard and worshipped.

◻ The traditional marriage of Bodo society is different. The groom does not go to the bride's house but a small group of relatives go to fetch the bride. After the ceremonial rituals of the marriage, the bridal party is offered with local delicacies.

Mishing Tribe

◻ The Mishings are one of the largest tribes in Assam with a population **more than 8 lakhs**. Traditionally known as **Miri**.

◻ The Mishing tribe is divided into two groups – Degdoong and Dagdok.

◻ They are mainly concentrated in the districts of Lakhimpur, Dhemaji, Dibrugarh, Jorhat and Sonitpur.

◻ Traditionally Mishing people inhabit the riverine areas and build 'Chang Ghar' with timber bamboo, thatch for comfort living.

☐ Their social structure is patriarchal and they have joint families. The eldest member of the family is highly respected.

☐ The Mishing women are expert weavers and also rear silkworms.

☐ The traditional attires of women are – Gasar(Sadar), Sampan. For men- Gonro ugon, Mibu galuk(Shirt), Dumer(Gamusa).

☐ The Mishings have their own language but they don't have their own script. Hence, they use the Assamese language for writing.

☐ The Mishing observe many festivals throughout the year. Ali ai Ligang, Po Rag, Nora Siga, Amrok are some of them.

☐ They believe the Sun as their mother and Moon as their father. In modern times, some of them have converted in Christianity whereas some sections have adopted the Eksharan Dharma established by Sankardeva.

☐ The Mishing community buries their dead ones and for every village there is a common burial place.

☐ There is no caste system or ideas of slavery in the Mishing society.

Deori Tribe

☐ Deoris are one of the four divisions of Chutiyas and they represent the priestly section of the whole Chutia community.

☐ The Deoris are believed to have come to the Sadiya region before the first century. The Deoris are nowadays settled mostly in Sibsagar, Jorhat, Dibrugarh, Lakhimpur and Sonitpur districts.

☐ Deoris are traditionally riverine tribes. Usually their houses are made in a similar pattern facing the river.

☐ Agriculture is the main source of their livelihood. They also domesticate animals like pigs, fowls, cows and buffaloes.

☐ The Deoris have their own language which is similar to the Bodo language.

☐ Two major festivals are observed by the Deori people- the 'Bohagiyo Bisu' and 'Maghaya Utsava'.

☐ A Deori male uses loincloth called 'Ikho' with a shirt for the upper body. The Deori women wear a skirt called 'Igo' which is wrapped tightly above the breast flowing down to their ankles. Deori women use a towel called the 'Gathiki' to cover their heads.

☐ The Deoris conform to both their primal beliefs and Hinduism(Vaishnavism). The Kundi- Mama, Pichsa dema, Gailrung kundi, are the supreme deities.

☐ Regarding the burial process, dead are generally cremated, but in some cases, death of young pregnant women or those dying in epidemics, the dead bodies are buried.

Rabha Tribe

 Rabha is one of the major tribes in Assam with a population around **3 lakhs**. They are widely scattered in Goalpara, Kamrup and Darrang districts.

 The Rabha society is patriarchal in character. It is believed that the Rabhas were once a matrimonial tribe. The structure of the Rabha tribe is based on 'Pandulipis' or the local customary laws. The Pandulipis were written on the basis of customs. Usages, traditions and religious beliefs.

 Agriculture is the main occupation of the Rabhas. Earlier they also practiced hunting and Jhum cultivation which have gradually disappeared.

 The 'Baikho' or 'Khosi Puja' is the most important festival of Rabhas and it is observed in the month of Baisakh. Rabha people also observe a number of Puja festivals- 'Kechaikhaiti' Puja, 'Langa' puja or Dinga Puja , Maeri puja etc, 'Hana Ghora' is a festival of merriment.

 There is no specific enumerated rule for death. The death body may be buried or cremated.

Tiwa or Lalung Tribe

 Tiwa is an indigenous tribe inhabiting the states of Assam and Meghalaya.

 They have two sub groups -Hills Tiwas, and Plains. The Hills Tiwas displaying contrasting cultural features. The Hills Tiwas live in the westernmost areas of Karbi Anglong. Plain Tiwas mostly inhabits Morigaon, Nagaon, Kamrup.

 The main occupation is rice cultivation, growing of other crops- sesame, mustard, ginger, chilies.

 They speak both Tiwa and Assamese languages.

 The main festivals of Tiwas are three Bisus, Barat Utsav, Sagra Misuana, Wansua,'Jon Beel' Mela.

 Lali-lai-Hilali is a popular folk song type of Tiwas.

 The Tiwa community is divided into several clans called Phoit(Wali) and Dilok. Historically Tiwa people are closely associated with the principality of Gobha Raja.

 The Tiwas have a traditional faith akin to the Hindu Shakta religion but the mode of worship is not the same. The Hill Tiwas worship stone images. Both cremation and burial are practiced.

 The Lalung families are a nuclear family.

 After the death of the father the land is divided equally among his children.

Dimasa Kachari Tribes

 The Kacharis are the most widely spread tribe in northeast India. They belong to the Indo-Mongoloid group which includes the Bodos and their allied tribes.

☐ The North Cachar Hills district has been renamed as Dima Hasao district after the Dimasa Tribe.

☐ Busu harvesting festival is the main socio-cultural festival of the Dimasa. 'Rajni' and 'Harni Gabra' are festivals related to productive work. In the 'Rajni' festival. The village people worship their presiding deity.

☐ The dance of Dimasa people is an extremely complex form and based on instrumental music. No songs are used. Khram(Drum) follows the rhythm of the 'Muri'(fife) and so do the dancers.

☐ An important institution of Dimasa village is 'Hangsao'. It is an association of unmarried boys and girls of the village.

☐ Throughout the year, members of the Hangsao work together in the Jhums. Cultivating by rotation an area of land at every member's field.

☐ The Dimasas are a very religious people. Their religion is a mixture of the Hindu and Bodo traditions. The main gods worshipped by the Dimasas are Siva Deo, Rajo, Naikhu, and so on. The Supreme God is 'Shibrai'.

Karbi Tribe

☐ The Karbis are one of the major Tribes in Assam. They are also known as Mikir. Racially they belong to the Mongoloid group.

☐ Karbis are the principal ethnic group of Karbi Anglong but they also inhabits in Nagaon, Morigaon, Golaghat, Sonitpur, Lakhimpur.

☐ 'Chintong', 'Ronghang' and 'Amri' – three main groups of Karbi people based on types of habitation.

☐ Their main occupation is agriculture and practicing Jhum cultivation. Apart from rice, they grow spices, maize and fruits.

☐ They have five clans- Ingti, Terang, Inghi, Teron and Timung. The Ingti is the priestly clan.

☐ Me is the Karbi village council where all social and family matters are discussed.

☐ The Karbi version of Ramayana is called Sabin Alun.

☐ 'Rongker' and 'Hacha Kekan' are two main festivals related to agricultural seasons. Rongker is celebrated before the Jhum cultivation starts in winter and again in summer just prior to the planting of rice.

☐ The traditional turban of Karbi men is called 'poho'. Karbi women wear a short mekhela called 'Pinicamflak' and other adornments 'Wankok', 'Pekok '.

☐ The traditional religious faith of the Karbis is animistic and based on ancient customs and various animals are offered to the deities. These days some Karbi people have adopted the Vaishnava and other Hindu faiths and also Christianity.

☐ 'Chomangkan' is a death ritual which is very unique.

 It is observed with great festivity. Large quantities of beer, pigs and rice is necessary for this ceremony.

Sonowal kachari Tribe

 The Sonowal kachari tribe is the sub group of the Kachari tribe.

 They mainly live in Dibrugarh, Lakhimpur, Dhemaji, Tinsukia, Jorhat and Golaghat districts.

 Traditionally their occupation is Gold washing and hence they are known as Sonowals.

 Cooperation is the salient feature of their social life. All villagers co-operates with others activities.

 They observe Rangali Bihu like Assamese people which falls in the month of January.

 They have nuclear families and the social structure is similar to non-tribal.

 The Sonowal Kachari follows Mahapurusha Baishnav dharma.

 They don't have their own dialect and speak Assamese as their language.

Kuki Tribe

 The kukis are a mixed group of tribes(around 37 tribes) who entered India through Burma and Central asia. They belong to the great Mongoloid group.

 In Assam, they inhabit the districts of Dima Hasao and Karbi Anglong.

 Agriculture is their main occupation and they are good horticulturists. They grow pineapples, Lemons, Gingers. Kuki males are good hunters.

 Kuki tribes are ruled by hereditary chiefs who possess considerable power.

 The main festivals of Kukis are Ai- San, Sel Bonchon, Lom KIvah etc. Ai San is related to hunting. Sel Bonchon is about wrestling with Mithun. A few young boys then wrestled with the Mithn and tried to excite the animal. Lom Kovah is another festival of Kukis from ancestor's time having – Kut is celebrated at the end of the harvesting season.

 Some of the traditional musical instruments of the Kuki tribe are- Kho'ng -pi(big drum), Dah-pi(Gong), Pe'ngkul(trumpet). Theile(flute), Se'lki(horn).

Mech Tribe

 The Mechs are small in number. They are of Tibeto-Burman origin. It is believed that Mechas and Kacharis are of the same origin.

 They are mostly found in Goalpara districts and some parts of Khowang area in Dibrugarh area and also in Karbi Anglong.

 Some of the Mech Family converted to Christianity and the others follow Hindu religion.

Tai Phake or Phakial Tribe

◻ Tai Phake is a Tai speaking tribe with a tiny population of around 2000 in Dibrugarh and Tinsukia districts.

◻ They entered Assam in the 18th century and established their village on the bank of Burhi Dihing river and their village is now known as Namphake village.

◻ They are Buddhists. The main features of their village are its traditional stilt houses, its Buddhist monastery and the symbolic Ashokan pillar.

◻ They speak both Tai and Assamese languages. Poi Sangken, Budha Purnima are their major festivals.

Rengma Naga Tribe

◻ The Rengma Naga is originally a Naga Tribe of Nagaland, however a section of Rengma Nagas migrated to Karbi Anglong and settled between Barpathar and Chokihola.

◻ Rengma Naga of Karbi Anglong are divided into eight clans.

◻ Originally they are animists but many of them adopted Christianity.

◻ Their festivals are associated with agriculture. Nyada. Pi pe, Lotsung Nga are their main festivals.

Zeme Naga Tribe

◻ The Zeme Naga is originally a Naga Tribe of Nagaland, however a section of Rengma Nagas migrated and settled down in the North East side of North Cachar Hills and Maibong.

◻ They have their own dialect.

◻ Six clans of Zeme Nagas are there- Napame, Nkuame, Heneume, Nriame, Sogame and Pnma.

Khamti Tribe

◻ The Khamti Tribe is a branch of the Tai race. They are found in Bihpuria and Narayanpur areas of Lakhimpur and also Sadia regions.

◻ In the past they have cultivated opium in large quantities.

◻ The Khamtis are followers of Buddhism.

◻ Some festivals of Khamti Tribes are Poi Changken, Poi Nen Hok, Paribot, Maico Chumfai, etc.

COMMUNITIES

Ahoms

◻ The Ahoms are descendants of Tai people who accompanied Chaulung Sukapha and entered the Brahmaputra valley in 1228.

◻ They are mostly concentrated in the Upper assam region.

◻ The present culture of Ahom people are amalgamation of their original Tai culture and different indigenous cultures of Assam.

◻ Most of the Tai Ahoms practice Hinduism and speak Assamese as their mother tongue.

Chutias

◻ The Chutias are of Mongoloid origin.

◻ Originally they inhabited the region of Sadia. Currently, they inhabit the districts of Sibasagar, Dibrugarh, Tinsukia, Lakhimpur in upper Assam.

◻ They have adopted the Assamese language and still retained their own languages and culture in rituals.

◻ The Chutias Absorbed into Hindu society and they are called Hindu Chutia, those of the Ahom society are called Ahom Chutia and those absorbed into Kachari society are called Barahi Chutia.

Koch Rajbongshi

◻ The Koch Rajbongshi are of mixed origin.

◻ People of different tribal groups after conversion into Hinduism were known as Rajbongshi or Koch.

◻ The Koches call themselves Rajbongshi due to their connection with the Koch king Naranarayan.

◻ In 1872, in Brahmaputra valley , 3,12,999 Koches were enumerated.

◻ The Koch Rajbongshi has the status of OBC and now are claiming the status of ST status.

Matak

◻ Mataks were originally known as Moamarias- followers of Vaishnavite sect of Assam and their Guru was Sri Aniruddha.

◻ They mainly inhabit the districts of Dibrugarh and Tinsukia.

◻ It is believed that the term Moamaria is derived from Vaishnava sect practiced in Mayamara Sattra.

◻ In the 18th century, the Moamarias revolted against the Ahom monarchy and established their control over Ahom capital for a few years. Later they made terms with Ahom king and settled in a territory that came to be known as Matak Rajya.

Tea Tribe

◻ The Tea Tribe of Assam is basically referring to the tea garden workers in Assam. They were originally brought to Assam during the 19th century by British planters from tribal dominated regions of present-day Jharkhand, Odisha, Telangana and Chhattisgarh to work as labourers in Tea Estates in Assam.

◻ The total population is around 60 lakhs(17% population of Assam).

◻ They are found mainly in Upper Assam and Northern Brahmaputra belt where there is high concentration of tea gardens such as Sonitpur, Golaghat, Jorhat, Sivasagar, Dibrugarh, Tinsukia.

◻ They mainly speak Nagpuri, Odia, Santhali, Mundari, etc.

- Tusu Puja and Kara,(festival) are two important festivals.
- Jhumur Dance is a famous folk dance of the Tea Tribe community.

5.7: AC-7: ASSAM'S CULTURAL & RELIGIOUS INSTITUTIONS

Sattras

- Sattras are religious and socio - cultural institutions associated with devotional practices of Neo- Vaishnavism faith propagated by Sankardeva.
- Sattras were initially established by Sankardeva and his disciples namely, Madhabdeva, Harideva, Damodardeva for the propagation of the Vaishnavite faith.
- With passage of time Sattras have gradually transformed into socio-cultural centres of numerous arts and culture including education, music, dance, drama, fine art, manuscript painting, etc.
- Sattras are mainly concentrated in Majuli and Barpeta.
- The Sattradhikari is the religious and the administrative head of the Sattra and all the devotees who stay permanently within the Sattra are called as Bhakat.
- The following are the components of Sattra- Batchora, Manikut, Hati(place where Bhakats stay), Boha.
- During Ahom rule, kings donated lands to the Sattras.

Sattras of Barpeta

- Patbaushi Sattra- It was founded by Srimanta Sankardeva and spent 18 years of life in this Sattra and propagated his faith, literature, art forms, culture to its fullest form. He completed remarkable works such as the composition of 'Kirtan Ghosa' and 20 invaluable Borgeets in this place.
- Ganakkuchi Sattra- It was founded by Sri Madhab Deva. Some of the items used by Sankardeva and Sachipat puthis are well preserved here.
- Barpeta Sattra- Sri Madhab deva founded the Barpeta Sattra and stayed here for 8 years. He appointed Mathura Das Burha Ata as the first Sattradhikari of the Sattra who systemized the administration of the Sattra.
- The main Kirtanghar is where prayers are performed. In the Bhajghar a lamp is continuously burning for more than 400 years that is called 'Akhay Banti'.
- Some other important Sattras of Barpeta are Jania Sattra, Baradi Sattra, Sattra Kanara.

Sattras of Majuli

- Originally there were 64 Sattras in Majuli and due to erosion caused by floods in Brahmaputra, many Sattras were shifted to Lakhimpur and other areas. Now 31 Sattras are there in Majulia and are recognised by the Majuli Cultural landscape Region Act, 2006.

☐ Dhunyahat or Belguri Satra- It was the first Sattra in Majuli established by Srimanta Sankardeva. The famous Manikanchan Shanjog took place in this Sattra.

☐ Later this Sattra was transferred to Lakhimpur (Kasikota) because of erosion.

☐ Kamalabari Satra- Founded by Bedulapadma Ata. It is the centre of art, culture, literature. It is known for Boat making craft.

☐ Auinati sattra- Founded by Niranjan Pathakdeva. It is famous for 'Paalnam' and 'Apsara Nritya'. It has a collection of Assamese jewellery and handicrafts.

☐ Garamurh Sattra- Founded by Lakshmikanta deva. During the Autumn end traditional Raasleela is performed. Some ancient weapons such as bartop(cannon) are also preserved here.

☐ Dakhinpat Sattra- It is famous for its Raasleela celebrations.

☐ Samaguri Sattra- It is famous for its art of Mask making.

Namghor

☐ Namghor is basically the place of prayer or worship of the followers of NeoVaishnavite faith propagated by Srmanta Sankardeva.

☐ Shekiakhowa Bornamghor- It was established by Sri Madhabdeva in 1528. It is located in Dhekiakhowa village of Jorhat.

☐ Athkheliya Namghar- It is in Bosa Gaon, Golaghat. The name comes from eight kuris nearby it which forms the word athkuriya which eventually becomes Athkheliya. Ahom king Gadapani constructed it in 1681.

☐ Bharali Naamghor- It is in Kaliabor (Nagaon) another old and historically important Naamghor.

Kamakhya Temple

☐ It is an ancient Shakti peeth situated In Nilachal Hills Guwahati.

☐ It finds mention in the inscription of Allahabad pillar of Samudragupta.

☐ Devotees from all over India come for pilgrimage during Ambubachi and Manasa Puja.

☐ Goddess Kamakhya is worshipped in the form of yoni inside a cave.

☐ The temple can be dated back to the 8th century. The present structure was rebuilt in 1565 by King Naranarayan after it was destroyed by Muslim invader Kalpahar.

☐ Kamakhya temple is surrounded by other temples dedicated to deities like Bhubaneswari, Kali, Tara, Chinnamasta and all of them collectively are known as Dasamahavidya.

Other temples

☐ **Daul Govinda**- It is located in the north bank of Brahmaputra ate Rajaduar in North Guwahati. The temple has two idols- Lord Shyamaray and Lord Govinda. It is a place of historic importance and copper plates and rock inscription were discovered around the temple.

☐ **Dirgeshwar temple**- Located in the north bank of Brahmaputra. It has several rockcut images of the 11th and 12th century. This is one of the few temples where Buffalo sacrifice is done during Durga Puja.

☐ **Aswaklanta Temple**- This temple was constructed by King Siva Singha in 1720 situated on the bank of Brahmaputra. It is said that Lord Krishna, who came to kill Narakasura, his horse got tired at this place.

- There are two images- one of Janardana and another of Anantasai Vishnu. The latter is a fine art specimen of the 11th century.

- There is one stone inscription on the body of the temple.

☐ **Navagraha temple**- Temple of the nine planets as the name suggests was a great centre of study of astrology and astronomy in the ancient times. It is situated in the heart of Guwahati at a hilltop.

☐ **Basistha ashram**- It is situated in Guwahati. It is said to have been the hermitage of Hindu sage Vaishishtha. Three small streams named Sandhya, Laita, kanta meet here. Janardana Devalaya dedicated to Lord Vishnu is also there.

☐ **Haleswar Temple**- Located in Tezpur. It is believed that a linga was found by a farmer(halowa) while he was ploughing the field and a temple was constructed initially on this linga. Later, Ahom king Rudra Singha constructed the temple in 1705.

☐ **Mahabhairab temple**- Located in Tezpur. As per belief, it was established by king Bana with a Shiva lingam. The ancient temple was destroyed and a new temple was constructed.

☐ **Bhairabi Devalaya**- Situated in a hillrock on the bank of Brahmaputra in Tezpur. It is believed that 'Usha', daughter of King Banasur, used to offer puja to Goddess Bhairabi regularly.

Islamic Religious Institutions

☐ **Ajan Peer Dargah Sharif**- It is located in Saraguri Chapari in Sivasagar district. It was established by Sufi poet and muslim Saint Ajan Fakir. On the day of URUS, thousands of devotees pay homage to Ajan Peer.

☐ **Poa Mecca**- It is a 16th century dargah located in Hajo, Kamrup. It was established by Ghiyasuddin Auliya.

5.8: AC-8: MCQs – ART & CULTURE (351-400)

HC 351- When was Srimanta Sankardev born?

a)   1439   b)   1449

c)   1459   d)   1469

Ans- b) 1449

HC 352- Where was Srimanta Sankardev born?

a)   Koch Bihar   b)   Narayanpur

c)   Bordowa   d)   Majuli

Ans- c) Bordowa

HC 353- When was Madhavdev born?

a)   1449   b)   1459

c)   1489   d)   1491

Ans- c) 1489

HC 354- Where was Madhavdev born?

a)   Koch Bihar   b)   Narayanpur

c)   Bordowa   d)   Majuli

Ans- b) Narayanpur

HC 355- Who wrote Naam Ghosa?

a)   Sankardev   b)   Madhavdev

c)   Haridev   d)   Bhattadev

Ans- b) Madhavdev

HC 356- Who was the founder of "Ekasarana Dharma"?

a)   Sankardev   b)   Madahvdev

c)   Haridev   d)   Damodhardev

Ans- a) Sankardev

HC 357- Who wrote Gunamala?

a)   Madhavdev   b)   Sankardev

c)   Damodhardev   d)   Bhattadev

Ans- b) Sankardev

HC 358- Which among the following is a great work of Sankardev?

a)   Kirtan Ghosa   b)   Naam Ghosa

c)   Katha Gita   d)   Bhakti Ratnavali

Ans- a) Kirtan Ghosa

HC   358- Ali-Aye-Ligang/Ali-Ai-Ligang   is   festival   by   which community?

a)   Bodo Community   b)   Mising Community

c)   Khasi Community   d)   Ahom Community

Ans- b) Mising Community

HC 359- Who is called the "Rupkonwar"?

a)   Jyoti Prasad Agarwala   b)   Laxminath Bezbarua

c)   Chandra Kumar Agarwala   d)   None of the above

Ans- a) Jyoti Prasad Agarwala

HC 360- Who directed the film "Joymati"?

a)   Jyoti Prasad Agarwala   b)   Laxminath Bezbarua

c)   Chandra Kumar Agarwala   d)   Bhupen Hazarika
Ans- a) Jyoti Prasad Agarwala

HC 361- When was the film "Joymoti" released?
a)   1934   b)   1935
c)   1936   d)   1937
Ans- b) 1935

HC 362- Who directed the film "Indramalati"?
a)   Chandra Kumar Agarwala   b)   Jyoti Prasad Agarwala
c)   Bhupen Hazarika   d)   None of the above
Ans- b) Jyoti Prasad Agarwala

HC 363- Who directed the film "Piyoli Phukan"?
a)   Jyoti Prasad Agarwala   b)   Chandra Kumar Agarwala
c)   Phani Sharma   d)   Bhupen Hazarika
Ans- c) Phani Sharma

HC 364- Who directed the film "Era Bator Sur"?
a)   Jyoti Prasad Agarwala   b)   Bhupen Hazarika
c)   Phani Sharma   d)   Laxminath Bezbarua
Ans-b) Bhupen Hazarika

HC 365- Who directed the film "Chameli Memsaab"?
a)   George Baker   b)   Phani Sharma
c)   Abdul Majid   d)   Bhupen Hazarika
Ans- c) Phani Sharma

HC 366- Name the largest village in Assam.
a)   Sarupathor   b)   Dergaon
c)   Sualkuchi   d)   Barnagar
Ans- c) Sualkuchi

HC 367- What was the first Assamese Newspaper?
a)   Dainik Batori   b)   Bengal Gazette
c)   Arunodoi   d)   Assam Daily
Ans- c) Arunodoi

HC 368- Bodo tribes called the Bihu As-
a)   Baisagu   b)   Ali-Aye-Ligang
c)   Bhasgi utsav   d)   Bhagi mela
Ans- a) Baisagu

HC 369- Poa Macca in Hazo is a holy palce of-
a)   Hindu   b)   Islam
c)   Christian   d)   Buddhist
Ans- b) Islam

HC370- The first Assam magazine Arunodoi published in year-
a)   1836   b)   1838
c)   1846   d)   1848

Ans- c) 1846

HC 371- Who composed the religious song "Zikir and Zari"?

a)   Shah Navi   b)   Azan Fakir

c)   Sankardev   d)   Madhavdev

Ans- b) Azan Fakir

HC 372- Who composed the song 'Chira Chenehi Mor Bhasa Janani'?

a)   Nilmani Phukan   b)   Padmanath Gohain Barua

c)   Mitradev Mahanta   d)   Laksminath Bezbarua

Ans- c) Mitradev Mahanta

HC 373- The first Assamese Magazine was published from Kolkata was-

a)   Jonaki   b)   Bahi

c)   Usha   d)   Bijuli

Ans- a) Jonaki

HC 374- The first Assamese newspaper was published by Assamese personality was-

a)   The Dainik Assam   b)   The Assam Bilasinee

c)   The Assam Mihir   d)   The Assam Bandhu

Ans- b) The Assam Bilasinee

HC 375- Who was the founder and chief editor of magazine"Prantik"?

a)   Dr. Bhupen Hazarika   b)   Dr. Hiren Gohain

c)   Surya Hazarika   d)   Dr. Bhabendranath Saikia

Ans- d) Dr. Bhabendranath Saikia

HC 376- The Doordarshan Kendra was established in-

a)   1981   b)   1983

c)   1982   d)   1990

Ans- c) 1982

HC 377- Which personality is known as "Lion Man" of Assam?

a)   Rudra Barua   b)   Jyoti Prasad Agarwala

c)   Kamalakanta Bhattachrya

d)   Radha Govinda Barua

Ans- d) Radha Govinda Barua

HC 378- Which personality from Assam is known as "DeshBhakta"?

a)   Rudra Barua   b)   Tarunram Phukan

c)   Kanaklata Barua   d)   Gopinath Bordoloi

Ans- b) Tarunram Phukan

HC 379- Which writer is known as Pitambar Rajmedhi?

a)   Rajmohan Nath   b)   Robin Dey

c)   Rudra Barua   d)   Hemchandra Goswami

Ans- a) Rajmohan Nath

HC 380- Tusu puja is observed by which community?

a)   Bodos   b)   Tea tribes

c)   Aadibasis   d)   Karbis

Ans- b) Tea tribes

HC 381- When Magh-Bihu is celebrated in Assam?

a)   Mid-January   b)   Mid-October
c)   Mid-June   d)   Mid-September

Ans- a) Mid-January

HC 382- Kushaan gaan is popular in which area?

a)   Barpeta   b)   Goalpara
c)   Dhubri   d)   Darrang

Ans- b) Goalpara

HC 383- What is "Haati"?

a)   A Satra   b)   A Monikut
c)   A living place   d)   An entrance to Satra

Ans- c) A living place

HC 384- What is Gumraag?

a)   Kind of music   b)   An instrument
c)   A sweet dish   d)   A kind of dance

Ans- d) A kind of dance

HC 385- Maho-ho is celebrated to terminate-

a)   Cold   b)   Mosquitoes
c)   Diseases   d)   Rats

Ans- b) Mosquitoes

HC 386- What is Fitra?

a)   An offering   b)   A type of Namaz
c)   A Mosque   d)   A kind of dress

Ans- a) An offering

HC 387- Which site is called the Khajuraho of Assam?

a)   Basistha Asram   b)   Sukreshwar
c)   Kamakhya   d)   Madan Kamdev

Ans- d) Madan Kamdev

HC 388- Where did Gandhiji stay during his visit in 1921?

a)   At circuit house   b)   Tarunram Phukan's house
c)   Poki   d)   Phani Sharma's house

Ans- Poki

HC 389- In which year Dr. Hazarika got Dadasaheb Phalke Award?

a)   1991   b)   1999
c)   1992   d)   1993

Ans- c) 1993

HC 390- Who wrote the first Assamese Novel?

a)   Laksminath Bezbarua   b)   Padmanath Gohain Barua
c)   Phani Sharma   d)   Braja Nath Sharma

Ans- b) Padmanath Gohain barua

HC 391- Who started 'Under Sal Tree Drama' festival?

a)   Bishnu Prasad Rabha   b)   Phani Sharma

c)   Birubala Rabha   d)   Sukracharya Rabha

Ans- d) Sukracharya Rabha

HC 392- When was Assam Sahitya Sabha established?

a)   1919   b)   1925

c)   1917   d)   1934

Ans- c) 1917

HC 393- The headquarter of Assam Sahitya Sabha is situated in-

a)   Jorhat   b)   Darrang

c)   Sivsagar   d)   Sadiya

Ans- a) Jorhat

HC 394- The first autobiography in Assamese is thought to be-

a)   Atma Jivan Charit   b)   Mur Jiwon Suworon

c)   Adhalikha Dostabej   d)   Jibon Britto

Ans- b) Mur Jiwon Suworon

HC 395- The first recipient of Assam valley literary award is-

a)   Birendranath Dutta   b)   Bhabendranath Saikia

c)   Mamoni Raisom Goswami d)   Nagen Saikia

Ans- b) Bhabendranath Saikia

HC 396- The Assam valley Literary Award is conferred by-

a)   Balmer Lawrie Literary Trust   b)   Tata Trust

c)   Williamson Magor Trust   d)   None of the above

Ans- c) Williamson Magor Trust

HC 397- Name the first Sahitya Akademi winner in Bodo-

a)   Anil Boro   b)   Mangalshingh Hazowary

c)   Rita Boro   d)   None of the above

Ans- b) Mangalshingh Hazowary

HC 398- Who formed the Yatra Party

a)   Achyut Lahkar   b)   Jyoti Prasad Agarwala

c)   Bishnu Prasad Rabha   d)   None

Ans- a) Achyut Lahkar

HC 399- Who is then editor of Abhiruchi?

a)   Homen Bargohain   b)   Balendra Mohan Chakravarty

c)   S.M Barua   d)   Jugal Luchan Das

Ans- b) Balendra Mohan Chakravrty

HC 400- What was the most popular Sports magazine in Assam?

a)   Sport-star   b)   Olympic

c)   Abhiruchi   d)   Khela

Ans- c) Abhiruchi

6. MISCELLANEOUS

M-1: Important Places
M-2: Awards & Honours
M-3: Important Events
M-4: Assam Agitation and Assam Accord
M-5: Some Eminent Personalities
M-6: Geographical Tagged Products from Assam
M-7: MCQs - Miscellaneous

6.1: M-1: Important Places

MAJULI

☐ Majuli is a river island in the Brahmaputra River, Assam and in 2016 it became the first island to be made a district in India.

☐ It had an area of 880 square kilometers (340 sq mi) at the beginning of the 20th century, but having lost significantly to erosion it covers 352 square kilometers (136 sq mi) as at 2014. Majuli has shrunk as the river surrounding it has grown.

☐ The island is formed by the Brahmaputra River in the south and the Kherkutia Xuti, an branch of the Brahmaputra, joined by the Subansiri River in the north.

☐ Majuli island is accessible by ferries from the city of Jorhat. The island is about 300–400 kilometers (186–249 mi) east from the state's largest city —Guwahati. It was formed due to course changes by the river Brahmaputra and its tributaries, mainly the Lohit. Majuli is the abode of the Assamese neo-Vaishnavite culture.

Sualkuchi

☐ It is a census town in Kamrup district in the Indian state of Assam. It is situated on the north bank of the river Brahmaputra, about 35 km from Guwahati, Sualkuchi is a block of Kamrup District. It has large number of cottage industry engaged in handloom, for which it is also known as the "Manchester of Assam".

☐ This is the textile center of Assam. Muga silk and Pat silk along with Eri silk and Endi cloth from this region is famous for its quality.

☐ Mekhela chadors and Gamosas made from this indigenous material is in demand throughout Assam as well as other parts of India.

☐ Its registered trademark is SUALKUCHI'S.

Jatinga

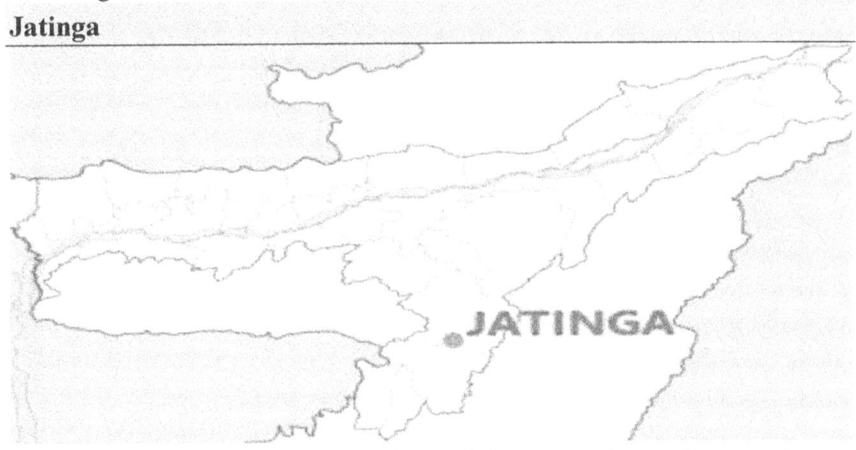

☐ It is a village on a ridge, is located in Dima Hasao district, Assam State in India. It is 330 kilometres (210 mi) south of Guwahati.

☐ At the end of the monsoon months especially on moonless and foggy dark nights between 6 p.m. and 9:30 p.m., birds are not disturbed by the locals but out of the dark northern skies will start to descend as they are attracted to lights. These dazed birds are captured using bamboo poles by the locals. The local tribal first took this natural phenomenon to be spirits flying from the sky to terrorize them.

☐ This phenomenon is not confined to a single species, with tiger bittern, black bittern, little egret, pond heron, Indian pitta, and kingfishers all being affected, as well as hill partridge, green pigeon, emerald dove, necklaced laughingthrush, black drongo. The birds are mostly juvenile, according to Assam's best known ornithologist, Anwaruddin Choudhury.

☐ The most recent description of the phenomenon and its comparison with similar incidents elsewhere in Malaysia, Philippines, and Mizoram is found in the book The Birds of Assam by Anwaruddin Choudhury. He concluded that the birds, mostly juveniles and local migrants, are disturbed by high velocity winds at their roost. When the disturbed birds fly towards lights as refuge they are hit with bamboo poles and killed or injured.

Stillwell road (Ledo Road)

☐ The Ledo Road (from Ledo, Assam, India to Kunming, Yunnan, China) was an overland connection between India and China, built during World War II to enable the Western Allies to deliver supplies to China and aid the war effort against Japan.

☐ After the Japanese cut off the Burma Road in 1942 an alternative was required, hence the construction of the Ledo road.

☐ It was renamed the Stilwell Road, after General Joseph Stilwell of the U.S. Army, in early 1945 at the suggestion of Chiang Kai-shek.

☐ It passes through the Burmese towns - Shingbwiyang, Myitkyina and Bhamo in Kachin state. Of the 1,726 kilometres (1,072 mi) long road, 1,033 kilometres (642 mi) are in Burma and 632 kilometres (393 mi) in China with the remainder in India.

☐ The road had the Ledo-Pangsau Pass-Tanai (Danai)-Myitkyina--Bhamo-MansiNamhkam-Kunming route.

6.2: M-2: Awards and Honours

Srimanta Shankardeva Award

☐ It is a national level award instituted by Government of Assam in 1986.

☐ It is given to persons of eminence in the field of Journalism, Art, Culture and Literature.

☐ It is only given to individuals of 50 years and above and associations are not eligible for it.

☐ The first receipient was Kirtinath Hazarika – 1986.

☐ The State government has nominated two personalities - Prof. Bhabaprasad Chaliha and noted Kathak artiste Jayanta Kastuar - for the Srimanta Sankardev Award, 2020. The award will be given away between January 3 and 10, 2021.

Few other national level awards instituted by Assam Government

Gopinath Bordoloi Award 1993

Ajan Peer Award 2004

Fakhruddin Ali Ahmed Award 2004

Sui KaPha Award 2005

Bir Chilarai Award 2006

K.K. Handique Award 2008

Madhavdeva Award 2009

Kalicharan Brahma Award 2009

6.3: M-3: Important Events

☐ Majuli Festival- Majuli Festival is celebrated in Majuli River Island on the bank of Brahmaputra. Usually it is a four day celebration from 21st – 24th of November. Cultural Programs showcasing various arts and cultures particularly of Satriya is the prime attraction.

☐ Assam tea Festival- It is organised in the month of November. Jorhat is the prime attraction during this festival. It is sponsored by Assam tourism.

☐ Kaziranga Elephant Festival- It is a yearly elephant festival held in Kaziranga National park of Assam for conservation and protection of Asiatic Elephants. It is jointly organised by the Forest Department and Tourism Department of Assam.

6.4: M-4: Assam Agitation and Assam Accord

Assam Agitation

☐ The Assam Movement or Assam agitation was a historic event in post independence Assam mainly led by students of Assam.

☐ This movement was started in 1979 under the leadership of All Assam Students Union (AASU) and All Assam Gana Sangram Parishad (AAGSP) and officially ended on 15th August 1985.

☐ Assam Agitation was a series protests and demonstration to compel the Government to identify and expel illegal (Bangladesh immigrants) and protect and provide constitutional safeguards to the indigenous Assamese people.

☐ Developments- In 1978, a by-elections in the Mangaldoi Lok Sabha constituency was to be held. By that time it was noticed that a sharp increase in the numbers of voters. Then AASU demanded that the elections be postponed till the names of foreign nationals were deleted from the electoral rolls and it was the genesis.

- On 27 November 1979, AASU-AAGSP called for a closure of all educational institutes and picketing in state and central government offices.

- At Barpeta, police attacked protestors and Khargeswar Talukdar – the general secretary of Barpeta AASU Unit was beaten to death. He was the first martyr of Assam Agitation.

Assam Accord

☐ The agitation lasted for Six years and 855 people sacrificed their lives.

☐ On 15th August 1985, a memorandum of understanding known as the Assam Accord 1985 was signed between Govt. of India and AASU.

☐ 24th March 1971 was made the deadline for identifying foreigners in Assam.

☐ Bridge over river Brahmaputra near Bogibeel, Numaligarh Refinery Limited, Assam Gas Cracker Project, IIT Guwahati, Tezpur University and Assam University – all these were set as an implementation of Assam Accord.

6.5: M-5: Some Eminent Personalities

Mahapurush Srimanta Sankardeva

- Vaishnava saint, great socio-religious reformer, propagated Neo Vaishnavism or Eksharan Bhagwati Dharma in Assam. Scholar, poet, playwright.
- Born in 1449 in Bordowa, Nagaon (Baro Bhuyan family)
- First pilgrimage- 1481, Second pilgrimage- 1550.
- Contribution to Assamese Culture- Sattriya Dance, Borgeet, Bhatima, Ankiya Nat, Bhaona, Kirtan Ghosa, Dasham.
- Cihna Yatra was the first Bhaona.
- Passed away in Bheladonga in 1568.

Lakshminath Bezbarua

- Literary stalwart of Assam and celebrated pioneer of modern Assamese literature.
- Written a number of plays , essay, fiction, poetry.
- Wrote sattires under the pen name of Kripabor Barbarua.
- 'Roxoraj' was the title given to him by Assam Sahitya Sabha (1931).
- Composed the state anthem- O mur apunar desh.
- His death anniversary is on 26th March and is observed as Sahitya Divas by asom Sahitya Sabha.
- His autobiography 'Mur Jiban Suworn' first assamese modern autobiography.

Jyoti Prasad Agarwala

- Assamese playwright, songwriter, poet, writer and film maker.
- Popularly called Rupkonwar.
- The songs he composed are called Jyoti Sangit.
- Directed and produced the first Assamese film Joymoti in 1935.
- Plays- Sonit Kunwori, Karengar Ligiri, Rupalim, Nimati Konya, Labhita, etc.
- His death anniversary 17th January is observed as Silpi divas (artist's day) in his honour.

Bishnu Prasad Rabha

- Well known cult figure from Assam well known for his literary and cultural contributions.
- He was known as Kala Guru- master of arts.

- His compositions are collectively known as Rabha Sangeet.
- He was a freedom fighter and was also influenced by Socialism.

Pratima Baruah Pandey

- Winner of Sangeet Natak Akademi and Padma Shree.
- Eminent Folk singer of Goalporiya Lokgeet.
- She belonged to the royal family of Gauripur.
- Awarded a documentary on her life and works named 'Hashtir Kanya' won a national award in 1997.

Bhupen Hazarika

- Stalwart of Assamese music renowned Assamese singer lyricist, musician, film maker.
- He was widely known as Sudhakantha.
- He received the National Film Award for Best Music Direction in 1975, the Sangeet Natak Akademi Award (1987), Padmashri (1977), and Padmabhushan (2001), Dada Saheb Phalke Award (1992), the highest award for cinema in India and Sangeet Natak Akademi Fellowship (2008), the highest award of the Sangeet Natak Akademi. He was posthumously awarded both the Padma Vibhushan, India's second-highest civilian award, in 2012, and the Bharat Ratna, India's highest civilian award, in 2019.
- Hazarika also held the position of the Chairman of the Sangeet Natak Akademi from December 1998 to December 2003.

Bhabendranath Saikia

- He was a novelist, short-story writer and film director from Assam, India.
- He won many literary awards, including Sahitya Academy (1976), and was also recognised with the Padma Shri.
- Saikia edited the Prantik an Assamese monthly magazine, and a children's magazine named Xaphura both in the Assamese language.
- He was also the president of the Jyoti Chitraban which was for a long time the only film studio in Assam.

Gopinath Bordoloi

- The first Chief Minister of Assam after independence.
- A renowned leader of the freedom struggle and follower of Gandhian principle.

☐ Governor of Assam Jayram Das Doulatram conferred him with the title 'Lokapriya'.

☐ The international airport in Assam (Guwahati) is named after him- Lokapriya Gopinath Bordoloi International Airport.

6.6: M-6: Geographical Tagged Products from Assam

☐ A **Geographical Indication (GI)** is a name or a tag used on certain products which corresponds to a specific geographical location or origin.

NAME OF THE PRODUCT	TYPE	APPROVING YEAR
Muga Silk	Handicraft	2007-08
Assam (Orthodox) Logo Tea	Agricultural	2008-09
Karbi Anglong Ginger	Agricultural	2014-15
Tezpur Litchi	Agricultural	2014-15
Boka Saul (Soft Rice)	Agricultural	2017-18
Kaji Nemu (Lemon)	Agricultural	2019-20

6.7: M-7: MCQs - Miscellaneous (401-450)

M-401. In which year Bhupen Hazarika has been awarded the DadaSaheb Phalke Award?

a) 1970   b) 1975

c) 1992   d) 2008

Ans- c) 1992

M-402. Barat utsav is a festival of which of the following tribes in Assam?

a) Tiwa   b) Karbi

c) Mishing   d) Rabha

Ans- a) Tiwa

M-403. Which among the following is the first daily newspaper of Assam?

a) Assam Mihir   b) Dainik Batori

c) Asam Bondhu   d) Orunodoi

Ans- b) Dainik Batori.

Explanation- Dainik Batori was first published in 1935.

M-404. Who is the first editor of the Journal Jonaki?

a) Hemchandra Goswami b) Lakshminath Bezbaruah

c) Padmanath Gohain Baruah d) Chandrakumar Agarwala

Ans- d) Chandrakumar Agarwala

M-405. In which year the Bodo language is recognised as a Scheduled language?

a) 1967 b) 2003

c) 2005 d) 2008

Ans- b) 2003

M-406. In which year the second Assamese film Indramaloti was released?

a) 1935 b) 1937

c) 1939 d) 1941

Ans- c) 1939.

M-407. Who was the author of Hara Gauri Samvad?

a) Ram Saraswati b) Hem Saraswati

c) Ananta Kandali d) Madhab Kandali

Ans- a) Ram Saraswati.

M-408. Who was the author of the novel Bhanumati?

a) Rajni Kanta Bordoloi b) Padma Nath Gohain Barua

c) Lakshminath Bezbarua d) Mahim Bora

Ans- b) Padma Nath Gohain Barua

M-409. The first Assamese sonnet 'Priyotomar Sithi' is written by?

a) Hemchandra Goswami b) Hiteswar Barbarua

c) Chandra Kumar Agarwala d) Jatindranath Duara.

Ans- a) Hemchandra Goswami

M-410. Which of the following is the first Assamese Women Magazine?

a) Srimayi b) Ghor Jeuti

c) Ramdhenu d) Bijuli

Ans-b) Ghor Jeuti

M-411. Who compiled and published the first Assamese Dictionary in 1867?

a) Miles Bronson b) Nathan Brown

b) Oilver Cutter d) Jaduram Dekabaruah

Ans- a) Miles Bronson

M-412. Who directed the Movie Village Rockstars?

a) Rima Das

b) Zubeen Garg

c) Munna Ahmed

d) None

Ans- a) Rima Das

M-413. Who is author of Gyanmalini, an anthology of poems?

a) Mafizuddin Ahmed Hazarika

b) Raghunath Choudhury

c) Dvakanta Barua

d) Navakanta Barua

Ans- a) Mafizuddin Ahmed Hazarika

M-414. Who wrote Naam Ghosa?

a) Madhavdev

b) Haridev

c) Sankardev

d) Damodhardev

Ans- a) Madhavdev

M-415. Madhavdev was born in the year__________.

a) 1489

b) 1449

c) 1452

d) 1472

Ans- a) 1489

M-416. What is the name of Second Assamese movie?

a) Joymati

b) Rupkowar

c) Indramalati

d) Manomati

Ans- c) Indramalati

M-417. Who wrote Kirtan Ghosa?

a) Madhavdev

b) Haridev

c) Sankardev

d) Damodhardev

Ans- c) Sankardev

M-418. Who was the fountainhead of Ankiya Naat?

a) Madhavdev

b) Haridev

c) Sankardev

d) Damodhardev

Ans- c) Sankardev

M-419. Srimanta Sankardev was born__________.

a) 1468

b) 1449

c) 1452

d) 1472

Ans- b) 1449

M-420. What is the name of First Assamese movie?

a) Joymati

b) Rupkowar

c) Indramalati

d) Manomati

Ans- a) Joymati

M-421. Who directed the Assamese Movie Joymati and Indramalati?

a) Pramatesh Baruah   b) Dr. Bhupen Hazarika

c) Jyoti Prasad Agarwala   d) Bishnu Prasad

Ans- c) Joyti Prasad Agarwala

M-422. Kirtan Ghosa by Sankardev is adaption from the __________.

a) Harivangsa   b) Bhagawat

c) Ramayan   d) Mahabharat

Ans- b) Bhagawat

M-423. "O Mur Aponar Desh", the state anthem of Assam was first published in which of the following magazine?

a) Jonbiri   b) Abahan

c) Jonaki   d) Bahi

Ans- d) Bahi

M-424. "O Mur Aponar Desh", the state anthem of Assam was written and composed by whom?

a) Pramatesh Baruah   b) Dr. Bhupen Hazarika

c) Lakshminath Bezbarua   d) Bishnu Prasad

Ans- c) Joyti Prasad Agarwala

M-425. Who composed the religious songs Zikr and Zari?

a) Shah Navi   b) Azan Fakir

c) Sankardev   d) Madhavdev

Ans- b) Azan Fakir

M-426. Name the first Assamese colour Feature Film?

a) Bhaity   b) Bhonti

c) Maina   d) Babala

Ans- a) Bhaity

M-427. Who is the first Female actress in Assamese film?

a) Bidya Rao   b) Aideo Handique

c) Jubili Rajkumari   d) Malaya Goswami

Ans- b) Aideo Handique

M-428. Who is the Muzic Director of the film Chameli Mem Sahab?

a) Jitu Tapan   b) Bishunu Prasad Rabha

c) Dr. Bhupen Hazarika   d) Phani Sharma

Ans- c) Dr. Bhupen Hazarika

M-429. In which year Dr. Bhupen Hazarika was born?

a) 8 Sep 1926

b) 19 Sep 1928

c) 11 Sep 1926

d) 21 Sep 1928

Ans- a) 8 Sep 1926

M-430. Who produced the movie Bulbul Can Sing?

a) Rima Das

b) Flying River Films

c) Jaya Das

d) Manabendra Das

Ans- b) Flying River Films

M-431. Who was the first recipient of Assam Valley Literacy Award?

a) Bhabendranath Saikia

b) Homen Borgogain

c) Syed Abdul Malik

d) Navakanta Baruah

Ans- a) Bhabendranath Saikia

M-432. Who directed the famous Assamese film Rang Police which begged the President's Silver Medal?

a) Nip Baruah

b) Brajen Baruah

c) Prabhat Mukherjee

d) Dr. Bhupen Hazarika

Ans- a) Nip Baruah

M-433. Who was the CM of first non-congress Government formed in Assam after Independence?

a) Tarun Gogoi

b) Gulap Borbara

c) Prafulla Kumar Mohanta

d) Anowara Taimur

Ans- b) Gulap Borbara

M-434. Name the person who was not a member of the Legislative Assembly when he became the Chief Minister of Assam?

a) Mahendra Mohan Choudhury

b) Bimala Prasad Chalia

c) Jogendranath Hazarika

d) Hiteswar Saikia

Ans- b) Bimala Prasad Chalia

M-435. Which administrative head has been given the power to implement the special power as mentioned in 6th Schedule of Indian Constitution?

a) President

b) Governor

c) Prime Minister

d) Chief Minister

Ans- b) Governor

M-436. Who was the first Martyr of the Freedom Movement from Assam?

a) Maniram Dewan

b) Kushal Konwar

b) Piyoli Phukan

d) Kanaklata

Ans- c) Piyoli Phukan

M-437. When was the Assam Accord signed?

a) 25th Aug 1979

b) 20th Aug 1989

c) 12th Aug 1984

d) 15th Aug 1985

Ans- d) 15th Aug 1985

M-438. Who elected the Speaker of State Legislative Assembly?

a) The Members of Assembly

b) Governor

c) Chief Minister

d) Judge of High Court

Ans- a) The Members of Assembly

M-439. Who was the first Assamese elected as the President the President of India?

a) Gopinath Bordoloi

b) Fakaruddin Ali Ahmed

c) Bishnuram Medhi

d) None

Ans- b) Fakaruddin Ali Ahmed

M-440. Who was the first Women Chief Minister of Assam?

a) Hemprava Saikia

b) Anowara Taimur

c) Mavish Dun

d) Renuka Devi

Ans- b) Anowara Taimur

M-441. How many members are there in the Gauhati Munipal Corporation?

a) 50

b) 60

c) 65

d) 70

Ans- b) 60

M-442. Who was the first Woman nominated as Minister in Assam Government?

a) Hemprava Saikia

b) Anowara Taimur

c) Mavish Dun

d) Banale Khangmen

Ans- d) Banale Khangmen

M-443. Who is the first Woman Deputy Speaker Legislative Assembly?

a) Hemprava Saikia

b) Anowara Taimur

c) Mavish Dun

d) Banale Khangmen

Ans- d) Banale Khangmen

M-444. The CAG of India is established under which Article of our Indian Constitiution?

a) Article 146

b) Article 147

c) Article 148

d) Article 149

Ans- c) Article 148

M-445. Excise Duty is a tax levied on the ___________.

a) Import of Goods

b) Export of Goods

c) Manufacturing of Goods

d) Sale of Services

Ans- c) Manufacturing of Goods

M-446. Goods and Services Tax (GST) is a tax on sale of Goods and Services was introduced first in France. By which Amendment GST was introduced in India.

a) 42nd Amendment Act

b) 76th Amendment Act

c) 101st Amendment Act

d) None

Ans- c)101st Amendment Act

M-447. Goods and Services Tax (GST) is a tax on sale of Goods and Services is a matter of which List under 7th Schedule of Indian Constitution?

a) Union List

b) State List

c) Concurrent List

d) None

Ans- c) Concurrent List

M-448. Under which Article GST Council was made?

a) Article 279A

b) Article 269A

c) Article 126 A

d) None

Ans- a) Article 279A

M-449. Assam Public Service Commission (APSC) is _______ body.

a) Constitutional

b) Fundamental

c) Statutory

d) Non-constitutional

Ans- a) Constitutional

M-450. The first receipient of Sankardev Award was Kirtinath Hazarika in 1986.

a) Dr. Bhupen Hazarkia

b) Krishna Kamal Das

c) Janmejoy Das

d) Kirtinath Hazarika

Ans- d) Kirtinath Hazarika

7. VARIOUS MAPS OF ASSAM

7.1: Political Map of Assam (now 35 Districts)

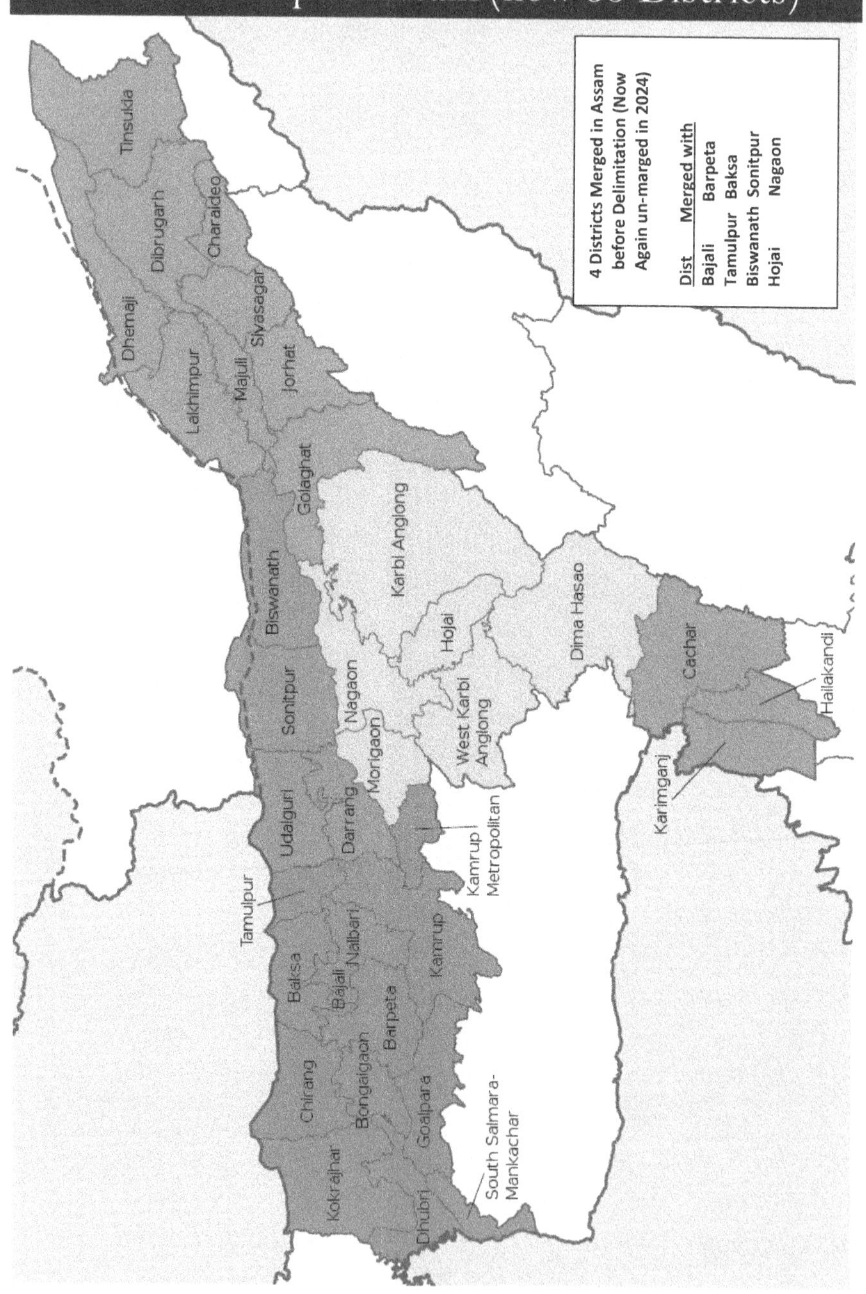

7.2: Blank Map of Assam

7.3: Political Map of Assam (now 35 Districts)

4 Districts Merged in Assam before Delimitation (Now Again un-marged in 2024)

Dist	Merged with
Bajali	Barpeta
Tamulpur	Baksa
Biswanath	Sonitpur
Hojai	Nagaon

7.4: Physical Map of Assam

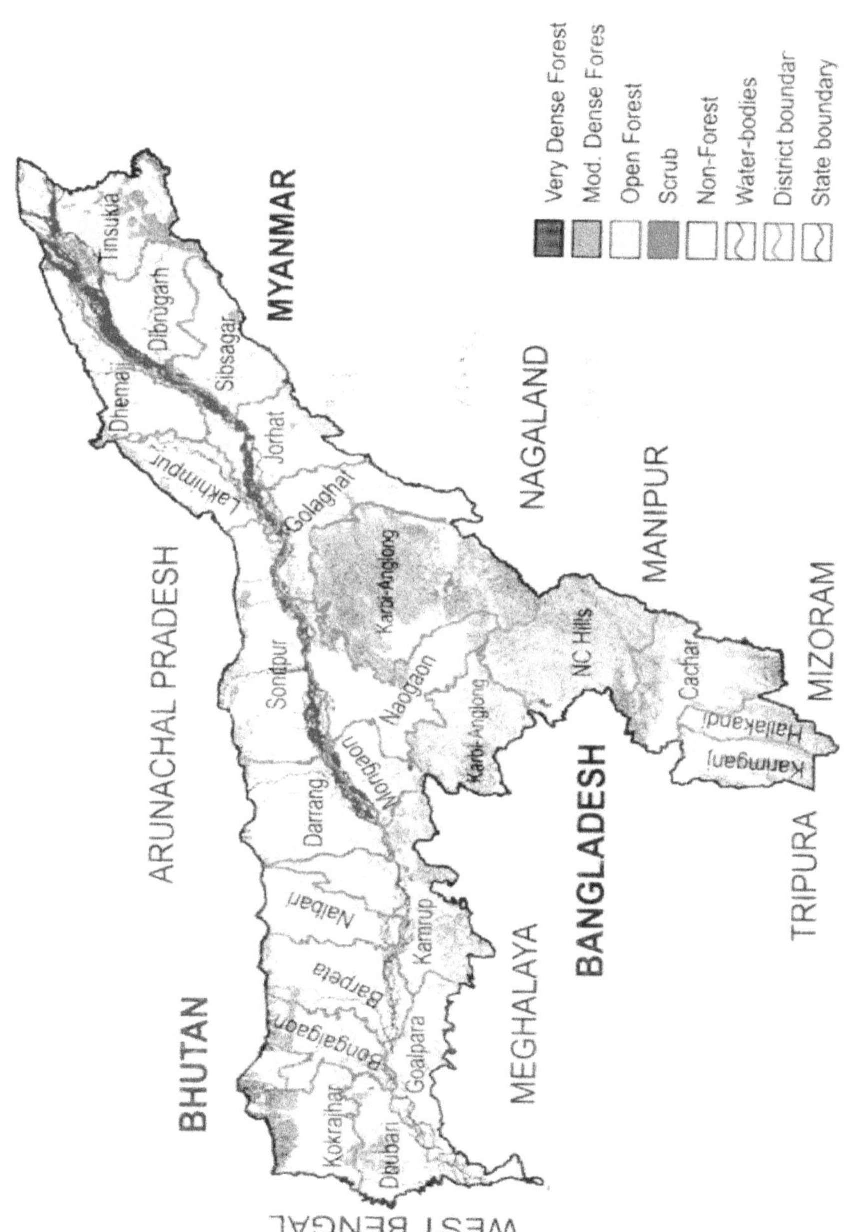

7.5: NP & WLS Map of Assam

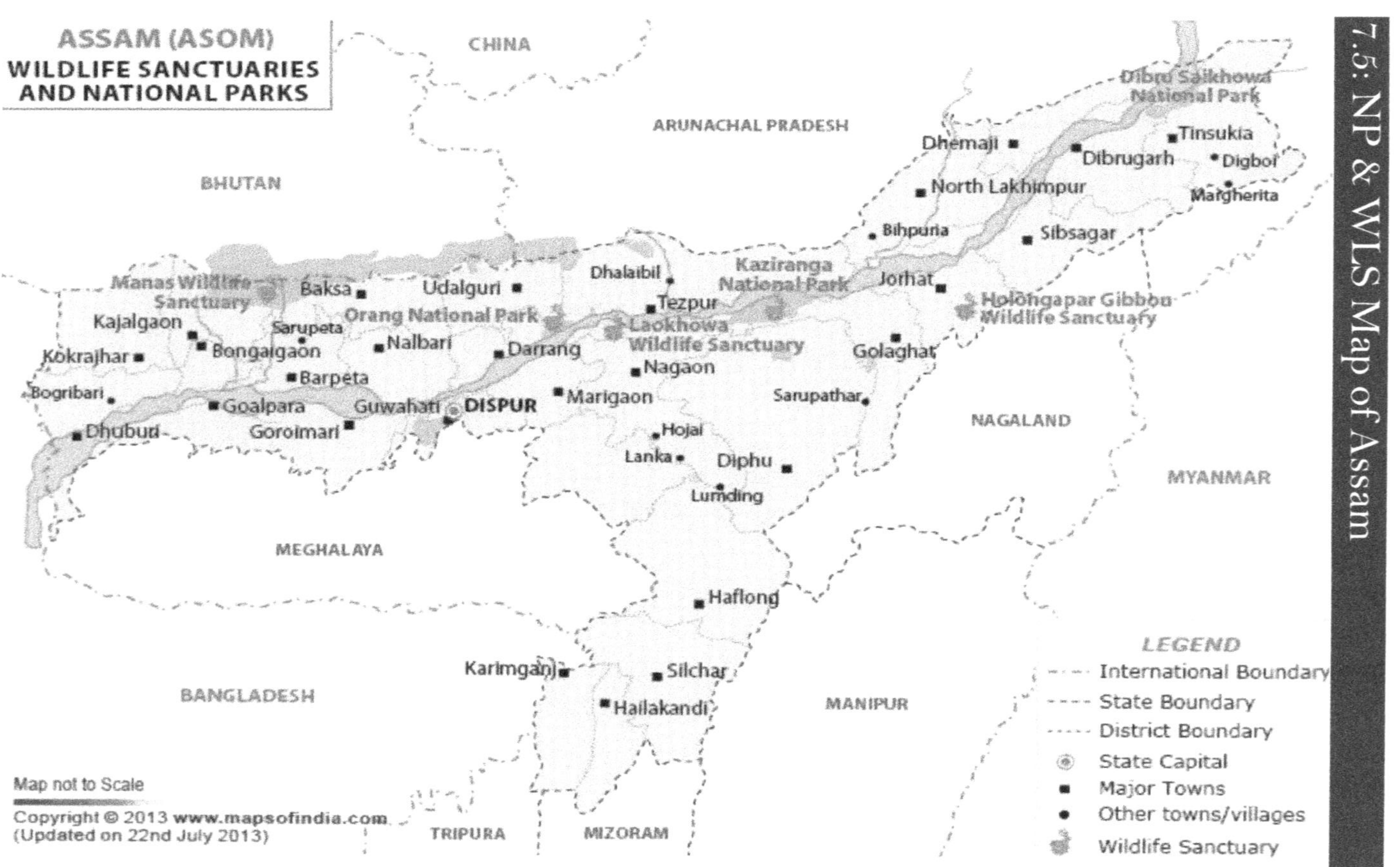